T0331185

Managerial Relationships and SMEs Internationalization

As the "backbone of the economy," small- and medium-sized enterprises (SMEs) are key players in the dynamics of local, regional, and global markets, and are often obliged to provide timely responses to the increasingly fierce cross-border competition. However, SMEs internationalization has temporarily been subject to a wait-and-see policy under the numerous uncertainties and global systemic disruptions. Despite the "new normal" brought about by the COVID-19 pandemic, recent studies show that the future still holds the potential to avail business performance opportunities to SMEs, and that the hopes of managers for the years to come are reasonably high.

Adopting a relationship-centric perspective, the book proposes a deeper analysis of the role of managerial relationship building and development and SMEs internationalization. In the networked economy, relationships are the invisible threads of the highly interconnected world. Either we call them connections, ties, bonds, or links, they are present everywhere marking the very essence of our lives, therefore claiming for wide consideration.

Giving way to a stepwise screening of relationships and SMEs internationalization, the book is simultaneously addressed to scholars from different fields of study (i.e., international management, international business, international relationship marketing, etc.) and worldwide decision-makers (i.e., entrepreneurs and managers) interested in conducting smart business abroad.

Elena-Mădălina Vătămănescu is a Full Professor at the Faculty of Management (SNSPA), Bucharest, Romania, Head of the Management Department, and Director of the Centre for Research in Management.

Andreea Mitan is a Lecturer at the Faculty of Management (SNSPA), Bucharest, Romania, Executive Director of the Centre for Research in Management, and CEO of the Norwegian–Romanian Chamber of Commerce.

Routledge Frontiers in the Development of International Business, Management and Marketing
Series Editors: Marin Marinov and Svetla Marinova

For more information about this series, please visit: https://www.routledge.com/business/series/RFDIBMM

Managerial Relationships and SMEs Internationalization

Un-weaving the Fabric of Business Performance

Elena-Mădălina Vătămănescu and Andreea Mitan

Routledge
Taylor & Francis Group

NEW YORK AND LONDON

First published 2024
by Routledge
605 Third Avenue, New York, NY 10158

and by Routledge
4 Park Square, Milton Park, Abingdon, Oxon, OX14 4RN

Routledge is an imprint of the Taylor & Francis Group, an informa business

© 2024 Elena-Mădălina Vătămănescu and Andreea Mitan

Library of Congress Cataloguing-in-Publication Data
Names: Vătămănescu, Elena-Mădălina, author. | Mitan, Andreea, author.
Title: Managerial relationships and SMEs internationalization :
un-weaving the fabric of business performance / Elena-Mădălina
Vătămănescu and Andreea Mitan.
Description: New York, NY : Routledge, 2024. | Includes bibliographical
references and index.
Identifiers: LCCN 2023018784 | ISBN 9781032556314 (hardback) |
ISBN 9781032558066 (paperback) | ISBN 9781003432326 (ebook)
Subjects: LCSH: Small business--Management. | Relationship marketing.
| International business enterprises--Management. |
Globalization--Economic aspects.
Classification: LCC HD62.7 .V383 2024 | DDC 658.02/2--dc23/eng/
20230628
LC record available at https://lccn.loc.gov/2023018784

ISBN: 978-1-032-55631-4 (hbk)
ISBN: 978-1-032-55806-6 (pbk)
ISBN: 978-1-003-43232-6 (ebk)

DOI: 10.4324/9781003432326

Typeset in Times New Roman
by MPS Limited, Dehradun

To my husband and son, my driving force, my roots into happiness and fulfilment, my strength and willingness to become a better person and human being.

To my mother, father, and brother, the anchors of my overall becoming and the tailors of the never-ending search for excellence. To my extended family, for fostering a loving and supporting climate.

To professor Constantin Bratianu, for opening new avenues toward self-achievement even before I have started walking. To my friend and Dean, Florina Pînzaru, for believing in me and for supporting me along all my professional ways. To all my fantastic friends and collaborators, Alexandra, Andreea, Andreia, Andrew, Aurora, Cristi, Elena, Elena-Alexandra, Gandolfo, Juan, Luminița, Mihai, Patrizia, Pedro, Simona, for all the lessons learned and great opportunities.

Mădălina

I would like to extend my deepest gratitude to my co-author, PhD coordinator, and friend Mădălina Vătămănescu, for being the best guide I could have asked for during the start of my journey into the academic realms of Management. Her drive, strategic thinking, and warm support have been immensely significant to me during the many years since we started working together.

My heartfelt appreciation goes to professors Constantin Bratianu, Florina Pînzaru, Cristian Paun, Dan-Cristian Dabija, and Valeriu Frunzaru, who have offered me the opportunity to discover new ways of looking at the world, and who have helped me carve out my professional path as a Management scholar.

To my family: thank you for always being there for me.

Andreea

Contents

Tables

Foreword

This book appears as a challenge for all of us involved in researching, designing, and developing managerial relationships in a world of business shaken by economic turbulences and global complex crises. The authors, who dedicated years of research on this topic, offer us a comprehensive analysis of the SMEs internalization process by changing the linear approach based on economic metrics with a new vision based on the paradigm of the global mindset and multidimensional metrics of assessing the organizational performance.

The architecture of the book is designed on a convergent dual perspective of zooming-out and zooming-in analyses. The logic is clear. Internalization is a process of transforming the potential physical and nonphysical capital of any SME into a successful enterprise beyond the domestic borders and over the barriers of the global business fabric. Understanding the dynamics between the internal and external business forces becomes a requisite of designing any strategy in the process of internalization. The authors remarked correctly on the challenges of SMEs having limited resources in achieving competitive advantage on the international market, especially those operating in emergent economies. However, managers with strategic thinking and a good understanding of business and intercultural phenomena can be successful in achieving sustainable development.

The authors reveal the power of the managers' global mindset in un-weaving the fabric of international business and designing their knowledge and business strategies based on entropic, nonlinear, and probabilistic ways of thinking in a complex world. The emergence of intellectual capital and the dominance of intangibles in the knowledge-intensive organizations lead toward an increasing role of knowledge management and developing new nonlinear performance metrics. The global mindset is promoting a new international vision based on cultural intelligence and multicultural leadership. The authors make a further step in proposing the 5Cs model for performing a successful internationalization, a model integrating the main five dimensions of this process: convergence, communality, compatibility, credibility, and connectivity.

The book challenges us with its new vision of SMEs internationalization and the new thinking architecture necessary for understanding the complexity of the changeable business environment, disrupted frequently by global crises. The emphasis is on understanding the dialectics of the global mindset and psychic distance and on developing new competencies for managers to design successful international business strategies.

Professor Emeritus Constantin Bratianu
UNESCO Department for Business Administration
Bucharest University of Economic Studies, Romania
President of the International Association
for Knowledge Management
Padua University, Italy

1   Introduction

The relationship-centric SMEs internationalization

During turbulent times, when change is expected and profuse, impacting many layers of the fabric of the world, the business environment, which needs relative social, economic, and political stability to thrive, is put to a test. Recent years have been particularly interesting in this regard, as the COVID-19 pandemic, a black swan that spread its wings over the world in the early 2020, acted as a catalyst for change, accelerating tendencies that were already present, bringing disruption to many industries all over the world, leading to a rearrangement of several markets and supply chains, and unexpectedly pressing Man toward embracing introspection. For months, if not years, humanity has been under siege due to a tiny, newly mutated, coronavirus. Man had to recognize the frailty of life and reassess his priorities. Man had to think about what he holds dear, and about what motivates him. Man understood his values better. And Man chose Life above Death. This choice has led to a reassessment of needs and wants, consequently impacting behaviors and businesses.

Following the governmental measures adopted to limit the spread of the virus, such as the lockdowns, consumer behavior changed. These changes impacted many industries, starting with commerce, as e-commerce and the demand for delivery services grew. Shifts in leisure and entertainment options and preferences took place. Live online shows became common, which increased streaming consumption; doing sports at home became more common; etc. Shifts in working arrangements appeared: work from home grew in importance, and flexible hours became widespread. Online teaching and learning replaced, for a while, face-to-face schooling and webinars, and other tech-enabled human interactions have been widely adopted. Travel and tourism were limited. New practices emerged: wearing masks, using various disinfectants, practicing social distancing, etc.

While the discourse on fast digitalization and authenticity was trending before the pandemic, it became almost obsolete by early 2022, as future and technology appear now to be intrinsically connected. The need for humanity to embrace novel ways of using Earth's resources in order to focus on survival, instead of focusing on the continuous growth in profits, gained a high rank on the world's public agenda. Sustainability and net zero carbon

DOI: 10.4324/9781003432326-1

emissions – regionally, European Union's (EU's) green energy goals – became the new guiding lights of the public opinion, directly or indirectly influencing all human activities.

For small and medium-sized enterprises (SMEs) in Europe, this newly imprinted direction – go green or lose business – joins the hot topics of the current times, which range from desiderates of survival to how to profitably elaborate on the surprisingly numerous business expansion opportunities that emerged in some sectors, for example, regionally relevant geopolitical shifts, such as the ones involving Ukraine, coupled with the already higher than usual average anxiety levels, leading to a rather gloomy current perspective on business development, seasoned with only a few examples of almost magical wins of some firms.

Within the EU, SMEs are defined according to EU Recommendation 2003/361. The criteria for classifying organizations as SMEs relate to the number of employees and turnover or total assets. Thus, according to Law No. 346 of July 14, 2004 as amended and supplemented, Art. 3, "Small and medium-sized enterprises are defined as those enterprises that cumulatively meet the following conditions: a) have an average annual number of employees of less than 250; b) have an annual net turnover of up to EUR 50 million, or have total assets not exceeding the equivalent of EUR 43 million, according to the last approved financial statement."

SMEs internationalization has temporarily been subjected to a *wait and see* policy, under the numerous uncertainties marking the systemic evolution at the national, regional, and even global levels. Nevertheless, as recent studies (Vătămănescu et al., 2019, 2020a, 2020b, 2021; Nicolescu, 2022) show, the future still has the potential to offering international expansion opportunities to SMEs, and the hopes of entrepreneurs for 2023 and beyond are reasonably high. In a world where competitiveness has become second nature to the organizational environment, the internationalization of SMEs with a view to increase business performance is thus emerging as a functional imperative. As the "backbone of the economy," SMEs are key players in the dynamics of local, regional, and global markets, and are often obliged to provide a relevant and timely response to the increasingly fierce cross-border competition.

To date, the influence of relationship building and development on international partnerships between SMEs has been addressed through various constructs and models, many of them considering relationship as a second-level factor in the understanding of the internationalization dynamics. Consequently, one of the goals of this work is to reposition the relevance of multifaceted relationships as a pillar of business performance in international markets and as key components of complex phenomena such as strategic networking, novel business model advancement, internationalization achievement, etc. The focus of the argumentation is on how manifold relationships (i.e., personal, social, business, economic, etc.) are established at the management level. The assumption is that the actors who have sustained and long-standing relationships are the ones creating the real market. Partnerships spring as key drivers for the internationalization of organizations, with business and interpersonal relationships between managers rising as propelling factors (Vătămănescu, 2020).

With the purpose of tapping into the intricacies of the SMEs internationalization processes, the argumentative structure of the book follows a deductive logic, from the exploration of the macro factors afflicting the SMEs environment toward the micro realities of such organizations. Each chapter is descriptive of the underlying relationships among varied entities, be they human, factors, strategies, models, or processes. In a networked society and networked economy, relationships are the more or less visible threads of the highly interconnected world. Either we call them connections, ties, bonds, or links; they are present everywhere marking the very essence of our lives. Relationships stand out as the fabric of the world, weaving multilayer strata and covering a wide spectrum of phenomena.

Adopting a processual approach, the book has been structured into two parts and six chapters. The first part – *Relationships and SMEs internationalization: A zoom-out perspective* – consists of three chapters designed as a preamble to the substantive issues concerning relationship building and development during the internationalization process. Their role is to address the main features of the current international environment, ranging from multifaceted macro factors toward phenomenological overviews of SMEs internationalization peculiarities in specific regions. These factors range from technological transformations related to the Fourth Industrial Revolution, to societal issues and energy-related transformations that imprint the world today, the recent evolutions of the economic system, the demise of capitalism and democracy to the shifting values, and cultural changes impacting Man today (Chapter 2).

Further, Chapter 3 addresses the main characteristics of the current international business environment, that is, the process of globalization and its consequences for SMEs, the opportunities and constraints of internationalization, the factors, forms, and models of SMEs internationalization, and the measurement of the internationalization performance. The focus is on the imperative for organizations to overcome the limitations of national or regional boundaries to achieve business performance.

Embracing a context-centric approach, Chapter 4 offers compelling insights into the process of internationalization of SMEs located in Central and Eastern European (CEE) region. The argumentative structure avails a discussion on multidimensional relationships, knowledge, and networks, showing that there are research gaps in the international business literature that could be filled through conducting research in the CEE region. The stake is to unravel phenomena specific to complex systems that have recently been impacted by changes that occurred on many levels: political, societal, cultural, demographic, and economic. The chapter underlines that the process of transition that the countries in the CEE region engaged in after the fall of the

communist regimes in the late 1980s and early 1990s has led to the emergence
of particularities regarding the behavior of the firms and of the behavior
and mindset of the managers, that could and should be studied in more
depth, in order to better understand the ways in which the business relationships may evolve in these countries, and how and to what extent are
firms, especially young SMEs and SMEs led by managers with a specific
cultural background (i.e., from former communist countries), enabled to
compete on the international markets.

The angle of investigation shifts from the general to the particular, from
the abstract to the concrete, from the reality and challenges of globalization.
Conceived as a macro environment-focused section, the first part of the book
sets the extra-organizational parameters that drive SMEs to move out of
their habitat and to tap foreign markets, engage in international relationships, and assume a cross-cultural logic.

The second part – *Relationships and SMEs internationalization: A zoom-in
perspective* – aims to bring to the fore the peculiarities of relationships
building under the aegis of the internationalization process. The three
chapters forming this part revolve around the importance and role of the
human capital in the dynamics of internationalization, with a special emphasis on the managerial level. The literature review highlights the nodal
points of research in the field, but also areas of vulnerability, i.e., topics of
study that still remain at an embryonic stage.

Once the research guidelines in the field of relationship marketing, in
general, are outlined, the focus shifts to two exponential models for the B2B
approach: the interaction-based B2B relationship marketing model and the
network-based B2B relationship marketing model. Processual highlights
are given of the enablers and inhibitors that act as moderators in the initiation, creation, development, and maintenance of international partnerships
(Chapter 5). The effects of culture and country of origin on international B2B
relationships are brought forward, hence anticipating the noteworthiness of
the managerial global mindset in today's interconnected world (Chapter 6).

The second part ends with the advancement of a relationship-driven
model – *The 5 Cs model of managerial relationship building* – which is
grounded in the main research directions in the field of business internationalization, international relationship marketing, and B2B marketing in
inter- and cross-cultural contexts. Chapter 7 aims to develop five interlinked
dimensions, building on strong and consistently valued strands of research by
members of the scientific, academic, and practitioner communities. A new
conceptual model is articulated (integrating the conditions, contexts, catalysts, consequences, and connections inherent in the construction of international relationships), rooted, however, in current themes of debate, which
confirms the topicality and relevance of such an approach.

The final chapter takes stock of the stepwise approach conducive to un-
weaving the fabric of SMEs internationalization and business performance
through the lens of intricate and ever-spanning relationships. By looking

backward at what has been done on the topic so far, a step forward is made as future research directions are availed by the existing knowledge gaps. A first endeavor toward the road ahead was reified by delving into the role of manifold relationships in the equation of internationalization. A broad spectrum of interpersonal, social, intercultural, transorganizational, micro, and macro relationships has been scrutinized with a view to unravel their configurations, influences, and outcomes in relation to business performance beyond national borders.

References

Nicolescu, O. (Ed.). (2022). Carta Albă a IMM-urilor din România. 20th edition. ProUniversitaria.

Vătămănescu, E.-M., Gorgos, E.-A., Ghigiu, A.M., & Pătruț, M. (2019). Bridging intellectual capital and SMEs internationalization through the lens of sustainable competitive advantage: A systematic literature review. *Sustainability*, *11*(9), 2510. 10.3390/su11092510

Vătămănescu, E.-M. (2020). *Internaționalizarea IMM-urilor și marketingul relațional: între convergență și conectivitate [The internationalization of SMEs and relationship marketing: Between convergence and connectivity]*. Pro Universitaria.

Vătămănescu, E.-M., Alexandru, V.-A., Mitan, A., & Dabija, D.-C. (2020a). From the deliberate managerial strategy towards international business performance: A psychic distance vs. global mindset approach. *Systems Research and Behavioral Science*, *37*(2), 374–387. 10.1002/sres.2658

Vătămănescu, E.-M., Cegarra-Navarro, J.-G., Andrei, A.G., Dincă, V.-M., & Alexandru, V.-A. (2020b). SMEs strategic networks and innovative performance: A relational design and methodology for knowledge sharing. *Journal of Knowledge Management*, *24*(6), 1369–1392. 10.1108/JKM-01-2020-0010

Vătămănescu, E.-M., Mitan, A., Andrei, A.G., & Ghigiu, A.M. (2021). Linking coopetition benefits and innovative performance within small and medium-sized enterprises networks: A strategic approach on knowledge sharing and direct collaboration. *Kybernetes*, *51*(7), 2193–2214. 10.1108/K-11-2020-0731

Part I

Relationships and SMEs internationalization

A zoom-out perspective

2 Macro factors influencing the SMEs sector

This chapter introduces some of the main issues that define the context in which we discuss today about the internationalization of small- and medium-sized enterprises (SMEs). We tackle some of the transformations that the modern civilization and economy currently undergo, in the wake of the Fourth Industrial Revolution, while facing disruptions linked to clean energy transition, climate change, and deepening inequalities.

Advancing theories and concepts stemming from recent works of leading economists, sociologists, geopolitics experts, and philosophers, the following pages address some of the significant overlapping crises the world faces today, and unravel contemporary perspectives on global economic, social, and political dynamics that nevertheless impact business development. While the shifts we present concern the entire human civilization, we focus, in the second part of this chapter, on why it is particularly relevant to study particularities of international business and the internationalization of SMEs. We argue that studying the prospects of business internationalization in the case of the SMEs is a fruitful effort that enables international business theory development, taking into consideration that internationalization stands out as a moving target and as a *living research laboratory*.

Energy-related factors and societal issues

Perhaps the most significant factors that determine the transformations that the macro-environment faces today are related to the evolution of technology and to the use of energy. These work as framing issues for several other transformations that we refer to in the following sections.

We shall start by introducing Frederick Soddy, winner of a Nobel Prize for chemistry in 1921, who wrote in his book *Money versus Man* (1931, p. 56) that "the flow of energy should be the primary concern of economists." Ecological economists build upon this assumption, and the popularity of the perspective today is not to be underestimated. We follow this thread by introducing the work of Vaclav Smil, Distinguished Professor Emeritus at the University of Manitoba, in Canada, who has dedicated his life work to interdisciplinary studies in energy, economic development, food, population,

DOI: 10.4324/9781003432326-3

public policy, environment, and history. He explains that energy is the only universal currency that humans have, and that people have built the current civilization by mastering energy transformations (Smil, 2017). Furthermore, he states that "every economic activity is fundamentally nothing but a conversion of one kind of energy to another, and monies are just a convenient (and often rather not representative) proxy for valuing the energy flows" (Smil, 2017, p. 448).

Contemporary human civilization is fossil-fuelled, argues Smil (2017), explaining how the modern civilization developed in relation to the energy sources that humans used, and showing how the use of fossil fuels, starting with the 19th century, enabled humans to transform great amounts of energy, a thing which was unimaginable before. Fossil-fuelled technology supported man to achieve massive progress in multiple areas, via agriculture, transportation, and industrialization, simultaneously accelerating urbanization, and dramatically improving the man's information and communication capabilities. The use of fossil-fuelled technologies leads to long periods of high rates of economic growth, to bettering the living conditions of many people, and to amassing affluence.

The transformations that improved the living standards of man took place very fast, underlines Smil (2017), who mentions that the Gross Domestic Product (GDP) of the United States of America (USA) doubled between 1880 and 1900, and that other industrializing societies of the 19th century were able to witness their economies growing with 20% to 60% in only one decade. High-energy service economies appeared not late afterwards, as a result of the multiple technical advancements and countless innovations that improved the lives of many people, while also creating inequalities and negatively impacting the environment. This is the reason why modern societies have grown to be dependent upon reliable sources of incessant and inexpensive fossil fuel and electricity, in a context in which the energy resources are distributed unevenly (Smil, 2017). These facts have intra- and international consequences. Among those, he mentions domestic and foreign political concerns and responses, which range from intolerance to corruption, from regional disparities to the emergence of violent political regimes, from the rising cost of the energy bills to issues connected to the control of the energy flow affecting the stability of economies and countries. We will address, in the following pages, some of these topics.

Now, the civilization of man has reached a stage that is defined as *the modern era*. The Renaissance and the Illuminist Age have made possible the modern times, with Great Britain acting as a forerunner of the industrialization and societal change (Aglietta, 2019). The modern era started to emerge in the 1500s, when the first signs of inanimate power use were made by man, planting the seeds of the First Industrial Revolution (Smil, 2022). The evolution of technology was gradual, and the changes in production became massive only in the late 1800s, accounting for major transformations in the societies, economies, and politics.

According to Smil (2022), in the 1500s, around 90% of the mechanic energy used by man was provided by animate power (manpower, animal power), and the thermal energy produced by mankind was linked to combusting plant fuels (wood, straw, dried dung), and charcoal. At the beginning of the 1800s, the muscle force of man and animal was still providing about 90% of the energy used in manufacturing, construction, and farming. Inanimate prime movers were able, around 100 years later, in the 1900s, to provide half of the mechanical energy used by man, via coal-fired engines, waterwheels, water turbines, windmills, steam turbines, and internal combustion engines (since the 1880s). In the 1900s, modern energy sources such as coal and crude oil were used to produce half of the primary energy, while traditional fuels such as charcoal, straw, and wood provided the other half. The 1950s were times of technical advancements, fossil fuels supplying (through coal) around 75% of the primary energy production. Over 80% of the mechanical energy was produced by using gasoline and diesel-fuelled internal combustion engines.

In the 2000s, wood and straw combustion still provided 12% of the world primary energy and 5% of the mechanical energy used by humanity was still derived from animate prime movers. As related to electricity production, water turbines, and hydro stations were used in the 1880s, followed by geothermal electricity and, after the Second World War, by solar and wind power. This evolution did not accelerate much in the next decades, as in 2020 about half of the electricity consumed on Earth was still generated through combustion of fossil fuels (mainly coal and natural gas). In the words of Smil (2022, p. 49), "during the past two centuries [...] [*humanity*] witnessed a rapid global substitution of primary energy sources, accompanied by the expansion and diversification of fossil energy supply, and the no less rapid introduction, adoption, and growth in capacity of new inanimate prime movers – first coal-fired steam engines, then internal combustion engines (piston and turbines). [...] [*We now live in*] a truly global society built and defined by mass-scale, stationary, and mobile conversions of fossil carbon, deployed everywhere but in some of the planet's uninhabited regions."

Previous civilizations, such as the ones of Sumer, Egypt, Greece and Rome, Caral-Supe, or Maya, among others (for analyses see Friedman, 1983, or Targowski, 2009), grew at slower paces, had their times of glory, and, on the basis of reaching their limits in technological advancement, on depleting the reserves of natural resources they were using, together with climate change issues, and war, entered their declining phases, ultimately being absorbed by other civilizations, or slowly disappearing. At the moment, the modern civilization powered by the four Industrial Revolutions is linked to the Western civilization, developed since the mid-20th century under the flagship of the USA, but is, in fact, planetary, and has started to face issues that point to it potentially reaching its limits and moving toward a declining phase.

Factors related to the evolution of modern civilization

Natural resources and the environment

After decades of change and growth, starting with the 1970s, *concern* became the keyword of many discussions covering the future of the economies, societies, and even the future of modern civilization. Debates regarding the exhaustion of fossil fuel deposits and the consequent demise of humanity, as a result of the unreasonable fast growth which depletes the energy resources of the planet, have been conducted. Fossil fuel reserves are indeed finite, and the constant civilizational growth based on using fossil fuels is not sustainable over many centuries, if not for the limited quantity of available resources, at least due to the negative effects using those resources has on the environment, most notably leading to average temperatures rising and to freshwater becoming scarce.

The members of the Club of Rome, through the volume *The Limits to Growth*, edited by Meadows et al. (1972), presented a neo-Malthusian perspective, underlining that equating economic growth with progress is deemed to bring to the fore limits that may pose a threat to the long-term well-being of man. The authors thought that by maintaining the growth rate in resource use, food production, industrialization, pollution, and population, mankind would engage in a quest to a rapid and disastrous decline by 2070s. They believed that the growth trends could be altered, without negatively affecting the possibility of covering the basic needs of humans, so that a state of *global equilibrium* would be reached. They militated for a speedy start in this regard, posing that it would have a greater chance to success.

Following this line of reasoning, Gates (2021) posits that all human activities (from agriculture to construction and transportation, let alone industry) still emit greenhouse gases that lead to changes in the atmosphere, affecting the living conditions of man as well as of all the living species, from plants and insects to animals, and that the only option for humanity to survive (!) is to adopt a net-zero policy toward carbon emissions and by this means limit global warming at 1.5 degrees Celsius.

The concerns regarding the depletion of natural resources and the climate change due to releasing too much carbon in the atmosphere add to the fear that, due to overheating the atmosphere via the greenhouse effect, draughts will become more prevalent, the level of planetary ocean would rise, destroying human settlements, and that clean water would become a scarce resource due to pollution, as well as lack of rain and iceberg melting (Magnason, 2021). All these concerns point to an apocalyptic perspective on the future, unless humanity changes its behavior very fast.

Smil (2022) portrays those fears and promises of change as exaggerated, taking into account that our civilization is based on a large, inertia-driven, complex system, that is unable to change fast. Steel, cement, ammonia, and plastic, says Smil (2022), are expected to remain the four material pillars of the human civilization for the next 20–30 years, and while innovations such as

3D printers are operational, revolutionary scale changes are not expected to take place, transportation is also not expected to relay much on other than refined liquid fuels, and Artificial Intelligence is also not expected to be able to bring to the fore working solutions for vital human concerns such as preventing a new deadly pandemic.

However, steps toward diminishing the negative impact of human activities on the environment are already being made, such as searching for alternate sources of energy and new ways to stock energy, saving and reusing drinking water, to decrease the consumption per capita, in areas where drought became a common occurrence (Gates, 2021), and a more nature-friendly approach to agriculture, by using natural fertilizers and non-GMO seeds (see the work of activist Vandana Shiva) is already being promoted for years.

Technology and innovation

Technology and innovation are expected to help building a better, more inclusive, and cleaner future for mankind, and are equally feared by tech-pessimists. Based on hope or fear, predictions on the future are abundant and cover many layers of the human experience. As new, disruptive technologies emerge; additional shifts are being expected in the wake of the Fourth Industrial Revolution: the lines between the biological sphere, the physical sphere, and the digital sphere already began to blur (Schwab, 2018). Man evolves to become the creator of a multi-level reality for himself. Discussions concerning the Metaverse, a man-made multiverse where Augmented Reality, Virtual Reality, and physical reality are expected to be woven together in the fabric of a new all-encompassing Multiplex stage system for human existence, lead many to ponder whether a dystopian future is to be expected.

As the frontrunners of the digital companies, such as Meta, focus on building the infrastructure for the Metaverse (Zuckerberg, October 28, 2021), we can still only guess how disruptive the process will prove to be for the people, and what areas of human experience would be impacted and how. Uncertainty still haunts the ones who think of the dynamics of the techno-logical advancement and the evolution of the artificial intelligence (AI), of the impact of the digitalization process and of the adoption of the Internet of things (IoT) (World Bank, 2016), of the innovations that change the limits of medicine and blur the lines between man and machine (Schwab, 2018), of the impactful use of computers and software in education and training, of the development of new business models, by using the new available technologies (the platform business model, the sharing economy), of the use of crowd-sourcing in order to harness the power of the collective intelligence, of the significant role that the instruments provided by the Internet and social networks, by the media and by the contemporary algorithms play in defining tailor-made worlds online, for targeted users (see the involvement of Cambridge Analytica in elections), together with the apparition of new communication pathologies such as the infodemic and fake news.

Politics

In the political arena, the emerging technologies and the market dynamics that lead to the growth of corporations and the rise of the digital couple with the pressures concerning the need to source energy in a cleaner way and to replace the use of fossil fuels, producing perceivable tension and announcing potential planetary power shifts. From a bird's eye view, systemic changes are visible, and they ask for pragmatic takes, as new power centers emerged (the digital corporations), challenging the extant world order. Their role evolves as the rate of worldwide Internet penetration and mobile phone adoption increases. Let us not forget that mobile phone adoption is high even in regions where people do not have access to electricity at home (World Bank, 2016).

The role of the digital corporations in coding information, in transporting information, and even in creating the context for information reception is of paramount importance. Alphabet (former Google), Apple, Amazon, Cambridge Analytica, Dell Technologies, Hitachi, Huawei, IBM, Lenovo, LG Electronics, Meta, Microsoft, Oracle, Samsung Electronics, Sony, are the largest known digital corps. Some of these companies have yearly turnovers that surpass the GDP of entire countries. For example, in 2020 Amazon had a turnover of 386 billion dollars (STATISTA, 2021), while Romania's GDP reached only 248.7 billion dollars (World Bank, 2021).

The interplay between technology, digital corporations, and politics and their impact on human existence already took the stage in the works of contemporary thinkers, leading to the launch of concepts such as surveillance capitalism (Zuboff, 2019), and persuasive technology (Fogg, 2002), and to the emergence of tech-empowered business models such as the social media platforms (Gawer, 2009; Choudary, 2013; Van Alstyne et al., 2016). The role of the big tech companies in molding the business environment today through AI and algorithms is known and has become even a film topic see The Social Dilemma, 2020.

Geopolitics and international business development

Geopolitics and international business are transforming too, and the changes have long-lasting impacts, considering that we live in times of greater than ever state interdependency. Apart from changing economic performances of various countries, multiple other factors came at play in recent years, influencing the world order: the Fourth Industrial Revolution leads to change in the job market and regulations, the financial crisis of 2008 fragmented societies and made people and business owners focus on internal markets more that during previous decades, central banks and states recently intervened more often into the national economies, as a consequence of the 2008 crisis, corporations now play a much more powerful role in relation to the state, influencing the decision-making processes of national governments, and the economic and industrial solidarity are recognized as key factors for the development of the military and technological arenas (Dăianu, 2021).

The Unites States of America played, after the Second World War, the role of the world champion of international trade, "as an expression of the functioning of the system based upon free market, and as an instrument of promoting their own interests," reflecting the belief that boundless globalization should be the guiding force behind international economic relations (Dăianu, 2021, p. 260). The global economic hegemon role of the USA is now eroded (Smith, 2015), and Asia, through China and India, became significant actors on the world economic arena. Stiglitz (2019a, 2019b) argues that the *malaise* the USA faces can only be treated through a deep change in the American values, embracing tolerance, morals, cooperation, care for the ones who are vulnerable, and through work toward diminishing social inequality, "economic, racial, and ethnic divides." This way, trust and stability can be restored, and the premises for saving capitalism from itself would be observed. For the moment, internationalism and free market neoliberalism are being replaced in the USA by protectionism and nativism, which cannot promote General Welfare, which is the goal that Americans should aim at (Stiglitz, 2019a, 2019b).

The Arab Gulf States (Bahrain, Kuwait, Qatar, Saudi Arabia, and the United Arab Emirates), major oil producers and key players in the fossil-fuelled economy are now deeply impacted by the fact that they need to reshape their economies to support the global energy transition, even though that is expected to happen during a number of decades, and perhaps finalize well after the mid-century (IISS, March 2022). Their relations to China and the United States are to be reframed in this new energy equation.

Moving to Asia, we witness a re-heating of historical conflicts and an emergence of crises that erode countries. Following decades of growth, China now faces multiple issues, starting with the collapse of the over-developed real estate sector, a job market collapse, and the undeclared but nevertheless real bankruptcy of many financial institutions that supported the real estate business (Financial Times, March 10, 2022). The job crisis accelerated during the many zero-COVID lockdowns and as a consequence of the massive layoffs, as the state launched a crackdown on tech companies (Weinland, November 8, 2021), and is sustained as the factory employment is decreasing. People in 24 of the 31 Chinese provinces recently boycotted mortgage payments for unfinished buildings, on the grounds that real estate developers worked on credit and are seemingly unable to deliver the properties they sold, and that the prices have declined since they signed their contracts (Gunya, July 21, 2022). Violent protests took place in front of banks from many Chinese regions, on the basis that the banks froze the accounts of their clients without explanation (Fan, July 11, 2022). The military actions that China recently organized near Taiwan (Palmer, August 10, 2022) and the tension between Beijing and New Delhi (India) (Detsch & Gramer, August 11, 2022) suggest increasing instability in Asia.

Additionally, pursuant to the COVID-19 pandemic, countries in the region that were dependent upon tourism, such as Sri Lanka, currently go through a financial crisis and political crisis, doubled by social unrest, as people faced an inflation of over 50% in June 2022, and food shortages (Perera, July 14, 2022).

Europe and the European Union witness times of particular significance and change too. After the Russian Federation invaded Ukraine in February 2022, Western Europe's dependency upon Russian gas became a topic of great concern for the leaders of the countries in the European Union. The on-going conflict in Ukraine has already been named "the largest armed conflict in Europe since World War II" (RAND, 2022), and its profound consequences are still to be underpinned, as the end of the conflict is not yet in sight at the moment we write this book. Economic consequences for the individuals in the European Union and in Romania are already visible and are expected to be even worse as winter approaches and heating capacities become vital for most European households. Among the consequence, we can already mention inflation, higher costs for credits, and much higher costs for energy. There is a tendency toward economic stabilization, but a return of inflation below 2% is expected to take place only in 2024 (Adrian Vasilescu, counselor to the Governor of the Romanian National Bank, interviewed in Neag, August 5, 2022).

The armed conflict in Ukraine is particularly relevant to Romania, as it takes place at its borders. And while Romania's economy did fare unex-pectedly well during the pandemic, facing a contraction of only 3.9% in 2020 (Roşu, February 16, 2021), in spite of the pessimistic estimates (European Commission, 2020), the more recent developments in the neighboring country gave rise to many concerns. *A country without a project*, as Radu and Dobrescu (2019) label it due to its structural weaknesses and brain drain issues, as well as its notorious lack of long-term country-level planning, Romania registered progress through structural reforms after the 2008 crisis. The industrial exports and agricultural harvests have supported a steady growth between 2013 and 2017, but there is yet a strong dependency to trade to the EU (accounting for roughly 70%), which is nonetheless leading to potential economic consequences during these times (CIA, n.d.).

The Middle East and Africa face multiple crises as well, which overimpose on the extant inequalities and difficulties related to the social, political, and economic conditions that can be seen in many of the countries in these regions. For example, not late after the SARS-CoV-2 pandemic, Lebanon became bankrupt. The Lebanese pound lost 90% of its value, and 80% of the population now lives below the poverty line, six out of ten inhabitants wishing to leave the country (DW, August 5, 2022). The energy crisis pur-suant to the 2022 Russo-Ukrainian conflict has consequences not only for the countries in Europe, but also for people in regions in Africa and the Middle East, which was dependent upon Ukrainian cereals, which now face a food crisis, says Vasilescu (interviewed in Neag, August 5, 2022).

Overall, in the post-pandemic period, we witness the four major trends that Keller, et al. (2020) mentioned: a de-globalization tendency and a change in the role that China played in relation to the global ICT value chain; a decrease in the international mobility of people, affecting the global GDP, tourism, and the migrant labor; an accelerated adoption of technology, leading to more automation and a leap forward in what concerns digitization; a growing pressure on companies and governments toward embracing green policies.

A report by McKinsey (Huber & Sneader, June 2021) highlighted a number of additional trends that are expected to shape the world economy during next years: innovation led by necessity, a change in the consumer behavior (e-grocery, investments in the home), increased efforts to mitigate the climate change risks through greening, a rise in demand for telehealth services and increased investments in healthcare and bio, a restructuring of corporate portfolios, with the top companies amassing more wealth and the bottom 20% of the companies losing clients, a relocation of around 25% of the supply chain links over five years, due to the US-China dynamics, and a slow recovery of the air travel sector. These trends happen in the context of greater governmental involvement in the economy, and greater governmental scrutiny, and are moderated by the fact that stakeholder capitalism is on the rise, asking companies to satisfy the needs and respect the interests of more than their shareholders.

Multifaceted factors affecting the economic system

Prior to the SARS-CoV-2 pandemic which started in late 2019, and pursuant to the 2008 crisis, some of the well-known analysts of the contemporary times, such as Arjun Appadurai (2017), Zygmunt Bauman (2017), Donatella Della Porta (2017), Nancy Fraser (2017), or César Rendueles (2017) among others, deemed appropriate to point to an apparent decline of the (especially Western) world as we knew it, in their essays published in the volume *The Great Regression*, edited by Geiselberger, a book which was simultaneously launched in fourteen countries. The Great Regression, as the authors of the volume put it, refers to a wide range of phenomena happening under the same umbrella: democracy and capitalism seem to have reached a moment of structural crisis. The symptoms are many and the implications they cite are far-reaching. Due to the purpose of this book, we will enumerate below only a few of those symptoms, which are particularly relevant to the Central and Eastern part of Europe, to Romania, and to its economy.

The crisis manifests at the level of meaning and legitimacy of the political representatives and public authorities (Geiselberger, 2017). For the countries in the CEE region, this can be read, for example, through the mistrust that the citizens seem to have toward politicians, most visible, perhaps, in case of turnouts. In the 2019 elections for the European Parliament, only roughly 40% of the voters from the CEE region decided to participate

(European Parliament, October 22, 2019). In the US, the crisis of legitimacy of institutions manifested more recently through events that were unbelievable one decade before, such as the Capitol riot, which took place in early January 2021 (Encyclopaedia Britannica, 2022).

Other forms of the current political and administrative crisis can be observed through the rise of authoritarian regimes, through the recrudescence of nationalist and fundamentalist tendencies, and through the rise of the illiberal ideology (see Laruelle, 2022, for a fine-grained description of illiberalism). Relevant manifestations include Viktor Orban's regime in Hungary, the Taliban's ruling of Afghanistan, peaking in 2021 with a human rights crisis, the yet present discrimination and human rights violations that take place in countries all over the globe, and also legislative changes such as the epochal overturning on June 24, 2022, by the US Supreme Court, of Roe v. Wade, "ending nearly 50 years of federally protected abortion rights" (Summers & Tavenner, 2022). These events are joined by modern uses of misinformation, and by the rise of the fake news phenomenon. All these occurrences influence the public agenda, and work as forces that weaken democracy and the social contract, by undermining the values that functioned as the pillars of the modern world (freedom, justice, respect, community, responsibility).

Other concerns related to the crisis touch on the issues of contemporary demographic dynamics and migrations. Speaking about dynamics that are highly relevant to the CEE countries, we should mention the European Union's *migration crisis* or the *Syrian refugee migration*, which started in 2015 (Almustafa, 2021), as well as the massive population migration following the Ukraine's invasion by Russian Federation in late February 2022. Both migrations lead to the displacement of millions of people, many of whom are now living in CEE states or have passed through these states while heading to other countries, most of them remaining in Europe, with almost 6.400.000 Ukrainians now living in other European states (UNHCR, August 10, 2022). What is to be noted, at this point, is that these events are now pressing millions of people to flee unemployment, famine, and death, leading to a humanitarian crisis, and that disruption in the economic flows in the belligerent countries, as well as generalized uncertainty, are observable.

Developments related to decreased political legitimacy, to authoritarianism, to illiberalism, to fundamentalism, and to issues related to population displacement and migration due to modern conflicts and economic reasons are undesirable consequences of the action of some of the forces that shaped the modern world: the free market fundamentalism, the liberal capitalism, globalization, financialization, followed by deindustrialization and digitalization (Geiselberger, 2017).

Pursuant to the demise of the USA as leading ship of the capitalist economy (Smith, 2015; Dăianu, 2021), several theories explaining why this happened and what the world might expect emerged. Robert Albritton (2015) posits in *A phase of transition away from capitalism* that capitalism, as the

USA has defined it to be after the Second World War, has come to face a deep accumulation crisis, which makes it compulsory for the system to embrace change in order to survive; otherwise, it would implode. The model change is compulsory, as the recent crisis of 2008–2009 did not do for the American economy what previous crises did (such as the Great Depression in the 1930s), namely it did not lead to the destruction of over-accumulated capital, and implicitly did not kill the companies that are named *too big to fall* (Ivanova, 2015). That, among other factors, points to the necessity of creating a new economic model, a new form of capitalism (Westra et al., 2015).

Alan Nasser (2018) discussed about the profound de-structuring of the world as we know it, in the quest for a *new normal*, labeling his time as the final days of an overripe American and global economy. He underlines that the 2008 crisis was indeed a milestone, marking the beginning of a systemic decline, and considers the responses given by the Obama administration and mainstream economists, at least for the United States of America, to having been rather ineffective. In his view, the US capitalist model, soon to be followed by the rest of the world, faces two options: to create an Age of Austerity by repressing the working people and trying to maintain the functionalities of the current system, or to shift to a society where public investment is key, where people have a much shorter work week and a much higher income, enabled by larger-scale government employment. The role of the state becomes crucial, as "capitalism's life can be prolonged only at the expense of democracy and of material and psychological security. [...] the course of capitalist development itself points to the feasibility and desirability of democratic socialism" (Nasser, 2018, p. 2).

The inevitable emergence of a new international regime or international ideology is the focus of several other current studies: the recent years have witnessed many authors trying to underpin what they envision as the *new capitalism*. Frase (2016) saw four possibilities of development after industrial capitalism: communism (based on equality and abundance, to which the introduction of the universal income would help make a peaceful slide), rentism (based on hierarchy and abundance), socialism (based on equality and scarcity), and exterminism (based on hierarchy and scarcity). Frase believed that regardless of the future model, it would certainly not be the same as industrial capitalism.

Back in the early 2000s, Wilson (2002) was pleading for a conservative take on the economic thought and practical matters, as he believed that a marriage between neo-conservatism and postmodernism would lead to an evolution that would be beneficial to man. Schweickart (2011) pleads for a socialist take on the future of the economy, calling for a revolutionary change of the world. Ditching the anti-globalist discourse, Schneider (2018) pointed out the need for a new global economy to emerge; recognizing that man should be the central figure of future economic models, Hirschfeld (2018) wrote about the need for a humane economy to be built; Opdebeeck (2018) went even further and connected economy and meaningfulness, his view stemming from even more philosophical concepts such as the Buddhist economy, the moral economy, or the trust economy. Stiglitz (2019a) wrote about the role and significance of stakeholder capitalism, Henderson (2020) advanced the concept of reimagined capitalism, and Stiglitz (2019a) launched the concept of *the Great Reset*.

Agreeing that the role played by the state in the new form of economy shall be significant, Mariana Mazzucato, in her book *Mission Economy. A Moonshot Guide to Changing Capitalism* (2021), stressed upon the need for building an entrepreneurial state, as well as a mixed economy. Trompenaars and Hampden-Turner (2021) stressed the role of public-private partnerships in the most recent pandemic-related crisis and suggest the proliferation of an economic system based upon this sort of collaborations, while Arietta (2022) pleads for a participatory social contract "that would restore inclusive growth" for all stakeholders.

Arietta and Espagne (2019) stated that the financial capitalism has advanced a growth trajectory which is not viable, linking it to the macroeconomic instability, to the social inequities exacerbation, to the concentration of power in the hands of the ruling elite, to the re-emergence of geopolitical rivalries, and to the relative decline of the global world order. Instability and insecurity, which are observable in the world today, as terrorism, cyber-attacks, hybrid wars, and uncertainty are prevalent, press the states to adopting measures that point to economic protectionism, and to embrace Realpolitik, authoritarianism, and state interventionism (Dăianu, 2021). During the following years, these are expected to impact both the states and the alliances they are part of, such as the European Union. Mariotti (2022) also observes that a "global protectionism" has been installed since the end of the 2008 crisis and adds that de-globalization and regionalization processes are to be expected, with nationalism and populism take over multilateralism. That would be similar to what happened during the period before the First World War, raising questions regarding the possibility for a global conflict to emerge (Dent, 2020).

During the Word Economic Forum that took place in Davos in 2021 Klaus Schwab (2021) underlined the current global relevance of the most recent edition of his book on stakeholder capitalism, in the quest for establishing a more resilient, more sustainable, and more inclusive global economy. Stakeholder capitalism (Schwab, 2021) would put the lights on the wellness of the people, instead of the maximizing profits of a few, and should correlate with a more sustainable approach toward the resources and the planet. It is to be noted, however, that there are many who do not believe that this version of capitalism would be able to bring the much-needed change on a global scale, so that each society would be a welfare society sooner or later. For example, Angelique Kidjo, UNICEF international Goodwill Ambassador, underlined during the same DAVOS Summit that, as presented, this new capitalism is still reinforcing a postcolonial stage of development, that has taken resources from Africa and helped Africa, but never empowered Africa to educate people, to fight the corruption of the local African leaders, to grow the local economies so that youngsters could get jobs in their native countries and not be chasing the mirage of Europe, risking their lives to escape poverty (Kidjo, January 25, 2021). While digitalization and technology might bring solutions to the more developed countries, there are, perhaps, still many regional disparities to be addressed if we are to discuss about a truly developed global society.

Cultural factors and the shifting values

Kate Raworth (2017) shows that the 21st century needs to foster economies that are built around promoting human prosperity, aiming at balance through distribution and regeneration, within the social and ecological conditioning "that underpin collective human well-being." Both Raworth (2017) and Stiglitz (2019a, 2019b) call for a change in the approach to the economy, understanding that *homo economicus*, the subject that has long been considered the agent in economy, selfish and self-serving, is nothing but a construction which leaves human values such as care or empathy to rust, and eliminate the idea of focusing on the well-being of others.

Following a similar rhetoric, the Commission on the Measurement of Economic Performance and Social Progress (CMEPSP) aimed, at the call of French President Nicholas Sarkozy, to assess the relevance of using GDP as the indicator of economic performance and social progress (Stiglitz et al., 2009). The CMEPSP pleaded for shifting the emphasis of the measurement system from economic production to the well-being of the people, in the context of sustainability. They voiced twelve recommendations, which jointly point in the direction of the significance of moving the focus from production to the human being, and its well-being. Well-being is seen as the central concept, and it shall be measured by referring simultaneously to "material living standards (income, consumption and wealth), health, education, personal activities including work, political voice and governance, social connections and relationships, environment (present and future conditions), insecurity, of an economic as well as a physical nature" (Stiglitz et al., 2009, pp. 14–15).

Now, after the COVID-19 pandemic, economies recover "at the expense of sharply deteriorating debt-to-GDP ratios," global public debt is at a high after the Second World War, world faces resurgent inflation and environmental issues, and, overall, mankind understands that GDP is not a good measure for progress, and that indicators such as happiness, biodiversity, and social cohesion could enrich the measuring of societal progress (Schwab & Malleret, 2020). Just a few months before, Tim Jackson (2021) published a book in which he names capitalism "a catalogue of system errors," which fostered the *casino economy* and the *age of irresponsibility*, where investors aimed at gaining fast.

To Jackson (2021), economic growth has been equated to well-being for too many years, making man forget about prudence and measure, and this shall be reverted, through disinvestment in unethical businesses, through prudence, and through *ecological investments* (which would support and protect the environment, the climate, the water, soil, nature), through *care investment* (which would help maintain life such as hospitals, homes, schooling, shops), and *creative investment* (which would create a fulfilling and durable human world such as meeting places, artistic venues, communal spaces, art).

Signs of shifting values can already be seen, as they accompany changes in the mindset of people. The relevant values in the Western world changed during the late 1800s and the 1900s to accommodate the shift from *Gemeinschaft* (community) to *Gesselschaft* (society) (Tönnies, 2001), allowing for individualism to become the highest-rated value, and leading to societal alienation and even to rewarding socially predatory behavior (Dutton, 2013). The *new normal* presses toward embracing a return to community, and to shift from individualism, competitiveness, and opulence toward general well-being, nurture, cooperation, nature, modesty. It is a sign of a profound change of focus from individual survival at all costs to survival of entire social organisms, from the masculine to the feminine, from the west to the east. An embrace of the Ubuntu (Zulu word for "I am because we are"). This is what Ng (2020) considers to be the appropriate take to a modern economy, which, he argues, shall be Buddhist in its nature, meaning that it should be "humanistic and genuinely care for the community and environment."

Artistic expression rides the waves of the times, pointing to the embrace of Man as the measure of things. Neo-minimalism, neo-humanism (Prabhat Ranjan Sarkar), altermodernism,[1] and post-postmodernism have already started to bloom, starting with the 80s. Figurative art, the quest for authenticity, a preference for clean, complex yet sophisticated designs and forms, a return to natural fabrics and materials, to the love of nature, the return of concern for community, the idea of caring for the other, of building durable things, of repurposing, DIY, of greening, along with a sort of pauperization (in comparison to the excess of the 1970s, see von Schönburg, 2016) mark the current times.

In June 2022, the Trilateral Commission launched *The Report of the Task Force on Global Capitalism in Transition.* The authors speak about the emergence of the capitalism's fifth stage, marked by climate change concerns, rising inequalities, and disruptions caused by the digital revolution. They argue that while capitalism is now the dominant economic system, having propelled humanity in an unprecedented way toward well-being, literacy, wealth, and increasing the life expectancy of many, it has also brought unprecedented challenges to humanity, concerning global warming, equality among people, and the access to the benefits of the digital technologies.

Recognizing the magnitude of the current phenomena influencing the trajectory of capitalism, the authors of the report underline that capitalism is a cultural system, which is molded by the most significant values of the people, expressing the *spirit of the age*, and following a set of rules that were agreed upon by the people. Some of the main rules refer to property rights, trade agreements and treaties, the rule of law, and various regulations, norms, and management practices.

For a smooth transition to this fifth stage of capitalism, which is deeply linked to the digital, they argue that investments in new technologies, infrastructure, and the development of new skills and working arrangements are key factors. They envision a future whereby 2050 people would live in the net-zero worlds, and they believe that this result can be achieved through a green transition, which encompasses ideas such as green innovation, innovation diffusion, green finance acceleration, green labeling, green businesses, and through integrating a concern for climate into corporate governance. The authors link the goal of harnessing the potential of the digital revolution to the equal access to data, to Internet and to devices, to skills and to scale, to the adoption of digital innovations, and to the transformation of the way in which governments operate, as well as to adopting antitrust laws that would regulate the digital age. Along the lines of equal access to the digital revolution benefits comes the necessity to offer to the people a fair start and the opportunity to achieve their potential, to address market concentration, to eliminate administrative burdens, and to tax consistently.

***

As presented in this chapter, a multitude of changes are currently unfolding at macro level, potentially leading to long-term and profound transformations concerning the environment in which firms evolve and relationships develop. Taking place on the geopolitical, the political, the economic, the technological, the social, and the cultural levels, these changes are expected to continue to unfold during the years to come. Hypotheses have been launched regarding the potential impact of some of these developments, yet the outcome is rather difficult to predict. We believe that, at the time we write this book, the best course of action, for researchers who investigate the dynamics of topics in the field of international business (IB), is to anchor their empirical endeavors through contextual analysis. For companies, the lens that the managers and other team members use to interpret the signals they receive regarding the evolutions of the environment in which the firm operates are highly significant, as they lead to different developmental routes for the company itself.

Note

1 Altermodernism refers to a sort of a new modernity based on translation, a movement that embraces creolization of cultures as well as the fight for autonomy, where cultural values of cultural groups are translated and connected through the world network, potentially producing singularities even though the world seems increasingly standardized (Nicolas Bourriaud in his keynote speech to the 2005 Art Association of Australia & New Zealand Conference).

References

Aglietta, M. (2019). *Capitalisme. Les temps de rupture*. Odile Jacob.

Albritton, R. (2015). A phase of transition away from capitalism. In R. Westra, D. Badeen, Dennis & R. Albritton (Eds.), *The future of capitalism after the financial crisis. The varieties of capitalism debate in the age of Austerity*, 151–170. Routledge.

Almustafa, M. (2021). Reframing refugee crisis: A "European crisis of migration" or a "crisis of protection"? *Environment and Planning C: Politics and Space*, 40(5). 10.1177/2399654421989705

Appadurai, A. (2017). Uzura democrației. [The wear of democracy] In H. Geisselberger (Ed.), *Marea Regresie. De ce trăim un moment istoric [The Great Regression: Why we witness a historical moment]*, 15–31). Editura Art.

Arietta, M. (2022). *The reform of Europe. Political guide to the future*. Verso.

Arietta, M., & Espagne, E. (2019). Quatrieme partie. Transformer la regime de croissance. In M. Arietta (Ed.), *Capitalisme. Le temps des ruptures*. Odile Jacob.

Bauman, Z. (2017). Simptome în căutarea unui obiect și a unui nume [Symptoms in the search for an object and a name]. In H. Geisselberger (Ed.), *Marea Regresie. De ce trăim un moment istoric [The Great Regression: Why we witness a historical moment]*, 32–51. Editura Art.

Choudary, S.P. (2013). Why business models fail: Pipes vs. platforms. *WIRED*. https://www.wired.com/insights/2013/10/why-business-models-fail-pipes-vs-platforms/

Dăianu, D. (2021). *Economia și pandemia. Ce urmează? [The economy and the pandemic, what is next?]*. Polirom.

Della Porta, D. (2017). Politică progresistă și politică regresivă în neoliberalismul târziu [Progressist Politics and Regressive Politics during the Late Neoliberalism]. In H. Geisselberger (Ed.), *Marea Regresie. De ce trăim un moment istoric [The Great Regression: Why we witness a historical moment]*, 52–70. Editura Art.

Dent, C. (2020). Brexit, Trump and trade: Back to a late 19th century future? *Competition&Change*, 24(3-4), 338–357. 10.1177/1024529420921481

Detsch, J., & Gramer, R. (August 11, 2022). *India's Beef with China Sizzles at Over 10,000 Feet*. Foreign Policy. https://foreignpolicy.com/2022/08/11/india-china-himalayas-us-military-exercise-border/

Dutton, K. (2013). *Înțelepciunea psihopaților. Din experiența de viață a sfinților, spionilor și criminalilor în serie*. Globo.

DW (August 5, 2022). Lebanon: An economic crisis and the aftermath of the Beirut port explosion. https://www.youtube.com/watch?v=RZuKyIYMSEw

Encyclopedia Britannica. (2022). United States Capitol attack of 2021. https://www.britannica.com/event/United-States-Capitol-attack-of-2021

European Commission. (May 11, 2020). https://ec.europa.eu/romania/news/20201105_previziunile_economice_toamna_romania_ro

European Parliament. (October 22, 2019). The turnout by country 2019. https://www.europarl.europa.eu/election-results-2019/en/turnout/

Fan, W. (July 11, 2022). Large Chinese bank protest put down with violence. *The Wall Street Journal*. https://www.wsj.com/articles/large-chinese-bank-protest-put-down-with-violence-11657543437

Financial Times. (March 10, 2022). Evergrande: the end of China's property boom | FT Film. https://www.youtube.com/watch?v=dnp_MxXY9qs

Fogg, B.J. (2002). *Persuasive technology using computers to change what we think and do*. Morgan Kaufmann Publishers.

Frase, P. (2016). *Four futures: Visions of the world after capitalism*. Verso.

Fraser, N. (2017). Neoliberalism progresist versus populism reacționar: o alegere a la Hobbson [Progressist neoliberalism versus reactionary populism: A choice a la Hobbson]. In H. Geisselberger (Ed.), *Marea Regresie. De ce trăim un moment istoric [The Great Regression: Why we witness a historical moment]*, 71–85. Editura Art.

Friedman, J. (1983). civilizational cycles and the history of primitivism. *Social Analysis: The International Journal of Social and Cultural Practice, 14*, 31–52. https://www.jstor.org/stable/23170415

Gates, B. (2021). *Cum să evităm un dezastru climatic. Soluțiile la îndemână și inovațiile necesare [How to avoid a climate disaster. The solutions we have and the break-throughs we need]*. Litera.

Gawer, A. (2009). Platform dynamics and strategies: From products to services. In A. Gawer (Ed.), *Platforms, markets and innovation*, 45–76. Edward Elgar Publishing.

Geiselberger, H. (Ed.) (2017). *Marea Regresie: de ce trăim un moment istoric [The Great Regression: Why we witness a historical moment]*. Editura Art.

Gunya, A. (July 21st, 2022). People are refusing to pay their mortgages in China. The protest could spill into the wider economy. Time. https://time.com/6198624/china-mortgage-boycotts/

Henderson, R. (2020). *Reimagining capitalism. How business can save the world*. Penguin Random House.

Hirschfeld, M.L. (2018). *Aquinas and the market. Toward a humane economy*. Harvard University Press.

Huber, C., & Sneader, K. (June 2021). *The eight trends that will define 2021–and beyond*. McKinsey Global Publishing. https://www.mckinsey.com/capabilities/strategy-and-corporate-finance/our-insights/the-eight-trends-that-will-define-2021-and-beyond

IISS (March 2022). The Arab Gulf states and the geopolitics of the energy transition. IIS vol. 28 https://www.iiss.org/publications/strategic-comments/2022/the-arab-gulf-states-and-the-geopolitics-of-the-energy-transition

Ivanova, M.N. (2015). Not just another crisis. How and why the Great Recession was different. In R. Westra, D. Badeen & R. Albritton (Eds.), *The future of capitalism after the financial crisis. The varieties of capitalism debate in the age of Austerity*, 171–183. Routledge.

Jackson, T. (2021). *Post growth. Life after capitalism*. Polity Press.

Keller, C., Shelepko, I., Sodhani, S., & Tan, B. (August 14, 2020). The post-COVID economy. Barclays. https://www.cib.barclays/our-insights/The-post-COVID-economy.html

Kidjo, A. (January 25, 2021). Speech regarding stakeholder capitalism in Africa, Stakeholder Capitalism: Building the Future | DAVOS AGENDA 2021. Moderator Edward Felsenthal, Editor-in-Chief and CEO TIME. https://www.youtube.com/watch?v=LQ3Q-CdoXlQ

Laruelle, M. (2022). Illiberalism: A conceptual introduction. *East European Politics, 38*(2), 303–327, 10.1080/21599165.2022.2037079

Magnason, A.S. (2021). *Despre Timp și Apă [About water and time]*. Litera.

Mariotti, S. (2022). A warning from the Russian–Ukrainian war: Avoiding a future that rhymes with the past. *Journal of Industrial and Business Economics*. 10.1007/s40812-022-00219-z

Mazzucato, M. (2021). *Mission economy. A moonshot guide to changing capitalism.* Alen Lane.

Meadows, D.H., Meadows, D.L., Randers, J., & Behrens III, W.W. (1972). *The limits to growth.* Potomac Associates.

Nasser, A. (2018). *Overripe economy. American capitalism and the crisis of democracy.* Pluto Press.

Neag, M. (August 5, 2022). INTERVIU. Omul care a stat 26 de ani în umbra lui Mugur Isărescu: „Omenirea are nevoie de lecții de istorie, pentru că 50 de ani a avut ochii închiși și urechile astupate" [INTERVIEW. The man who stood for 26 years in the shadow of Mugur Isarescu: „Mankind needs history lessons, because for 50 years it had its eyes closed and its ears covered"]. https://www.libertatea.ro/stiri/adrian-vasilescu-consilier-bnr-omenirea-are-nevoie-de-lectii-de-istorie-pentru-ca-50-de-ani-a-avut-ochii-inchisi-si-urechile-astupate-4230803

Ng., E.C.H. (2020). *Introduction to Buddhist economics. The relevance of Buddhist values in contemporary economy and society.* Palgrave Macmillan. 10.1007/978-3-030-35114-4

Opdebeeck, H. (2018). *The economy and meaningfulness. A Utopia?* Peter Lang.

Palmer, J. (August 10, 2022). Why doesn't China invade Taiwan? *Foreign Policy*. https://foreignpolicy.com/2022/08/10/china-taiwan-invasion-reunification-risk/

Perera, A. (July 14, 2022). Sri Lanka: Why is the country in an economic crisis? BBC. https://www.bbc.com/news/world-61028138

Radu, L., & Dobrescu, P. (2019). *Țară fără proiect. Dezvoltare inegală, subdezvoltare structurală. [A country without a project. Unequal development, structural under-development].* comunicare.ro.

RAND (2022). Russia's War in Ukraine: Insights from RAND. https://www.rand.org/latest/russia-ukraine.html

Raworth, K. (2017). *Doughnut economics. Seven ways to think like a 21st-century economist.* Random House Business Books.

Rendueles, C. (2017). De la recesiunea globală la contramișcările capitaliste [From global recession to capitalist counter-movements]. In H. Geisselberger (Ed.), *Marea Regresie. De ce trăim un moment istoric [The Great Regression: Why we witness a historical moment]*, 220–238. Editura Art.

Roșu, R., (February 16, 2021). Surpriză: Economia României a scăzut în 2020 cu numai 3,9%, un rezultat foarte bun în condițiile în care previziunile de la începutul crizei indicau o cădere de 7-8%. În T4 PIB-ul a crescut cu 5,3% față de T3 [Surprise: Romania's Economy only went down 3.9% in 2020, a very good result comparing to the forecasts that announced it would go down by 7-8%. In the fourth trimester it went up 5.3% comparing to the third strimester]. https://www.zf.ro/companii/surpriza-economia-romaniei-scazut-2020-numai-3-9-rezultat-foarte-bun-19919684

Schneider, M. (2018). *Everything for everyone. The radical tradition that is shaping the next economy.* Nation Books.

Schwab, K. (2021). Stakeholder Capitalism: Building the Future | DAVOS AGENDA 2021. https://www.youtube.com/watch?v=LQ3Q-CDoXlQ

Schwab, K. (2021). *Stakeholder capitalism. A global economy that works for progress, people, and planet.* Wiley.

Schwab, K., & Malleret, T. (2020). *COVID-19: The great reset.* Forum Publishing.

Schwab, K. (2018). *Shaping the future of the Fourth Industrial Revolution.* Currency.

Schweickart, D. (2011). *After capitalism.* Rowman & Littlefield Publishers, Inc.

Smil, V. (2017). *Energy and civilization: A history.* The MIT Press.

Smil, V. (2022). *How the world really works. A scientist's guide to our past, present, and future.* Penguin.

Smith, T. (2015). The end of one American century … and the beginning of another? In R. Westra, D. Badeen & R. Albritton (Eds.), *The future of capitalism after the financial crisis. The varieties of capitalism debate in the age of Austerity,* 79–95. Routledge.

Soddy, F. (1931). *Money versus man.* Elkin Mathews & Marrot.

STATISTA. (2021). Annual net income of Amazon.com from 2004 to 2020. https://www.statista.com/statistics/266288/annual-et-income-of-amazoncom/

Stiglitz, J.E. (2019a). Is Stakeholder Capitalism Really Back? https://www.project-syndicate.org/commentary/how-sincere-is-business-roundtable-embrace-of-stakeholder-capitalism-by-joseph-e-stiglitz-2019-08

Stiglitz, J.E. (2019b). *People, power and profits. Progressive capitalism for an age of discontent.* W.W. Norton & Company.

Stiglitz, J.E., Sen, A., & Fitoussi, J.-P. (2009). Report by the Commission on the Measurement of Economic Performance and Social Progress. www.stiglitz-sen-fitoussi.fr

Summers, K., & Tavenner, E. (June 29, 2022). What Do You Need to Know about the Overturning of Roe v. Wade? https://www.american.edu/sis/news/20220629-what-do-you-need-to-know-about-the-overturning-of-roe-v-wade.cfm

Targowski, A. (2009). *Civilization life cycle: Introduction.* IGI Global.

Tönnies, F. (1887/2001). *Community and civil society.* Cambridge University Press.

Trompenaars. F., & Hampden-Turner, C. (2021). *Culture, crisis and COVID-19: The great reset.* Cambridge Scholars Publishing.

UNHCR [The UN Refugee Agency]. (August 10, 2022). https://data.unhcr.org/en/situations/ukraine.

Van Alstyne, M.W., Parker, G.G., & Choudray, S.P. (2016). Pipelines, platforms, and the new rules of strategy. *Harvard Business Review.* https://hbr.org/2016/04/pipelines-platforms-and-the-new-rules-of-strategy.

von Schönburg, A. (2016). *Arta de a renunța cu stil sau mai puțin înseamnă mai mult [The art of quitting in style or less means more].* Baroque Books & Arts.

Weinland, D. (November 8, 2021). Xi Jinping's crackdown on Chinese tech firms will continue. *The Economist.* https://www.economist.com/the-world-ahead/2021/11/08/xi-jinpings-crackdown-on-chinese-tech-firms-will-continue

Westra, R., Badeen, D., & Albritton, R. (Eds.) (2015). *The future of capitalism after the financial crisis. The varieties of capitalism debate in the age of Austerity.* Routledge.

Wilson, H.T. (2002). *Capitalism after postmodernism. Neo-conservatism, legitimacy, and the theory of public capital.* Brill.

World Bank. (2016). World Development 2016. *Digital Dividends.* https://www.worldbank.org/en/publication/wdr2016

World Bank (2021). World Development Indicators. https://datatopics.worldbank.
  org/world-development-indicators/
Zuboff, S. (2019). *The age of surveillance capitalism. The fight for a human future at the
  new frontier of power*. Public Affairs.
Zuckerberg, M. (October 28, 2021). Connect 2021: Our vision for the metaverse.
  https://www.facebook.com/zuck/videos/1898414763675286

3 Toward further contextualization of SMEs internationalization

This chapter is intended to bring to the fore the basic premises of a globalized, interconnected world, in which the variables of business internationalization are part of a multiple system of relationship-driven approaches, each of them marking the choice of optimal strategies in a different way. Its role is all the more important as the specificity of the internationalization strategies and models adopted by organizations prescribes the managerial vision of relationship building with actors from distinct socio-cultural and national spaces, often difficult to understand and manage effectively. For this reason, a proper understanding of the internationalization variables, forces, and defining factors in the managerial decision to go international is a prerequisite for accurately contextualizing the subsequent processes. Gradual emphasis is laid on the macro-environmental factors and micro-organizational forces, setting the parameters that drive small and medium-sized enterprises (SMEs) to move out of their domestic habitat and to tap foreign markets, engage in international relationships, and assume a cross-cultural logic.

Globalization and global relationships: Backstage catalysts of business internationalization

Globalization and new socio-economic and cultural factors are profoundly influencing the way managers and leaders approach their businesses. Staying local and thinking local have become a threat to organizational survival in today's dynamic global market. Economic resorts and the profit drivers have pushed the organization out of its domestic space and placed it in the midst of global currents. Going global is no longer seen as an imperative only for the development of corporations or large organizations, but as an adaptive requirement for SMEs that need to pass the test of competitiveness (Birnleitner, 2013; Cantet al., 2015; Hagen et al., 2012).

The fundamental changes in the contemporary socio-economic environment have a strong impact on individuals, groups of people, global, and local contexts. The transformation of localities into "globalities" (in terms of de-territorialization), changes in our natural environment, the relativization of former points of reference, the influence of remote political and economic

DOI: 10.4324/9781003432326-4

phenomena on local settings, multiculturalism as a continuous pressure, intensive mobility, and the penetration of new media into our domestic spaces are more than a promise of the future, they have become a prerequisite for adaptation to the new global context.

Mattelart (2007) notes that deterritorialization and transnational mobility have become for most scholars the keys to interpreting the contemporary world. Deterritorialization defines the experience of a life lived in another area where individuals can recognize realities from their home environment (Tomlinson, 1999). Deterritorialization is experienced by international students, workers working abroad, European officials, businesspeople, showbiz artists, etc. The mobility paradigm shows that all places are interconnected in the form of different networks of relationships. Although mobility today has its roots in the migrations of a hundred years ago, Sheller and Urry (2006) speak of a new paradigm of mobility brought about by globalization, a process that attracts the attention and research interests of many analysts, theorists, and practitioners.

A simple view of globalization focuses on the inexorable, unprecedented integration of markets, nation-states, and technologies in a way in which individuals, businesses, and nation-states benefit from the opportunity to interact faster, deeper, and cheaper than in the past (Friedman, 2008, p. 30). According to Friedman (2008), a prerequisite for globalization is the existence of open economies, free trade, and competition that foster the expansion of free market capitalism, a view shared by Sahay (2013), Tuca (2013), Gurgul and Lach (2014), and Tue (2014). In this context, one of the major actors and beneficiaries of globalization is the corporation which, thanks to the opening of the market, has gone beyond the limits of the state in which it is legally registered to expand its activity anywhere in the world, becoming a multinational company. Crane et al. (2008) consider that globalization should not be seen as a historical fact, but as a constructed phenomenon that offers new dimensions to corporations. They not only influence the process of globalization but also indirectly determine or transform individuals in the global era. The authors attribute a defining role to technology and, in particular, to the accessibility that enables the communication of information, the movement of capital, and the management of resources and products in real time (Crane et al., 2008, p. 170).

Moderate approaches to globalization propose a careful reading of reality that emphasizes the rapid changes in modern society and stresses the processes related to globalization, such as the massive restructuring of societies, governmental institutions, and the global order. In other words, globalization generates "new patterns of social stratification" within and between states, stimulating the emergence of new forms of relationships, interactions, and socialization that transcend political boundaries – the territorial boundaries of national cultures and social spaces are blurred by the emergence of recent technologies based on modern values such as speed, instantaneity, and universality (Dobrescu, 2007).

A similar view is espoused by Nye and Keohane (1989), the originators and promoters of the concept of "complex interdependence" which explains the use of multiple channels of action in inter-state, trans-state, and transnational relations and the prioritization of issues based on their overall, global impact. The new international and global relations are driven by the constant reconfiguration of contemporary global issues such as terrorism, imperialist and dominationist tendencies of some world powers, environmental problems, health and social crises (i.e., COVID-19), organized crime, etc. The complexity and extent of these international issues lead to an increasing openness to cooperation, to effective collaboration between states and between people, putting into practice the principle of a single voice on the international stage.

Globalization has constantly highlighted interdependence and interconnectedness, transforming them into societal alternatives of being and acting. According to Sklair (2007, p. 98), the architects of globalization are part of the transnational capitalist class (TCC). Transnationality has two meanings: its members have a global rather than a local perspective and operate transnationally in accordance with their current professional activity. Thus, the TCC has four central dimensions: the corporate dimension (includes those who own or control multinational companies and their subsidiaries), the state dimension (includes bureaucrats and supra-state politicians), the technocratic dimension (includes professionals who act globally), and consumerist dimension (includes the media and traders). Individuals migrate between the four dimensions, but together they form the power elite or the power of the elite. As an overview, the transnational character of the capitalist class is determined by the economic interests of its members becoming increasingly globally interconnected and outweighing nationally contextualized interests. Ownership and shares held within corporations are also becoming global following the logic of profit growth for all shareholders (Amaeshi & Olufemi, 2009, p. 225).

In Sklair's (2007) conception, the only concept that matters in this vein is the market in which the company operates, which often no longer corresponds to the territory of a particular state. The TCC seeks to exert economic control at the level of the workplace, national and international politics, and everyday life through consumerist practices and rhetoric. Members of the TCC also have similar lifestyles and attend business schools in Western Europe or North America, which ensures the formation of uniform ideologies and a preference for exclusive clubs and destinations. They see themselves as citizens of their home country as well as of global society and migrate between the four dimensions with ease, the glue being the "cultural ideology of consumerism," a fundamental value that keeps the system intact and allows for a variety of alternatives. "The four dimensions of the TCC perform complementary functions for integration in each region, country, city, company or community. Achieving these goals is facilitated by national agencies and organizations connected in a complex web of junctions" (Sklair, 2007, p. 100).

In Stiglitz's view (2008, p. 165), transnational corporations are not only rich, but also hold political power. The weapon used by corporations against governments is relocation, which entails the loss of the benefits of globalization in developing countries: technology transfer, direct investment, better prices, higher quality of products, higher living standards, lower inflation, and interest rates. At this point, a pertinent question is how the damage can be minimized and the net contribution to host countries maximized, especially as globalization must lead to development, not just in rich countries, but in all countries.

Stiglitz (2008, p. 180) believes that certain measures should be implemented especially in the home countries of corporations, i.e., in industrialized and advanced countries to limit potential abuses by corporations: reducing the level of corruption by adopting and enforcing national laws that sanction any immoral corporate behavior in international operations; eradicating banking secrecy that creates a tax haven for illegal gains; improving corporate law by holding corporate leaders accountable for their actions, so that they no longer hide behind the corporate name, etc.

SMEs internationalization at the crossroads: Opportunities versus constraints

Since the 1990s, "the transnational approach has provided a new analytical framework that sheds light on the increasing intensity and scope of circular flows of people, goods, information and symbols enhanced by international labour migration" (Vertovec, 2009, pp. 13–14). Transnational activities bring together global media consumption, transnational communication via the Internet, joining transnational networks of professionals, starting transnational businesses, activating in transnational organizations, participating in transnational events, cross-border cooperation between organizations, the emergence of cross-border social capital, labor relations, and international social relations (Pulignano, 2009). These transnational activities are either regular or occasional, their importance being associated with the degree to which they produce significant transformations, in the sense of social and cultural change of those involved in transnationalism, immigrants or indigenous people, communities, or nations (Vertovec, 2009).

In recent literature, transnationalism is defined in terms of specific everyday activities, business and capital flows, networks of cross-border relations, reconstruction of space, and identity beyond the nation-state (Brüggemann & Königslöw, 2009; Mattelart, 2007; Vertovec, 2009). Adjacent to this, transnationalism targets social space in the sense of multiple, multidimensional, and interconnected networks of social relations through which ideas, practices, and resources are unevenly exchanged, organized, and transformed (Levitt & Glick Schiller, 2004). In the context of flow dynamics, national borders do not implicitly overlap with social borders. In this sense, socio-economic and communication sciences have the task of defining the transnational social space that connects actors internationally, directly and indirectly, through a broad spectrum of economic, political, and social processes. In the view of Portes et al. (1999), there are three main forms of transnationalism: economic (corporations and transnational elites), political (migrants and non-state organizations), and socio-cultural (other transnational activities and practices), all of which are organized as a dyad: bottom-up transnationalism (designates activities of ordinary people) and top-down transnationalism (includes state and non-state agents).

In the same vein, the typology proposed by Vertovec (2009, pp. 1–4) includes: transnationalism at the top (global political, media, and capital institutions) *versus* transnationalism at the bottom (grassroots, local activities); narrow transnationalism comprising institutionalized and continuous activities *versus* broad transnationalism occasioned by spontaneous links; large transnationalism which includes the state and the economy *versus* small transnationalism which targets the family and household level; linear transnationalism based on emotional ties to fellow citizens *versus* resource-based transnationalism that focuses on the opportunities and constraints offered by the global labor market and the accumulation of economic resources needed for cross-border activity; extended transnationalism which includes both regular and occasional activities *versus* strict transnationalism which includes only regular participation; central transnationalism which assumes specific and predictable participation around an area of social life *versus* generalized transnationalism which targets occasional practices across a wide range of spheres of interest.

While the transnationalism of large corporations has often been seen as a fundamental point of globalization, there has recently been a shift in perspective due to the important role that SMEs have to play in an unprecedentedly dynamic globalized economy. Thus, the dichotomy between globalization and internationalization of business should not be seen in terms of a static delimitation, but as two dynamic elements and processes with the same frame of reference.

From a conceptual perspective, both globalization and internationalization are multidimensional constructs, expressed in multiple forms at the organizational level. As early as 1996, Julien noted that 85% of small firms were operating with a strategy that was in line with the new conditions of market globalization (p. 57). In this respect, he gave examples from various studies he had conducted which highlighted purchases and sales of goods and services from or in other foreign countries, investments in other countries, and cross-border collaborations between organizations. Julien (1996, pp. 57–59) supported the idea that internationalization strategies of SMEs were an inherent part of the logic of globalization, while Ocloo et al. (2014, p. 2) considered SMEs to be "the backbone of the private sector at all levels of developing countries."

In the current period, SMEs have become a milestone in the analysis of international relations, with the requirement for international conduct stemming from the very desire of the organization to survive or progress. Versatile business contexts have begun to call for prompt adaptive measures to preserve competitiveness, lower costs, and expand the market (Cannon & Perreault, 1999). The global marketplace plays a key role in the emergence and growth of international business relationships as it challenges organizations to act appropriately in the transnational arena. A simple glance at the literature shows that there is a vast array of incentives for SMEs to internationalize their businesses (Cannon & Perreault, 1999; Harvie, 2008; Nicolescu & Nicolescu, 2016; Vătămănescu et al., 2014a, 2014b): access to large or developing markets; exploiting first-mover advantage in a new market; the opportunity to follow the competition closely; access to better, cheaper, more resources; reducing production or distribution costs; collaboration within transnational business networks that can generate a major competitive advantage; avoiding customs duties, etc. These factors range from what Wyer and Smallbone (1999) called the "opportunistic behavior" of SMEs, to the approach of Majocchi and Zucchella (2003) who stress the importance of careful analysis of the risks specific to new markets.

On this point, Majocchi and Zucchella (2003) have insisted that the acceptance of SMEs as mere clones of large organizations should be avoided. Moreover, the authors believe that SMEs focus on markets that are similar or have geographical proximity, which allows them to understand and manage them in an efficient way. Managers running SMEs, however, have to carefully manage different pressures in the context of resource scarcity (Harvie, 2008; Majocchi & Zucchella, 2003): the major costs of internationalization (e.g., personnel costs, logistics, management of new locations, etc.); the need for continuous professionalization (management is a profession, a science in itself, not just the art of management); the need for control, informed market choice (management must first develop extensive research-documentation to properly understand the specifics of new markets); policy and asset adaptation (management must demonstrate flexibility and adaptability in terms of marketing strategies, product, pricing, promotion, distribution policies); monitoring of operational flows (management should monitor and evaluate international flows accordingly, especially in the early stages of internationalization); and contingency management (management must have the ability to react quickly to unforeseen situations and even proactively address potential risk situations).

In conclusion, SMEs are likely to manage similar challenges as large organizations and corporations, even though they do not have the same resources. In this regard, Hampton and Rowell (2010, 2013) have analyzed the rationale for internationalization of small businesses, highlighting that they have to deal with the opportunities and risks generated by a highly competitive international business environment in a constant manner.

In the same vein, Senik et al. (2014, pp. 35–36) propose a categorical approach to the constraints that SMEs (especially those in developing countries) frequently face: lack of resources (qualified human resources, skills and knowledge needed for R&D projects on new markets, tools to reach new customers); financial constraints (inability to acquire state-of-the-art technology, insufficient funds available, difficulty and length of time to access loans); the attitudes of entrepreneurs or managers (negative attitudes generated by blaziness, fear of risk, low intrinsic and extrinsic motivation, lack of enthusiasm for new challenges, self-sufficiency in relation to the status quo); limited firm capacity (morally worn out, unsound products, physically worn out technology, lack of R&D departments to innovate products and types of services); political interference (trade barriers imposed by the countries concerned, unstimulating legislation, heavily regulated industries); managerial incompetence (difficulty in generating credibility, lack of managerial skills in an international context, mobility of the workforce, including managers); psychological distance (cultural, linguistic, social, and value differences); differences in government policy (between home and target countries, poor information from foreign authorities, major policy changes, bureaucracy); parallel management of local and international operations (paradigm shifts and adjustments in thinking patterns, greater need for documentation and knowledge, proactivity and action); competition with other firms (the need to innovate, to create competitive products and services, to position oneself in relation to the competition).

It has become obvious that modern SMEs are facing dramatic changes and innovation flows that can influence and even determine the progress of the business environment (Nicolescu & Nicolescu, 2012). In this sense, the management model of SMEs is progressively changing in line with the logic of both local and global markets, under the pressure of fierce competition. As the business environment evolves, so does the business model adopted by modern managers. The ability and art of managing and adapting to contemporary changes in outlook should no longer be seen as a challenge, but as a survival valve for most businesses. In other words, SMEs are at the crossroads between external forces and internal changes, and a proactive attitude and harmonization with the pace of the global market are necessary conditions for creating or maintaining a competitive advantage. Going beyond national borders and cultural differences is a prerequisite for staying in the game, in the league of the organizations willing and doing their best to succeed.

SMEs internationalization through the lens of knowledge (and) networks

The emergence of the knowledge-based economy, globalization, and its economic intricacies, coupled with EU's objective to developing a strong Single Market for the EU Member States to operate on, are factors that push SMEs from the EU to look outside of the national borders and domestic markets to do business, thus becoming subject to internationalization.

As a result, the internationalization of SMEs is a highly relevant topic for the EU's economy and supports its mission, being mentioned as such in the most recent programmatic documents regarding the EU-27 economy SME growth. The objectives EU-27 have regarding SME internationalization are connected to facilitating access to the Single Market to more SMEs from all the State Members, and to fostering exports to non-EU states, in order to diminish the dependency of European SMEs to the Single Market (European Commission, 2020).

In becoming effective internationally, SME managers need to deal with transnational and multicultural experiences, build relationships, create and extract value, listen and observe, coordinate others so as to be competitive in a turbulent environment. The activities they will carry out must subscribe to creativity, innovation, and the quality of strong but flexible strategies and projects that are likely to ensure the long-term effectiveness of organizations (Gomes et al., 2010).

The literature defines internationalization as a process that companies undertake, expanding their operations from their domestic markets to one or more foreign markets (Javalgi et al., 2003). The purpose of internationalization is business growth (Ghauri & Buckley, 1993). Thus, internationalization is an "increasing involvement in international operations" (Welch & Luostarinen, 1988, p. 84), and it impacts the company's activity, structure, and resource use, strategy, as, in the process of internationalization, the company must adapt to new environments (Calof & Beamish, 1995).

For SMEs, which are usually first developed in a single country, the process of internationalization poses unique challenges and has unique features (Ruzzier et al., 2006). Perhaps the most significant of these features refers to the fact that, for SMEs, internationalization is considered an entrepreneurial activity (Knight, 2001; Korsakienė & Tvaronavičienė, 2012; Lu & Beamish, 2001).

SMEs internationalization is defined at EU-level through a *Guide for supporting the SMEs in their internationalization endeavors* (European Union, 2014, p. 10), as encompassing all the activities that place an SME in a significant relationship to a foreign partner: exports, imports, direct foreign investments, international subcontracting, and international technical cooperation. The partners may be both from the EU or not. An SME associated with licensing and franchising services or products, with doing export or import, with direct investments on foreign markets, with attracting foreign investors, with collaborating with foreign partners for R&D, with being part of a national or global value chain, with the purpose of becoming active on foreign markets is considered as having international activity, thus being enrolled in internationalization (DIW ECON, July 27, 2018). Similarly, Manolova et al. (2002) advanced the following types of international activities that an SME can perform, which are synonyms to its operation mode: import, direct export, export through an intermediary, solo venture direct investment, joint venture direct investment, licensing of a product or service, contracting, franchise, and other international activities.

On a theoretical level, during the last decades, studying SMEs internationalization has been one of the focal points of the international business (IB) research community, as well as of the entrepreneurs and policymakers (Amal & Filho, 2010). SMEs are considered adaptable and agile, both characteristics leading scholars to conclude that these companies can manage knowledge at organizational and individual levels in a successful manner, and to respond in appropriate ways to the challenges of the business environment (Handzic, 2006).

However, it is known that SMEs compete with various players on the global market, many of which being multinational enterprises (MNEs) who have access to unique resources ranging from technology and knowledge to people, and to finances, that are impossible for SMEs to attain, or at least impossible to amass on a comparable scale (Gabrielsson et al., 2008a, 2008b; Gorgos et al., 2019; Hutchinson & Quintas, 2008; Vătămănescu et al., 2016, 2017a).

A report by OECD (2017, p. 5) mentions the "access to strategic resources, such as skills, knowledge networks, and finance, and on public investments in areas such as education and training, innovation and infrastructure" as the main constraints of SMEs that aim at conquering foreign markets. The scarcity of resources in strategic areas, ranging from finance to management skills and employees, is also mentioned by Maldonado-Guzmán et al. (2017).

To be competitive in the international arena, SMEs need to access strategic knowledge, and to develop internal structures and procedures that would support their innovative endeavors and aid them in solving the complex issues that are prone to appear in the business environment (Kianto et al., 2018; Kim & Lui, 2015; Le, 2017). This is a daring task, as SMEs usually do not collaborate with education and training institutions (OECD, 2015), and SMEs managers usually need to develop their managerial skills and expertise in unique ways, to respond to the particularities of operating in foreign markets (OECD, 2017). The *Annual Report on European SMEs 2017/2018* (European Commission, 2018a) explains that SMEs in the EU often had to face substantial difficulties, as they did not have the necessary knowledge, on many hierarchical levels, including the management, and they also did not know how to capitalize the knowledge they had to develop. Accessing the best practices related to the knowledge repertoire poses a tremendous difficulty to SMEs that seek to embark in international ventures (Vătămănescu et al., 2019), and the lack of effective management systems and tools – prevalent in the SME sector – give rise to additional concerns (Garagorri, 2016; OECD, 2013; Pauw & Chan, 2018).

SMEs depend upon access to networks and partners to innovate (OECD, 2017, p. 7). Giannacourou et al. (2015) mention that the lack of resources pushes SMEs that want to access the opportunities offered by the markets to put an emphasis on becoming members of networks and to embrace informal relationships, with the underlying desire of innovating at the structural level. Partnering with other private companies can lead SMEs to having an increased business performance and help lower the environmental risk (Pauw & Chan, 2018). Kmieciak and Michna (2018) further explain that alliances with business partners support the actors' innovative capabilities and help them integrate the knowledge they acquire. Knowledge-sharing mechanisms among business partners are catalysts of performance and welfare for all SMEs involved (Chen et al., 2010; Lee et al., 2013; Vătămănescu & Alexandru, 2018; Wang & Lin, 2013).

Factors, forms, and models of SMEs internationalization

Factors

The propensity of SMEs to tap international markets is based on both external and internal factors. External factors are related to the extra-organizational environment, while internal factors are influenced by the specific characteristics of the organization assessing the possibility to internationalize. At this point, the management's decision to open up to international collaborations is directly related to the organization's mission and objectives, their effective fulfillment, and the possibility to benefit from a conducive international environment and optimal conditions in the targeted markets (Birnleitner, 2013; Harrison, 2011).

Among the major elements ("vault" factors) that determine the decision to internationalize business are the rationality of organizations, the changing international environment, and the indicators of the target countries (Harrison, 2011, pp. 4–6). For most SMEs, profitability is at the top of the decision-making equation. The opportunity to make a profit by selling products in a foreign market can become attractive, especially when the domestic market has a low growth trend, is saturated, or there are regulatory barriers (Jones & Coviello, 2005). Therefore, significant growth of a business can only take place by expanding internationally, which allows the organization to gain a solid international reputation. Profitability is highly dependent on competitiveness, so the internationalization strategy is likely to become a form of cost-cutting in a competitive international market (Birnleitner, 2013; Ravelomanana et al., 2015). Implicitly, it can lead to increased output and lower unit cost. Access to international production allows sourcing components and raw materials from foreign markets, relocating production operations, outsourcing business functions that can be performed at a lower cost outside the home country (*offshoring*) (Brassington & Pettitt, 2000; Búrca et al., 2004; Cant et al., 2015).

Interested in schematically capturing the logic and characteristics of SMEs internationalization, Senik et al. (2014) developed a descriptive scheme that presents the main defining factors in the internationalization process. In their opinion, there are two classes of factors impacting the internationalization of SMEs: breaking factors and catalyst factors. Breaking factors include internal factors, such as organizational capabilities, the entrepreneurs'/general managers'/entrepreneurial capabilities, company-specific location, government incentives and support, and barriers and challenges, which consist of resources (inside the firm), rules and laws, government policies, standards and requirements, attitude, willingness of entrepreneurs/key managers, business guidelines (in the local market). Catalyst factors are further divided in two categories: external factors and internal factors. The former comprise Industrialization programmes, government policies, attractiveness of foreign markets, demand from other markets, economic integration, and barriers and challenges, which refer to International standards – adequacy and preparedness; host countries which cover rules, laws, policies, requirements; psychic distance referring to cultural, social, linguistic, faith-related, and business behaviors and practices. The latter mainly encompass the organizational capacity and the human, material, financial and informational resources of the firm. The internal and external factors influence networking, a factor which refers to governmental and non-governmental institutions, other organizational players, personal contacts, and entrepreneurs/general managers build business networks. Networking allows the company to engage in international learning, knowledge, and awareness. The dynamics between the breaking factors and the catalytic converters (or factors) create the basic conditions for the internationalization process of SMEs. These conditions include motivational factors, market coverage, internationalization patterns, and market entry decisions.

As highlighted, SMEs choose to embrace internationalization due to many factors (Belniak, 2015). Bartlett and Ghoshal (2000a, 2000b) list traditional motivations and emerging motivations. Traditional motivations include the need to secure scarce raw materials and other supplies, the desire to access low-cost production factors, and the need to conquer other markets, to leverage their existing intrinsic competitive advantage. The emerging motivations of internationalization press companies to develop their international operations to survive in a particular sector, and derive from economic, social, and technological developments.

A model proposed by Daszkiewicz and Wach (2014) cites the existence of push factors, pull factors, chance factors, and entrepreneurial factors. To them, *the push factors* refer to the saturation of the domestic market, which stimulated the company to seek new potential customers, outside of its traditional environment, but may also refer to the intensity of the competition on the domestic market, or to the overproduction. *The pull factors* are specific to companies that seek to make use of economies of scale, in search for more profits. *The chance factors* refer to the fortuitous situation when a foreign company places an order, expanding the market for the company without the company seeking foreign clients, and *the entrepreneurial factors* are considered to manifest as a natural step in the development of the company, after conquering the domestic market. Another noticeable conceptualization of the factors that propel an SME on the international market is advanced by Hollensen (2007), who mentions the following decisive factors: internal factors, desired mode characteristics, transaction-specific factors, and external factors.

For Belniak (2015), the basic factors favoring the internationalization of businesses shall be presented as:

1 external factors, including domestic environment factors, regional factors, and international environment factors. The theoretical approach of international marketing is the most suitable to study those factors;
2 intermediate factors, including the industry-related factors (which shall be studied through a strategic approach), and the role of formal and informal networks in the internationalization process (which shall be studied through the networking approach);
3 internal factors, including enterprise specifics (to be studied under the demographic, biographic, and ethnographic approaches in management), the firm resource and competences – including resources *stricto sensu*, innovation potential, and competences and capabilities (to be investigated under the resource-based and competences approach), organizational structure and its changes (structural approach), the internationalization strategy (strategic approach), and the attitude and skills of the entrepreneur/manager (international entrepreneurship approach).

The changing international environment takes into account the socio-cultural, economic, political, geopolitical, and legal context of the 21st century. Dynamism and permanent adjustments at the international and even global levels have reconfigured the opportunities for SMEs to grow with catalysts such as the reduction of trade barriers between countries and the gradual liberalization of national trade and investment policies (Aldakhil & Nataraja, 2014; Birnleitner, 2013; Bo Bernhard, 2007). Correlatively, significant developments in manufacturing and information technology have brought substantial benefits for the generalization of economic growth, including in developing countries.

Hollensen (2007, p. 298) mentions four factors that influence the entry mode decision: internal factors, external factors, desired mode, and transaction-specific factors. Internal factors include firm size, its international experience, the product's complexity, and the product's differentiation advantage. These factors play a positive influence on the entry mode decision. External factors such as market size and growth, direct and indirect trade barriers, and the small number of relevant export intermediaries available can act as drivers of internationalization, while the sociocultural distance between home and host country, the country risk/demand uncertainty, and the intensity of competition may play out as reverse forces. Internationalization is also supported by the desired mode, when it takes the form of a desire for control, and negatively impacted when we observe risk aversion and a propensity toward flexibility. Transaction-specific factors such as the tactic nature of know-how, the opportunistic behavior of the firm, and their interest in transaction costs also bear a positive influence on the company's internationalization efforts.

If the international environment influences internationalization decisions generically, the choice of a particular country as a destination market is based on the conditions it offers. Among the most important factors to consider are economic and political stability, culture, and available institutions and resources (Búrca et al., 2004; Harrison, 2011; Hollensen, 2001; Roberts, 2005). Both tangible values of the country, such as transport and communication infrastructure, and intangible values, such as education and skills, technology and innovation capacity, intellectual property, and business networks, are considered. The comparison of alternative locations, both between and within countries, also takes into account government policies, such as the level of taxes or financial incentives that the state can offer to foreign investors, bureaucratic obstacles, corruption, and mafia activities. All of these are likely to drive away foreign investors who want to develop their businesses in a balanced environment, without sudden and unfounded moves.

In terms of factors specific to SMEs, attracting new markets (in large developed countries or emerging economies with growth potential) can be a defining factor in the internationalization process (Dong & Glaister, 2007). A potential example of this can be the establishment of manufacturing units within a regulated economic region (such as the European Union) which facilitates access to the entire market of that region (Harrison, 2011). In some cases, entering a market with an emerging economy brings first mover advantages and the possibility to dominate the market before rivals establish themselves in the same segment. However, situations are not excluded where the best strategy is to follow direct competition so as not to be left irreversibly behind.

Another important factor for choosing a foreign market is access to resources that can be natural, social, cultural, and human (Bo Bernhard, 2007; Ravelomanana et al., 2015). However, there is an important trend in the modern world, namely that resources are considered a secondary catalyst for the internationalization of business as highly transferable knowledge and technology have gained in value over natural resources in very many industries. For SMEs, intellectual capital (human, structural, and relational) is one of the fundamental catalysts for internationalization as they are often materially and financially constrained (Bell et al., 2007; Nicolescu et al., 2015; Vătămănescu et al., 2019).

Reducing costs by outsourcing operations internationally or by relocating production units of SMEs has become common practice (Cant et al., 2015). However, cheap labor is not an attraction for all types of businesses, especially where highly skilled employees are needed in certain areas but would not be willing to work for low wages in the context of a global business and organizational infrastructure.

Forms

Focusing on the forms of international expansion, these range from direct and indirect export and import, foreign direct investment, licensing and franchising, joint ventures, strategic alliances, and collaborative strategies, to internationalization of production – outsourcing of services or relocation of production capacities (Gomes et al., 2010; Harisson, 2011; Wild et al., 2003). In a more detailed approach, Hill (2007, pp. 320–323) considers that there are three major decisions that management must consider before entering an international market: (a) which market is most suitable for its approach in terms of attractiveness and balance of benefits, costs, and risks; (b) when international expansion should take place: some SMEs are pioneers in their sector/industry, while others internationalize later, after other similar firms have taken this step; in general, SMEs that are pioneers have higher operating costs due to lack of experience in a foreign market, while SMEs that expand internationally later benefit from the lessons learned and best practices of the former; (c) the extent to which international expansion should take place (level of expansion): SMEs can expand into several markets at once from the outset, or they can opt for just one foreign market at first to limit uncontrolled exposure to more risks and to learn progressively about foreign markets.

Correlating the three variables, Hill (2007, pp. 624–631) discusses six different forms of internationalization that are at the discretion of managers, stating that there is no right or wrong way to internationalize, only a rational way based on internal or external factors that influence the work of organizations (e.g., age and size of the firm, available resources, constraints of economic, political, social, cultural, technological environments). These forms of internationalization are exports, turnkey projects, licensing, franchising, joint ventures, and representative offices. Of these, turnkey projects, franchising, and representative offices are most commonly found in corporations as they require the mobilization of substantial human, material, and financial resources when entering a foreign market; the creation of operational teams of experts contracted for the medium and long term; and the possession of superior know-how and a rapid response capacity to manage the opportunities and risks associated with internationalization (Hill, 2007, p. 627). At the antipode, exporting, licensing, and joint ventures allow for lower initial investment and greater flexibility, as shown in the SME-specific forms summarized in Table 3.1.

Table 3.1 SME-specific forms of internationalization (adapted from Hill, 2007)

No.	Form of internationalization	Features
1.	**Export**	• It is the most common internationalization strategy for SMEs, given the constraints of resources, knowledge, experience, and skills.
		Advantages:
		• allows to avoid production costs in the host country;
		• the company benefits from new markets for the goods produced or services provided;

(*Continued*)

Table 3.1 (Continued)

No.	Form of internationalization	Features
		• the company will progressively gain knowledge and experience in the host market. **Disadvantages:** • transport and distribution costs are higher; • protectionist policies of host countries (tariff barriers, protectionist laws) can be objectified.
2.	**Licensing**	• It is a form of arrangement whereby one entity grants another entity the right to use an intangible asset for a specified period of time for a predetermined fee. • For example, it is found in the pharmaceutical field where patents, inventions, and formulas are most commonly encountered. **Advantages:** • is a suitable foreign market entry route for firms that do not have the capital to produce outside their home country or where government policies prevent them from entering a particular market. **Disadvantages:** • little control of the licensor over production, marketing, product development, and sales strategies; • often prevents a firm from coordinating its strategic transnational actions by exploiting profits earned in one country to support competitive strategies in another; • the know-how of the licensing firm can be used later as a competitive advantage by the other entity.
3.	**Joint enterprise**	• Represents an entity formed by two or more independent firms working together. The firms agree to work together, sharing revenues and costs as well as control of the new entity. **Advantages:** • can be conceived as a project or as a long-term relationship whereby the component companies pool complementary skills; • the commitments made by each party are established at the outset, with the internationalizing firm benefiting from the knowledge of the host country firm (competition, culture, language, political and business systems) and the costs and risks are shared. **Disadvantages:** • can be affected by conflicts between component parts when differences of opinion arise over development strategies.

Models

Internationalization is one of the most complex strategies that a company can undertake (Fernández & Nieto, 2005). Studying the internationalization strategies of SMEs has been the usual centerpiece of the literature on the subject (Solberg & Durrieu, 2006; Tuppura et al., 2008). The strategies employed by SMEs focus on developing their international businesses and the approaches vary (Ruzzier et al., 2007), but numerous recent studies (Bennet et al., 2015; Edvardsson & Durst, 2013; Ferraris et al., 2017; Le, 2017; Vătămănescu, Gorgos, & Alexandru, 2018; Vrontis et al., 2017) focus on the paramount role of capitalizing intangible assets within SMEs.

Regardless of the operation mode and of the chosen internationalization strategy, the decisions regarding the expansion are taken after a process of learning about the targeted markets, while the success in the current activities helps build the engagement for developing the business on each market (Johanson & Vahlne, 1977). There is no consensus in the literature regarding the ways in which the expansion of a company's operations from one market to more markets takes place (Dominquez, 2018), yet it is widely accepted that today markets are networks of relationships where companies are connected with each other through invisible wires; the place that a company occupies in that network being the one that determines the degree of success of its operations, while establishing trust-based relationships and creating knowledge being key elements to understanding the process (Johanson & Vahlne, 2009).

Building on the various forms of SME internationalization outlined above, the literature has advanced multiple models of internationalization. The development of new models started from the identification of areas of vulnerability of previous models that require more complex interpretative parameters in line with the dynamics and continuous reconfiguration of reference environments (Birnleitner, 2013). From this perspective, the existing studies have proposed several taxonomies that classify internationalization models according to distinct criteria (objective vs. subjective view, static vs. dynamic view, planned vs. action orientation, etc.).

According to Sorensen (1997, pp. 4–5), there are three groups of models specific to business internationalization: progressive, contingency, and interactive models. The central features of each model have been centralized by Sorensen and are the subject of Table 3.2.

A closer look at the taxonomy proposed by Sorensen (1997) brings to the fore some lineaments of internationalization patterns. These perspectives fundamentally differ in what concerns the conceptualization of the internationalization phenomenon and may be broadly classified as theories that consider internationalization as a gradual process, and theories that consider internationalization to be a strategic choice, implying that the company chooses to move on the fast lane toward international exposure, without a correlation to the age of the company's development or to its previous experience on the domestic market being present.

Table 3.2 Main coordinates of internationalization models (adapted from Sorensen, 1997)

Groups of scientific models/dimensions	A. Progressive models	B. Contingency models	C. Interactive model
Sub-groups	A1. The Uppsala Model	B1. Transaction cost model	C1. Network-based model
	A2. Product cycle model	B2. The eclectic model	
Objective vs. subjective vision	Objective	Objective	Subjective
Static vs. dynamic perspective	Static comparison	Static	Dynamic
Planned orientation vs. action	Planned	Planned	Interaction

The progressive models of business internationalization start from the premise that internationalization is a gradual process, taking place over several stages. This category includes the Uppsala model, based on learning and knowledge, which argues that lack of knowledge at organizational level, is a major barrier to initiating and growing international action. On this level, openness to the assimilation of new knowledge and to coherent learning programmes is a major factor for the international expansion of organizations (Lakomaa, 2009).

The classic theory on internationalization is broadly known as the Uppsala model, or the gradual internationalization, and was developed in the early 1970s. The Uppsala model considers that companies begin to expand internationally by irregularly exporting through independent representatives, then by establishing overseas subsidiaries to take care of sales, and eventually by opening production units abroad (Johanson & Wiedersheim-Paul, 1975). The theory was updated a few times: by Johanson and Vahlne in 1977 and 2009 and by Vahlne and Johanson in the 1990s in 2013 and 2017. Gradual internationalization (Johanson & Vahlne, 1977; Welch & Luostarinen, 1988) is a result of the organic development of the company and takes shape as the company accumulates knowledge by learning through experience (Zahra et al., 2000) and by leveraging the work experience of the managers, including their experience in management positions with other countries, as well as resource fungibility (Sapienza et al., 2006).

Overall, the Uppsala model is characterized by three key aspects. First, the model is a benchmark for analyzing how companies manage to learn and share information during the internationalization process. The knowledge assimilated is both objective and market-specific and is acquired through constant experience and the exploitation of opportunities on a global scale. Second, the model shows that sound knowledge limits the risks of entering new markets and strengthens access to opportunities in as yet untapped markets. Third, the model explains which points are relevant in the selection of target markets as the internationalization of business is usually gradual, starting from investigating countries with psychological and geographical proximity and continuing with testing unknown markets.

The I-model is similar to the U-model and differs only through the number of steps that the internationalization process is expected to take, Bilkey and Tesar (1977) arguing for six phases, while Reid (1983) identifying eight. Following the steps of classic internationalization theory, Coudounaris (2018) proposes six pathways for business internationalization, based on the attitudes of top management, arguing that the internationalization model adopted by a company is strongly impacted by the managerial attitudes toward international activity. The pathways envisage non-exporters (NEs), traditional small exporters (TSEs), traditional medium exporters (TMEs), accelerated medium exporters (AMEs), born globals (BGs), and declining exporters (DEs).

The second sub-category within the progressive models of business internationalization is the product cycle model. The foundation of this theoretical perspective is the association between the successive stages of internationalization and those of the product cycle. According to Sorensen (1997), the product cycle model has three phases – the new product phase, the developed product phase, and the standardized product phase. Exceeding a certain phase entails better knowledge and cost reduction. For this reason, going through all phases of the process makes it easier for small and medium-sized companies to gain valuable experience and additional skills for expanding into new markets.

The second major category of business internationalization models concerns contingency models which include two sub-categories – the *transaction cost model* and the *eclectic model* (Hollensen, 2008, p. 35). These argue that the process of business internationalization is based on the forces of foreign markets, which makes it difficult for an organization to approach exiting an international market in a static manner. The imperative that contingency models put forward is that businesspeople need to treat their organizations as open systems and need to ensure that they have more options. Management has a critical role to play in addressing new markets, leveraging the strength of their own business. At this level, the ability to analyze the configuration of the business environment and the appropriate internationalization alternatives is an indispensable requirement for optimal decisions taken by SME managers.

The basic premise is that the internationalization of the firm arises from both proactive and reactive foundations (Hollensen, 2008, p. 35). Among the proactive reasons, suitable for SMEs, the following can be mentioned: profitability and growth targets; technological skills/unique products; economies of scale in production; cost reduction; foreign market opportunities; managerial ambition; access to resources.

The reactive motives that catalyze the internationalization drive of SMEs can be structured as follows (Hollensen, 2008, p. 35): competitive pressures in the domestic market; a small and saturated domestic market; decrease in sales; overproduction/overcapacity; the lighter regulations of other markets; expanding sales of seasonal products; proximity to desirable customers.

Focusing on the transaction cost model, it is assumed that the SME will internationalize if the transaction cost (cost of coordination, contracting, documentation, etc.) is within the profitability limits, with the actual prices of the goods or services provided being evaluated in the context of all the costs assumed for internationalization (Hollensen, 2008). The transaction cost is driven by the divergent interests and opportunistic behavior of exporters. Thus, the decision to internationalize is made after a meaningful analysis of transaction costs. When the analysis indicates that trading in a foreign market has a lower cost, the organization will outsource through different modes of entry into the target market (export, licensing, subcontracting, joint venture). When partners can be integrated into the internal structure of the organization at a low cost, the organization will resort to mergers and acquisitions (Hollensen, 2008; Sorensen, 1997).

In turn, the eclectic model makes explicit the conditions of SME internationalization when foreign direct investment is used instead of exporting. A company's propensity to engage in international production is enhanced by the advantages of management, location, and ownership of the internationalization project (Rubaeva, 2010; Hollensen, 2008).

The third category is represented by interactive business internationalization models. The assumption is that it is the actors who have sustained and longstanding business interactions and relationships that actually form the real market. In the interpretative framework specific to this category of models, business networks are a key driver for the internationalization of organizations, with business and personal relationships between businesspeople being a key stimulating factor. The place that a particular organization occupies within the network has an important impact on the network model and the access that the organization has to network resources (Rubaeva, 2010).

The process of internationalization as understood by business networks is carried out through three different strategies: expansion, penetration, and coordination (Hollensen, 2008; Sorensen, 1997). *Expansion* refers to the fact that the organization establishes links with organizations and networks in new markets, *penetration* focuses on developing relationships as a prerequisite for joining the international network, while *coordination* aims to improve links within different networks and markets. At this level, the internationalization of a particular business or organization is determined by the position it gains within the network and the global context.

According to Hollensen (2008), from the perspective of when SMEs decide to internationalize, there are certain differentiating characteristics that mark their path to foreign markets. As an *"early starter,"* the organization has no established business links with foreign organizations. It is likely to take gradual exploratory action in relation to foreign markets through an agent or by setting up a local subsidiary. As a *"lonely international,"* the organization has already gained sufficient experience in foreign countries, but its competitors and customers still have a low degree of internationalization (DOI). At this point, the organization's mission is to develop new business relationships and strengthen existing ones.

As a *late starter*, the organization is still locally focused, while competitors in the market have already joined international business networks and established partnerships with foreign players. The disadvantage for late starters lies in the difficulty of identifying as yet untapped partners and establishing a competitive position in an already coagulated market. As an international among *others*, the organization has the opportunity to take advantage of its position in a given network to approach new networks and establish new partnerships. As international business networks evolve at a rapid pace, organizations need to be flexible enough to adapt to changes in their markets. Thus, a good coordination of members within networks of interest should be considered as an added value for the organization's gains.

Bell et al. (2001) have developed another empirical study showing different patterns of internationalization of SMEs. They showed that, after a good position in the domestic market, some companies focused all their attention on internationalization. They had no specific interest in operating in foreign markets until a critical incident occurred. Sudden internationalization is due to significant events that bring additional resources to the firm and facilitate a focused internationalization process (Bell et al., 2003). The authors have termed these companies "globally reborn," most likely because the most common event leading to rapid internationalization was a change in ownership and/or management. Therefore, we can say that those companies that internationalize late have been reborn as global firms focusing on international markets. Globally reborn firms differ from "globally born" firms in the following aspects: globally reborn firms internationalize much later, are well positioned in the local market, and have developed tangible resources that can be used for international expansion (Tuppura et al., 2008).

From a bird's eye view, both the traditional model and that of the "globally reborn" organizations refer to SMEs with a long history in the market, which internationalize slowly and are different in terms of the way they operate in foreign markets and their revenues from international sales. Similar to globally born SMEs, globally born SMEs are likely to have a high volume of international sales, despite different timing of internationalization. Both target foreign markets beyond the criterion of psychological distance. However, globally reborn SMEs accumulate more tangible resources to use for better positioning in target markets (Bell et al., 2003) (see Table 3.3).

From a chronological standpoint, the modern or the Born Global (BG) approach to internationalization was coined in the early 1990s (Rennie, 1993). It is said that when an SME aims to follow the accelerated internationalization route, the lack of direct experience of the company, which would have generated an amount of knowledge accumulation, needs to be compensated through attracting and retaining employees or talents, and not only managers, who already have the necessary knowledge (Sapienza et al., 2006).

Table 3.3 Characteristics of different internationalization models (patterns) (Bell et al., 2003)

	Traditional models	The "Born Global" model	The "Global Reborn" model
Basic features	• older firm • traditional productive industries • step-by-step entry and commitment to foreign markets • without global interest • reactive • gradual internationalization	• new firm • knowledge-intensive industries, global niche markets • simultaneous penetration of foreign markets • to create • proactive • radical and assumed internationalization	• older firm • traditional productive industries and services (e.g., retail) • internationalization caused by a critical incident • reactive • radical and assumed internationalization
Countries (geographical coverage)	• development of the internal market first • successive international development in markets that are psychologically and/or geographically close • concentration on a single market	• simultaneous development on the local and international market • global operations, focused on core markets • focus on several markets at the same time	• first internal market development • global operations • focus on several markets at the same time
Performance scale	• is not a main feature • small or medium volume of international sales	• high volume of international sales more than 25% (in small economies even more than 50%)	• high volume of international sales
Modes of operation in foreign markets (structural scale)	• increasing engagement throughout the collaboration; • no regular export activities; exports through agents, sales offices, production	• flexibility in market entry • different approaches • range from exports to modes of collaboration and foreign direct investment	• flexibility in market entry • different approaches • better defined operating modes thanks to rich resources
Time to market	• late	• early • from three to ten years from the time of the creation of the company	• late

Born Global companies have been named rapid internationalizers (Hurmerinta-Peltomaki, 2004), instant internationals (Fillis, 2001; Melen & Nordman, 2009), born internationals (Kundu & Katz, 2003), international new ventures (Oviatt & Mcdougall, 1994), innate exporters (Ganitsky, 1989), global start-ups (Oviatt et al., 1995), or high technology start-ups (Jolly et al., 1992). However, the Born Global denomination is more often used (Çavusgil & Knight, 2009; Knight, 1997; Madsen & Servais, 1997; Rennie, 1993; Sharma & Blomstermo, 2003).

Born Global SMEs, who adopt an accelerated and steady internationalization strategy, who define a global vision for the company since the beginning, and who offer unique products to the market, obviously have a deliberate strategy of accumulating knowledge, which is translated into their network affiliations and into their human resources policies (Gabrielsson et al., 2008a, 2008b). The Born Global have gained more space into the IB literature recently, authors such as Axinn and Matthyssens (2002), Bell et al. (2001), Chetty and Blankenburg Holm (2000), Macharzina and Engelhard (1991), Oesterle (1997), and Pedersen et al. (2002) covering previously ignored firm behavior. The Born Global approach is said to be particularly relevant to high-tech small companies (Li et al., 2012).

The U-model, the I-model, and the Born Global theory were criticized throughout the years (Vissak, 2010), based on embracing a narrow perspective on the phenomena involving companies doing business on foreign markets. The U-model is said to overemphasize the significance of domestic market knowledge, to exclude hybrid entry modes, to not explain de-internationalization and leapfrogging in internationalization (stage skipping), to ignoring the beginning of the internationalization process, and to being relevant mostly to companies that sell products, not services. The I-model was criticized for its focus on exports, but without explaining how exports develop, for its lack of relevance for some industries, for not explaining or predicting firm behavior, for being static and deterministic, and for not allowing for individuals to make strategic choices.

The Born Global theory was considered to suppose that all entrepreneurs act similarly despite working in different geographical places and was criticized for not explaining what instant internationalization means for the firm in terms of future international developments, and for not explaining the entry mode choice and the development stages that follow the export initiation. Vissak (2010) shows that, in fact, internationalization is a nonlinear process, many companies engaging in behaviors that involve de-internationalization, re-internationalization, or being born-again globals or born-again internationals. Vissak (2010) argues that the linear internationalization is just a particular case of a nonlinear process, and that the literature should take into account the dynamics of firm behavior, which are essentially fluctuating, especially when we discuss the activity of SMEs, which are more often than MNEs subject to environmental pressures. Late Starters are, according to Vissak (2010), just Born Global companies that have chosen to focus on the domestic market for many years, only to bloom as fast international markets conquerors at a given time.

Likewise, analyzing the existing models in a critical manner, Hampton and Rowell (2013) consider that the classical models of business internationalization are prone to be relativized by the current international context. This perspective had previously been nuanced by Malhotra et al. (2003) and Kuivalainen et al. (2007) who proposed the development of a collective research direction on the essential factors of business internationalization. In their view, international linkages and partnerships should be placed within an updated and dynamic framework that uses traditional theories of business internationalization as premises, but which targets the strategic and synergistic nature of internationalization.

Measuring the internationalization of SMEs

Internationalization has been studied from multiple perspectives. Several authors addressed the relation between internationalization and business performance (Carneiro et al., 2011; Contractor, 2007; Dean et al., 2000; Naik & Reddy, 2013; Pangarkar, 2008; Papadopoulos & Martin, 2010; Prange & Verdier, 2011; Singla & George, 2013). Other researchers discussed about the barriers that a company has to overcome in its internationalization process (Acs et al., 1997; Baursmichmidt et al., 1985; Karagozoglu & Lindell, 1998; O'Grady & Lane, 1996).

One stream of studies reveals the connections between the DOI and the performance of the firm (Loncan & Nique, 2010; Lu & Beamish, 2001; Ruigrok et al., 2007; Tallman & Li, 1996; 2004; Thomas & Eden, 2004). The *degree of internationalization* of a company has been used as a synonym to *the level of internationalization of a firm*, and of *the intensity of internationalization*, with internationalization being considered an intermediary step between national development stage and global development stage, exporting being the firm activity which was more often considered the main vector of internationalization (Jankowska, n.d.).

The field literature mentions various indicators that can be used to assess business internationalization. UNCTAD (1998) proposed the Transnationality Index-TNi, while Ietto-Gillies (1998) proposed the Transnationally Spread Index-Tsi. Sullivan (1994) considered that the DOI has been measured in a speculative, arbitrary manner for a long time, the extant literature from the 1970s, 1980s, and early 1990s bringing to the fore the financial performance of the company, and the FSTS (foreign sales to total sales ratio) as sole indicators. Sullivan's study refers to MNC, not SMEs, but we consider some of his observations highly relevant to understanding the DOI of SMEs.

Sullivan (1994) understood that the DOI of a firm needed to be measured on three levels: performance, structure, and attitudinal. Consequently, Sullivan asked assessors to refer to a wider range of indicators when looking at DOI, including FSTS, FPTP (Foreign Profits as a Percentage of Total Profits), RDI

(Research and Development Intensity, as a means to innovate and maintain innovative performance on foreign markets), AI (Advertising Intensity – on foreign markets), ESTS (Export Sales as a Percentage of Total Sales), FATA (Foreign Assets as a Percentage of Total Assets), OSTS (Overseas Subsidiaries as a Percentage of Total Subsidiaries), TMIE (Top Managers' International Experience – "tallying the cumulative duration of top managers' international assignments, as identified by the firm and as summarized in each manager's company-reported career history. We then weighted this sum by the reported total number of years of work experience of the top management team of the firm as identified by the firm" – Sullivan, 1994, p. 332), PDIO (Psychic Dispersion of International Operation – measured by "calibrating the dispersion of the subsidiaries of a firm among the ten psychic zones of the world" as identified by Ronen and Shenkar in 1985, and presented in Sullivan, 1994, p. 333).

According to Sullivan (1994), the formula for calculating DOI for an MNC is:

$$DOI_{INTs} = FSTS + FATA + OSTS + TMIE + PDIO$$

De Clerq et al. (2005) added to this measurement FETE (number of exports employees/total employees), while Moen and Servais (2002) and Chetty et al. (2014) spoke about the need to include a *speed factor* in measuring the DOI, which would measure the number of years between the year the firm was founded and the year the firm started to engage in exporting activity. Luo et al. (2005) describe the *speed factor* as incremental, slow, and as cumulative of experience.

Özdemir et al. (2017) summarized the indicators used in the literature to measure DOI and proposed the following indicators, assessed on a scale from 1 to 5 (1 = 1–20%; 2 = 21–40%; 3 = 41–60%; 4 = 61–80%; 5 = 81–100%, equivalent of very low, low, medium, high, and very high):

1 **FSTS**: Foreign sales/Total sales
2 **FATA**: Total foreign assets/Total assets
3 **OSTS**: Number of foreign offices/Total number of offices
4 **TMIE**: Experience of exports managers/Total experience of all managers
5 **PDIO**: Number of countries of export/Total number of countries in the market
6 **FETE**: Number of exports employees/Total employees
7 **FIRST EXPO** (speed of conducting the first foreign sales) = Current year – first year of foreign sales/Years in operation
8 **COUNTRY** (geographical expansion of foreign sales) = Number of countries of export/Years in operation.

Ramaswamy et al. (1996) argued that the "index measure of the internationalization construct is superior to single-variable measures," as proposed by

Sullivan (1994) and developed as presented above, yet they believe and show that the meaning of each individual variable is lost by the aggregated index, leading to errors. They underline that measuring internationalization must be conducted in such a manner that would reflect the multidimensionality of the construct. To them, FSTS (performance attribute) can be linked to FATA and OSTS (structural attributes), but can hardly be considered connected to TMIE and PDIO (attitudinal attributes). They believe that TMIE has an intrinsic flaw: Sullivan (1994) considered that a top manager's experience in international teams equates with the overall performance of the MNC, the longer the manager's experience, the better the internationalization level of the MNC, which is not necessarily correct. More so, PDIO seems based upon the supposition that an MNC present on markets from whose cultural profile their psychic distance is higher, as being more internationalized, which is false. Ramaswamy et al. (1996, p. 173) mention that the cultural particularities of the destination countries shall not be forgotten, yet that a simple count of the number of different countries in which the organization has subsidiaries and/or sales may offer a more justifiable measure of the firm's international dispersion than PDIO.

While the ideas advanced by the authors were noted by the IB community, the DOI is still largely measured by referring to foreign revenues over total revenues (Riahi-Belkaoui, 1998), or by foreign revenues over total revenues and foreign assets over total assets (Riahi-Belkaoui, 1998). Bordean and Borza (2014) assessed the degree of international involvement of the companies they researched through two dimensions: propensity for export, and export intensity, and concluded that companies that are listed on the stock exchange are more prone to internationalization than the companies who are not.

When measuring the internationalization of Romanian SMEs, the authors of *Carta Albă a IMM-urilor* (Nicolescu, 2022) advance a different set of indicators to be used: the level of production/ services destined for import/ export (scale: better, the same, inferior, much worse); the import coverage ratio (scale: under 25%, 25–50%, 51–75%, over 75%); the export coverage ratio (scale: under 25%, 25–50%, 51–75%, over 75%); the efforts made by the SME to promote their offers internationally through attending fairs, exhibitions, diplomatic missions.

According to Miller et al. (2015), internationalization has a multifaceted nature, which asks for approaching it from three angles: international intensity, international diversity, and international distance. International intensity reflects the proportion of sales a firm makes to customers outside of its home country Miller et al. (2015); international diversity refers to the number of countries in which the firm does business (Hitt et al., 1997), and international distance encompasses the economic, institutional, cultural, and geographic characteristics that mark differences between the home country of the firm and the countries in which the firm has established subsidiaries (Ghemawat, 2001; Goerzen & Beamish, 2005).

To Nummela, Puumalainen and Saarenketo (2005), the internationalization of a firm shall be measured in relation to market characteristics (globalness of the market, turbulence on the market), to management experience (international education of the manager, international experience of the manager), to the subjective performance of the firm (qualitative and quantitative measures), and to the objective performance of the firm (development of the turnover, share if foreign partners, share of foreign customers, number of export markets). In a chapter from 2018, Torkkeli, Nummela, and Saarenko add that SMEs internationalization shall also be measured by referring to objective and subjective criteria of performance.

***

We have shown in this chapter that the internationalization of the firm is a non-linear process, which is influenced by internal factors pertaining to the firm, and to external factors. There is a bias in the academic community concerning the gradual internationalization of the firm as a norm, with companies being generally expected to perform well in the country where they were founded, and then gradually conquer new markets. The measurement models used to assess business internationalization are dependent on this perspective, in general, considering that indicators such as the ones measuring exports, the number of foreign customers, the number of employees working for exports, the assets of the firm in other countries, and the number of foreign offices are relevant for the researcher who desires to understand the internationalization level of a firm. There is no consensus regarding what indicators shall be used to assess how well does a firm perform internationally, yet several authors recognize the need to measure both objective and subjective aspects concerning the international activity of the firm.

References

Acs, Z.J., Morck, R., Shaver, J.M., & Yeung, B. (1997). The internationalization of small and medium-sized enterprises: A policy perspective. *Small Business Economics*, 9(1), 7–20. https://doi.org/10.1023/A:1007991428526

Aldakhil, A.M., & Nataraja, S. (2014). Environmental factors and measures that affect the success of international strategic alliances. *Journal of Marketing and Management*, 5(1), 17–37.

Amaeshi, K., & Olufemi, O.A. (2009). Corporate social responsibility in transnational spaces: Exploring influences of varieties of capitalism on expressions of corporate codes of conduct in Nigeria. *Journal of Business Ethics*, 86(2), 225–239.

Amal, M., & Filho, A.R.F. (2010). Internationalization of small-and medium-sized enterprises: A multi case study. *European Business Review*, 22(6), 608–623. https://doi.org/10.1108/09555341011082916

Axinn, C.N., & Matthyssens, P. (2002). Limits of internationalization theories in an unlimited world. *International Marketing Review*, 19(5), 436–449. https://doi.org/10.1108/02651330210445275

Bartlett, C.A., & Ghoshal, S. (2000a). Going global: Lessons from late movers. *Harvard Business Review, 78*(2), 132–141. https://hbr.org/2000/03/going-global-lessons-from-late-movers

Bartlett, C.A., & Ghoshal, S., (2000b). *Transition Management: Text, Cases, and Readings in Cross-border Management* (third edition). Irwin McGraw-Hill.

Baursmichmidt, A., Sullivan, D., & Gillespie, K. (1985). Common factors underlying barriers to export: Studies in the US paper industry. *Journal of International Business Studies, 16*(3), 111–123. https://doi.org/10.1057/palgrave.jibs.8490802

Bell, J., Loane, P.S., Njis, E., Nijs, I., & Phillips, J. (2007). Internationalization of European BioTech firms: A comparative study of Dutch, German & UK SMEs. In *Conference Proceeding at the International Council for Small Business (ICSB)* – 52nd ICSB World Conference, Turku, Finland. http://www.ecsb.org/doc/Tukkk_ICSB_2Ann.

Bell, J., McNaughton, R., & Young, S. (2001). "Born-again global" firms. An extension to the "born global" phenomenon. *Journal of International Management, 7*(3), 173–189. https://doi.org/10.1016/S1075-4253(01)00043-6

Bell, J., McNaughton, R., Young, S., & Crick, D. (2003). Towards an integrative model of small firm internationalization. *Journal of International Entrepreneurship, 1*(4), 339–362.

Belniak, M. (2015). Factors stimulating internationalization of firms: An attempted holistic synthesis. *Entrepreneurial Business and Economics Review, 3*(2), 125–140. https://doi.org/10.15678/EBER.2015.030209

Bennet, D., Bennet, D., & Avedisian, D. (2015). *The Course of Knowledge: A 21st Century Theory.* MQI Press.

Bilkey, W.J., & Tesar, G. (1977). The export behavior of smaller Wisconsin manufacturing firms. *Journal of International Business Studies, 8*(1), 93–98. https://doi.org/10.1057/palgrave.jibs.8490783

Birnleitner, H. (2013). Influence of macro-environmental factors to the process of integrating a foreign business entity. In *Proceedings of the 14th Management International Conference.* http://www.fm-kp.si/zalozba/ISBN/978-961-266-148-9/papers/MIC1119.pdf.

Bo Bernhard, N. (2007). Determining international strategic alliance's performance: A multidimensional approach. *International Business Review, 16,* 337–361.

Bordean, O.-N. & Borza, A. (2014). Board of directors and the internationalization process: The case of Romania. *The International Journal of Management Science and Information Technology, 9,* 72–85. http://hdl.handle.net/10419/97878

Brassington, F., & Pettitt, S. (2000) *Principles of Marketing.* 2nd ed. Harlow: Financial Times Management.

Brüggemann, M., & Kleinen-von Königslöw, K. (2009). Let's talk about Europe: Why Europeanization shows a different face in different newspapers. *European Journal of Communication, 24*(1), 27–48.

Calof, J.L., & Beamish, P.W. (1995). Adapting to foreign markets: Explaining internationalization. *International Business Review, 4*(2), 115–131. https://doi.org/10.1016/0969-5931(95)00001-G

Cannon, J.P., & Perreault Jr., W.D. (1999). Buyer-seller relationships in business markets. *Journal of Marketing Research, 36*(4), 439–460.

Cant, M.C., Wiid, J.A., & Kallier, S.M. (2015). Product strategy: Factors that influence product strategy decisions of SMEs in South Africa. *The Journal of Applied Business Research, 31*(2), 621–630.

Carneiro, J., Rocha, A.D., & Silva, J.F.D. (2011). Determinants of export performance: A study of large Brazilian manufacturing firms. *BAR-Brazilian Administration Review, 8*(2), 107–132. https://doi.org/10.1590/S1807-76922011000200002

Cavusgil, S.T., & Knight, G. (2015). The born global firm: An entrepreneurial and capabilities perspective on early and rapid internationalization. *Journal of International Business Studies, 46*(1), 3–16. https://doi.org/10.1057/jibs.2014.62

Chen, C.-J., Huang, J.-W., & Hsiao, Y.-C. (2010). Knowledge management and innovativeness. The role of organizational climate and structure. *International Journal of Manpower, 31*(8), 848–870. https://doi.org/10.1108/01437721011088548

Chen, G., Kirkman, B.L., Kim, K., Farh, C.I.C., & Tangirala, S. (2010). When does cross-cultural motivation enhance expatriate effectiveness? A multilevel investigation of the moderating roles of subsidiary support and cultural distance. *Academy of Management Journal, 53*(5), 1110–1130.

Chetty, S., & Blankenburg Holm, D. (2000). Internationalization of small to medium sized manufacturing firms: A network approach. *International Business Review, 9*(1), 77–93. https://doi.org/10.1016/S0969-5931(99)00030-X

Chetty, S., Johanson, M. & Martín, O.M. (2014). Speed of internationalization: Conceptualization, measurement and validation. *Journal of World Business, 49*(4), 633–650. https://doi.org/10.1016/j.jwb.2013.12.014

Contractor, F.J. (2007). Is international business good for companies? The evolutionary or multi-stage theory of internationalization vs. the transaction cost perspective. *Management International Review, 47*(3), 453–475. https://doi.org/10.1007/s11575-007-0024-2

Coudounaris, D.N. (2018). Typologies of internationalization pathways of SMEs: What is new? *Review of International Business and Strategy, 28*(3/4), 286–316. https://doi.org/0.1108/RIBS-12-2017-0119

Crane, A., Matten, D., & Moon, J. (2008). *Corporations and Citizenship.* Cambridge University Press.

Daszkiewicz, N., & Wach, K. (2014). Motives for going international and entry modes of family firms in Poland. *Journal of Intercultural Management, 6*(2), 5–18. https://doi.org/10.2478/joim-2014-0008

De Búrca, S., Brown, L., & Fletcher, R. (2004). *International Marketing: An SME Perspective,* 1st ed. Harlow: Financial Times Prentice Hall.

De Clercq, D., Sapienza H.J. & Crijns, H. (2005). The internationalization of small and medium-sized firms. *Small Business Economics, 24,* 409–419. https://doi.org/10.1007/s11187-005-5333-x

Dean, D.L., Mengüç, B., & Myers, C.P. (2000). Revisiting firm characteristics, strategy, and export performance relationship: A survey of the literature and an investigation of New Zealand small manufacturing firms. *Industrial Marketing Management, 29*(5), 461–477. https://doi.org/10.1016/S0019-8501(99)00085-1

DIW ECON. (July 27, 2018). SMEs Performance Review 2017/2018. Methodological Note on WP 3. www.diw-econ.com.

Dobrescu, P. (2007). *Globalizare şi Integrare Europeană [Globalization and European Integration].* Comunicare.ro.

Dominguez, N. (2018). *SME iNternationalization Strategies. Innovation to Conquer New Markets.* John Wiley & Sons, Inc.

Dong, L., & Glaister, K. (2007). National and corporate culture differences in international strategic alliances: Perceptions of Chinese partners. *Asia Pacific Journal of Management, 24,* 191–205.

Edvardsson, I.R., & Durst, S. (2013). The benefits of knowledge management in small and medium-sized enterprises. *Procedia – Social and Behavioral Sciences, 81*, 351–354. https://doi.org/10.1016/j.sbspro.2013.06.441

European Commission. (2018a). Annual Report on European SMEs 2017/2018. The 10th Anniversary of the Small Business Act. SME Performance Review 2017/2018, EASME/COSME/2017/031, European Union.

European Commission (2020). Entrepreneurship and small and medium-sized enterprises (SMEs). https://ec.europa.eu/growth/smes/support/networks_en

European Union. (2014). Sprijinirea internaționalizării IMM-urilor. http://publications. europa.eu/resource/cellar/dd69f968-fea2-4034-90d5-7a648574618f.0002.01/DOC_1

Fernández, Z., & Nieto, M.J. (2005). Internationalization strategy of small and medium-sized family businesses: Some influential factors. *Family Business Review, 18*(1), 77–89. https://doi.org/10.1111/j.1741-6248.2005.00031.x

Ferraris, A., Santoro, G., & Dezi, L. (2017). How MNC's subsidiaries may improve their innovative performance? The role of external sources and knowledge management capabilities. *Journal of Knowledge Management, 21*(3), 540–552. https://doi.org/10.1108/JKM-09-2016-0411

Fillis, I. (2001). Small firm internationalization: An investigative survey and future research directions, *Management Decision, 39*(9), 767–783. https://doi.org/10.1108/00251740110408683

Friedman, T.L. (2008). *Lexus și Măslinul [Lexus and the Olive Tree]*. 2nd edition. Polirom.

Gabrielsson, M., Kirpalani, V.H.M., Dimitratos, P., Solberg, C.A., & Zucchella, A. (2008a). Conceptualizations to advance born global definition: A research note. *Global Business Review, 9*(1), 45–50. https://doi.org/10.1177/097215090700900103

Gabrielsson, M., Kirpalania, V.H.M., Dimitratos, P., Solberg, C.A., & Zucchella, A. (2008b). Born globals: Propositions to help advance the theory. *International Business Review, 17*(4), 385–401. https://doi.org/10.1016/j.ibusrev.2008.02.015

Ganitsky, J. (1989). Strategies for innate and adoptive exporters: Lessons from Israel's case. *International Marketing Review, 6*(5). https://doi.org/10.1108/EUM0000000001523

Garagorri, I. (2016). SME vulnerability analysis: A tool for business continuity. In K. North & G. Varvakis (Eds.), *Competitive Strategies for Small and Medium Enterprises*, 181–194. Springer.

Ghauri, P.N., & Buckley, P.J. (Eds.). (1993). *The Internationalization of the Firm: A Reader*. Academic Press.

Ghemawat, P. (2001). Distance still matters. The hard reality of global expansion. *Harvard Business Review*. https://hbr.org/2001/09/distance-still-matters-the-hard-reality-of-global-expansion

Giannacourou, M., Kantaraki, M., & Christopoulou, V. (2015). The perception of crisis by Greek SMEs and its impact on managerial practices. *Procedia – Social and Behavioral Sciences, 175*, 546–551. https://doi.org/10.1016/j.sbspro.2015.01.1235

Goerzen, A., & Beamish, P.W. (2005). The effect of alliance network diversity on multinational enterprise performance. *Strategic Management Journal, 26*(4), 333–354. https://doi.org/10.1002/smj.447

Gomes, L.F.A.M., Moshkovich, H., & Torres, D. (2010). Marketing decisions in small businesses: How verbal decision analysis can help. *International Journal of Management Decision Making, 11*(1), 19–36.

Gorgos, E.-A., Alexandru, V.-A., & Vătămănescu, E.-M. (2019). Romanian SMEs under lens: Multifaceted instruments for developing the intellectual and financial capital. In V. Dinu (Ed.), *Basiq International Conference: New Trends in Sustainable Business and Consumption*, 143–151. ASE.

Gurgul, H., & Lach, L. (2014). Globalization and economic growth: Evidence from two decades of transition in CEE. *Economic Modelling, 36*(1), 97–107.

Hagen, B., Zucchella, A., & DeGiovanni, N., (2012). International strategy and performance-clustering strategic types of SMEs. *International Business Review, 21*(3), 396–382.

Hampton, A., & Rowell, J. (2010). Leveraging integrated partnerships as a means of developing international capability: An SME case study. *International Journal of Knowledge, Culture and Change Management, 10*(6), 19–30.

Hampton, A., & Rowell, J. (2013). An evolution in research practice for investigating international business relationships. *Management Dynamics in the Knowledge Economy, 1*(2), 161–178.

Handzic, M. (2006). Knowledge Management in SMEs. Practical guidelines. *CACCI Journal, 1*, 1–11. https://www.researchgate.net/publication/254287009_Knowledge_Management_in_SMEs_Practical_guidelines

Harrison, A. (2011). International entry and country analysis. A Lecture Programme delivered at the Technical University of Košice. https://www.coursehero.com/file/12014444/TUKE-Lectures-2011-12/.

Harvie, C. (2008). The role and contribution of SMEs to economic growth, development and integration in East Asia, Murdoch Business School Seminar at Murdoch University, South Street, Western Australia.

Hill, C.W.L. (2007). *International Business Competing in the Global Marketplace*. McGraw Hill.

Hitt, M.A., Hoskisson, R.E., & Kim H. (1997). International diversification. Effects on innovation and firm performance in product-diversified firms. *Academy of Management Journal, 40*(4), 767–798. https://doi.org/10.2307/256948

Hollensen, S. (2001). *Global Marketing: A Market-responsive Approach*, 2nd edition, Financial Times Prentice Hall.

Hollensen, S. (2007). *Global Marketing: A Decision-oriented Approach*, 4th edition. Pearson Education.

Hollensen, S. (2008). *Essential of Global Marketing*. Pearson Education.

Hurmerinta-Peltomäki, L. (2004). Conceptual and methodological underpinnings. In M.V. Jones & P. Dimitratos (Eds.), *The Study of Rapid Internationalizers, Emerging Paradigms In International Entrepreneurship*, 64–88, The McGill International Entrepreneurship Series.

Hutchinson, V., & Quintas, P. (2008). Do SMEs do knowledge management? Or simply manage what they know? *International Small Business Journal, 26*(2), 131–154. https://doi.org/10.1177/0266242607086571

Ietto-Gillies, G. (1998). Different conceptual frameworks for the assessment of the degree of internationalization: An empirical analysis of various indices for the top 100 transnational corporations. *Transnational Corporations, 7*(1), 17–40.

Jankowska, J. (n.d.). Measures of company internationalization. *Financial Aspects of Organizational Management*, 419–429. http://repozytorium.wsb-nlu.edu.pl/bitstream/handle/11199/7471/Jankowska%20Justyna%2C%20Measures%20of%20company%20internationalization.pdf?sequence=1

Javalgi, R.G., Griffith, D.A., & White, S.D. (2003). An empirical examination of factors influencing the internationalization of service firms. *Journal of Services Marketing, 17*(2), 185–201. https://doi.org/10.1108/08876040310467934

Johanson J., & Wiedersheim-Paul F. 1975. The internationalization of the Firm-Four Swedish cases. *Journal of Management Studies, 12,* 305–322. https://doi.org/10.1111/j.1467-6486.1975.tb00514.x.

Johanson, J., & Vahlne, J.E. (1977). The internationalization process of the firm-a model of knowledge development and increasing foreign market commitments. *Journal of International Business Studies, 8*(1), 23–32. https://doi.org/10.1057/palgrave.jibs.8490676

Johanson, J., & Vahlne, J.E. (2009). The Uppsala internationalization process model revisited: From liability of foreignness to liability of outsidership. *Journal of International Business Studies, 40*(9), 1411–1431. https://doi.org/10.1057/jibs. 2009.24

Jolly, V.K., Alahuhta, M., & Jeannet, J.P. (1992). Challenging the incumbents: How high technology start-ups compete globally. *Journal of Strategic Change, 1*(2), 11–26. https://doi.org/10.1002/jsc.4240010203

Jones, M.V., & Coviello, N.E. (2005). Internationalization: Conceptualizing an entrepreneurial process of behavior in time. *Journal of International Business Studies, 36*(3), 284–303.

Julien, P.A. (1996). Globalization: different types of small business behavior. *Entrepreneurship and Regional Development, 8*(1), 57–74.

Karagozoglu, N., & Lindell, M. (1998). Internationalization of small and medium-sized technology-based firms: An exploratory study. *Journal of Small Business Management, 36*(1), 44–59.

Kianto, A., Hussinki, H., Vanhala, M., & Nisula, A.-M. (2018). The state of knowledge management in logistics SMEs: Evidence from two Finnish regions. *Knowledge Management Research & Practice, 16*(4), 477–487. https://doi.org/10.1080/14778238. 2018.1488523

Kim, Y., & Lui, S.S. (2015). The impacts of external network and business group on innovation: Do the types of innovation matter? *Journal of Business Research, 68*(9), 1964–1973. https://doi.org/10.1016/j.jbusres.2015.01.006

Kmieciak, R., & Michna, A. (2018). Knowledge management orientation, innovativeness, and competitive intensity: Evidence from Polish SMEs. *Knowledge Management Research & Practice, 16*(4), 559–572. https://doi.org/10.1080/14778238.2018. 1514997

Knight, G. (1997). *Emerging Paradigm for International Marketing: The Born Global Firm, Doctoral Dissertation, E.* Michigan State University. https://d.lib.msu.edu/etd/26402

Knight, G.A. (2001). Entrepreneurship and strategy in the international SME. *Journal of International Management, 7*(3), 155–171. https://doi.org/10.1016/S1075-4253(01) 00042-4

Korsakienė, R., & Tvaronavičienė, M. (2012). The internationalization of SMEs: An integrative approach. *Journal of Business Economics and Management, 13*(2), 294–307. https://doi.org/10.3846/16111699.2011.620138

Kuivalainen, O., Sundqvist, S., & Servais, P. (2007). Firms' degree of born globalness, international entrepreneurial orientation and export performance. *Journal of World Business, 42*(3), 253–267.

Kundu, S.K., & Katz, J.A. (2003). Born-international Smes: Bi-level impacts of resources and intentions. *Small Business Economics*, *20*(1), 25–47. https://doi.org/10.1023/A:1020292320170

Lakomaa, E. (2009). *Models for Internationalization. A Study of the Early Steps of the Internationalization of Scandinavian Media Companies*. Stockholm School of Economics.

Le, T. (April 1, 2017). *Investigation into Knowledge Management in SMEs: Case of a Finnish Telecomunications Company*. Helsinki Metropolia University of Applied Sciences.

Lee, V.-H., Leong, L.-Y., Hew, T.-S., & Ooi, K.-B. (2013). Knowledge management: A key determinant in advancing technological innovation? *Journal of Knowledge Management*, *17*(6), 848–872. https://doi.org/10.1108/JKM-08-2013-0315.

Levitt, P., & Glick Schiller, N. (2004). Conceptualizing simultaneity: A transnational social field perspective on society. *International Migration Review*, *38*(145), 595–629.

Li, L., Qian, G., & Qian, Z. (2012). Early internationalization and performance of small high-tech "born-globals". *International Marketing Review*, *29*(5), 536–561. https://doi.org/10.1108/02651331211260377

Loncan, T. & Nique, W.M. (2010). Degree of internationalization and performance: Evidence from emerging Brazilian multinational firms. *GCG Georgetown University – Universia*, *4*(1), 40–51. https://doi.org/10.3232/GCG.2010.V4.N1.02

Lu, J.W. & Beamish, P.W. (2001). The internationalization and performance of SMEs. *Strategic Management Journal*, *22*(6-7), 565–586. https://www.jstor.org/stable/3094321

Lu, J.W. & Beamish, P.W. (2004). International diversification and firm performance: The S-curve hypothesis. *Academy of Management Journal*, *47*(4), 598–609. https://doi.org/10.2307/20159604

Luo, Y., Hongxin Zhao, J. & Du, J. (2005). The internationalization speed of e-commerce companies: An empirical analysis. *International Marketing Review*, *22*(6), 693–709. https://doi.org/10.1108/02651330510630294

Macharzina, K., & Engelhard, J. (1991). Paradigm shift in international business research: From partist and eclectic approaches to the GAINS paradigm. *Management International Review*, *31*(4), 23–43. https://www.jstor.org/stable/40213888

Madsen, T.K., & Servais, P. (1997). The internationalization of born globals: An evolutionary process? *International Business Review*, *6*(6), 561–583. https://doi.org/10.1016/S0969-5931(97)00032-2

Majocchi, A., & Zucchella, A. (2003). Internationalization and performance – Findings from a Set of Italian SMEs. *International Small Business Journal*, *21*(3), 249–268.

Maldonado-Guzmán, G., Garza-Reyes, J.A., Pinzón-Castro, S.Y., & Kumar, V. (2017). Barriers to innovation in service SMEs: Evidence from Mexico. *Industrial Management & Data Systems*, *117*(8), 1669–1686. https://doi.org/10.1108/IMDS-08-2016-0339

Malhotra, N.K., Aggarwal, J., & Ulgado, F.M. (2003). Internationalization and entry modes: A multitheoretical framework and research propositions. *Journal of International Marketing*, *11*(1), 1–31.

Manolova, T.S., Brush, C.G., Edelman, L.F. & Greene, P.G. (2002). Internationalization of small firms: Personal factors revisited. *International Small Business Journal: Researching Entrepreneurship*, *20*(1), 9–31. https://doi.org/10.1177/0266242602201003

Mattelart, T. (Ed.) (2007). *Médias, Migrations et Cultures Transnationales*. De Boeck.
Melén, S., & Nordman, R.E. (2009). The internationalization modes of born globals: A longitudinal study. *European Management Journal*, *27*(4), 243–254. https://doi.org/10.1016/j.emj.2008.11.004
Miller, S.R., Lavie, D., & Delios, A. (2015). International intensity, diversity, and distance: Unpacking the internationalization–performance relationship. *International Business Review*, 2015, 1–14. https://doi.org/10.1016/j.ibusrev.2015.12.003
Moen, Ø. & Servais, P. (2002). Born global or gradual global? Examining the export behavior of small and medium-sized enterprises. *Journal of International Marketing*, *10*(3), 49–72. https://doi.org/10.1509/jimk.10.3.49.19540
Naik, S.S. & Reddy, Y.V. (2013). Structuring the prediction model of export performance of selected Indian industries: A comparative analysis. *Open Access Scientific Reports*, *2*(3), 1–7. https://doi.org/10.4172/scientificreports667
Nicolescu, L., & Nicolescu, C. (2012). Innovation in SMEs – Findings from Romania. *Economics & Sociology*, *5*(2a), 71–85.
Nicolescu, L., & Nicolescu, C. (2016). The evolution of the Romanian SMEs' perceptions over the last decade. In O. Nicolescu, & L. Lloyd-Reason (Eds.), *Challenges, Performances and Tendencies in Organization Management*, 261–271. World Scientific Publishing.
Nicolescu, L., Vătămănescu, E.-M., Andrei, A.G., & Pînzaru, F. (2015). Towards a sustainability framework for relationship marketing. An insight into European steel pipe businesses. In *BASIQ 2015 International Conference "New Trends in Sustainable Business and Consumption"* (pp. 449–456). Editura ASE.
Nicolescu, O. (Ed.). (2022). *Carta Albă a IMM-urilor din România*. 20th edition. ProUniversitaria.
Nummela, N., Puumalainen, K., & Saarenketo, S. (2005). International growth orientation of knowledge-intensive SMEs. *Journal of International Entrepreneurship*, *3*(1), 5–18. https://doi.org/10.1007/s10843-005-0350-z
Nye, J., & Keohane, R. (1989). *Power and Interdependence: World Politics in Transition*. Little, Brown and Company.
Ocloo, C.E., Akaba, S., & Worwui-Brown, D.K. (2014). Globalization and competitiveness: Challenges of small and medium enterprises (SMEs) in Accra, Ghana. *International Journal of Business and Social Science*, *5*(4), 1–10.
OECD. (2013). *Skills Development and Training in SMEs*. OECD Publishing.
OECD. (2015). *Skills and Learning Strategies for Innovation in SMEs, Working Party on SME and Entrepreneurship*, CFE/SME(2014)3/REV1. OECD Publishing.
OECD. (2017). *Enhancing the Contributions of SMEs in a Global and Digitalised Economy. Meeting of the OECD Council at Ministerial Level, Paris, 7–8 June 2017*. OECD Publishing.
Oesterle, M.-J. (1997). Time span until internationalization: Foreign market entry as built-in mechanism of innovation. *Management International Review*, *37*(2), 125–149.
O'Grady, S., & Lane, H.W. (1996). The psychic distance paradox. *Journal of International Business Studies*, *27*(2), 309–333. https://doi.org/10.1057/palgrave.jibs.8490137
Oviatt, B., & McDougall, P. (1994). Toward a theory of international new ventures. *Journal of International Business Studies*, *25*(1), 45–64. https://doi.org/10.1057/palgrave.jibs.8490193
Oviatt, B., McDougall, P., & Loper, M. (1995). Global start-ups: Entrepreneurs on a world-wide stage. *The Academy of Management Executive (1993-2005)*, *9*(2), 30–44. https://www.jstor.org/stable/4165256

Özdemir, E., Altıntaş, H.M., & Kılıç, H.S. (2017). The effects of the degree of internationalization on export performance: A research on exporters in Turkey. *Business and Economics Research Journal*, 8(3), 611–626. https://doi.org/10.20409/berj.2017.69

Pangarkar, N. (2008). Internationalization and performance of small-and medium-sized enterprises. *Journal of World Business*, 43(4), 475–485. https://doi.org/10.1016/j.jwb.2007.11.009

Papadopoulos, N. & Martín, O.M. (2010). Toward a model of the relationship between internationalization and export performance. *International Business Review*, 19(4), 388–406. https://doi.org/10.1016/j.ibusrev.2010.02.003

Pauw, W.P., & Chan, S. (2018). Multistakeholder partnerships for adaptation: The role of micro, small and medium enterprises. In C. Schaer & N. Kuruppu (Eds.), *Private-sector action in adaptation*, 98–109. UNEP DTU Partnership.

Pedersen, T., Petersen, B., & Benito, G.R.G. (2002). Foreign operation mode change: Impetus and switching costs. *International Business Review*, 11(3), 325–345. https://doi.org/10.1016/S0969-5931(01)00063-4

Portes, A., Guarnizo, L., & Landolt, P. (1999). The study of transnationalism: Pitfalls and promise of an emergent research field. *Ethnic and Racial Studies*, 22(2), 217–237.

Prange, C. & Verdier, S. (2011). Dynamic capabilities, internationalization processes and performance. *Journal of World Business*, 46(1), 126–133. https://doi.org/10.1016/j.jwb.2010.05.024

Pulignano, V. (2009). International cooperation, transnational restructuring and virtual networking in Europe. *European Journal of Industrial Relations*, 15(2), 187–205.

Ramaswamy, K., Galen Kroes, K., & Renforth, W. (1996). Measuring the degree of internationalization of a firm: A comment. *Journal of International Business Studies*, 27(1), 167–177. http://www.jstor.org/stable/155377

Ravelomanana, F., Yan, L., Mahazomanana, C., & Miarisoa, L.P. (2015). The external and internal factors that influence the choice of foreign entry modes at Wuhan Iron and Steel Corporation. *Open Journal of Business and Management*, 3(1), 20–29. https://doi.org/10.4236/ojbm.2015.31003.

Reid, S. (1983). Firm internationalization, transaction costs and strategic choice. *International Marketing Review*, 1(2), 44–56. https://doi.org/10.1108/eb008251

Rennie, M. (1993). Born Global. *Mckinsey Quarterly*, 4, 5–52.

Riahi-Belkaoui, A. (1998). The effects of the degree of internationalization on firm performance. *International Business Review*, 7(3), 315–321. https://doi.org/10.1016/S0969-5931(98)00013-4

Roberts, G.H. (2005). Auchan's entry into Russia: Prospects and research implications. *International Journal of Retail & Distribution Management*, 33(1), 49–68.

Rubaeva, M. (2010). *Internationalization of Western Retail Company Eastwards: Metro Group Case*. The Aarhus School of Business.

Ruigrok, W., Amann, W., & Wagner, H. (2007). The internationalization-performance relationship at Swiss firms: A test of the S-shape and extreme degrees of internationalization. *Management International Review*, 47(3), 349–368. http://www.jstor.org/stable/40658212

Ruzzier, M., Antoncic, B., Hisrich, R.D., & Konecnik, M. (2007). Human capital and SME internationalization: A structural equation modeling study. *Canadian Journal of Administrative Sciences*, 24(1), 15–29. https://doi.org/10.1002/cjas.3

Ruzzier, M., Hisrich, R.D., & Antoncic, B. (2006). SME internationalization research: Past, present, and future. *Journal of Small Business and Enterprise Development*, *13*(4), 476–497. https://doi.org/10.1108/14626000610705705

Sahay, V.S. (2013). Globalization, urbanization and migration: Anthropological dimensions of trends and impacts. *The Oriental Anthropologist*, *13*(2), 297–304.

Sapienza, J.H., Autio, E., George, G., & Zahra, S.A. (2006). A capabilities perspective on the effects of early internationalization on firm survival and growth. *Academy of Management Review*, *31*(4), 914–933. https://doi.org/10.2307/20159258

Senik, Z.C., Isa, R.M., Sham, R.M., & Ayob, A.H. (2014). A model for understanding SMEs internationalization in emerging economies. *Jurnal Pengurusan*, *41*(2014), 25–42.

Sharma, D.D., & Blomstermo, A. (2003). The internationalization process of born globals: A network view. *International Business Review*, 12(6), 739–753. https://doi.org/10.1016/j.ibusrev.2003.05.002

Sheller, M., & Urry, J. (2006). The new mobilities paradigm. *Environment and Planning*, *38*(1), 207–226.

Singla, C. & George, R. (2013). Internationalization and performance: A contextual analysis of Indian firms. *Journal of Business Research*, *66*(12), 2500–2506. https://doi.org/10.1016/j.jbusres.2013.05.041

Sklair, L. (2007). A transnational framework for theory and research in the study of globalization. In I. Rossi (Ed.), *Frontiers of globalization research: theoretical and methodological approaches*, 93–108. Springer.

Solberg, C.A., & Durrieu, F. (2006). Access to networks and commitment to Internationalization as precursors to marketing strategies in international markets. *Management International Review*, *46*(1), 57–83. http://www.jstor.org/stable/40836072

Sorensen, J.O. (1997). The Internationalization of Companies. Different Perspectives of How Companies Internationalize. *International Business Economics*, Working Paper Series, 23.

Stiglitz, E.J. (2008). *Mecanismele globalizării [The Mechanisms of Globalization]*. Polirom.

Sullivan, D. (1994). Measuring the degree of internationalization of a firm. *Journal of International Business Studies*, *25*(2), 325–342. https://doi.org/10.1057/palgrave.jibs.8490203

Tallman, S. & Li, J. (1996). Effects of international diversity and product diversity on the performance of multinational firms. *Academy of Management Journal*, *39*(1), 179–196. https://doi.org/10.2307/256635

Thomas, D.E. & Eden, L. (2004). What is the shape of the multinationality-performance relationship? *Multinational Business Review*, *12*(1), 89–110. https://doi.org/10.1108/1525383X200400005

Tomlinson, J. (1999). *Globalization and Culture*. Polity.

Torkkeli, L., Nummela, N., & Saarenketo, S. (2018). A global mindset – Still a prerequisite for successful SME internationalization? Key success factors of SME internationalization: a cross-country perspective. *International Business & Management*, *34*, 7–24. https://doi.org/10.1108/S1876-066X20180000034001

Tuca, S. (2013). The evolution of economic globalization during the current global crisis. *CES Working Papers*, *4*(4), 645–653.

Tue, L.M. (2014). Does globalization put developing countries at the risk of increasing poverty and inequality? A brief overview. *MDE 20*. University of Economics, HCMC.

Tuppura, A., Saarenketo, S., Puumalainen, K., Jantunen, A., & Kyläheiko, K. (2008). Linking knowledge, entry timing and internationalization strategy. *International Business Review, 17*(4), 473–487. https://doi.org/10.1016/j.ibusrev.2008.02.003

UNCTAD. (1998). *World Investment Report 1998*. Trends and Determinants. United Nations.

Vătămănescu, E.-M., Alexandru, V.-A., & Gorgos, E.-A. (2014a). The five Cs Model of Business Internationalization (CMBI) – A preliminary theoretical insight into today's business internationalization challenges. In C. Bratianu, A. Zbuchea, F. Pînzaru, & E.-M. Vătămănescu (Eds.), *STRATEGICA. Management, Finance, and Ethics* (pp. 537–558). Tritonic.

Vătămănescu, E.-M., Pînzaru, F., Andrei, A.-G., & Alexandru, V.-A. (2014b). Going international versus going global. The case of the European steel pipe SMEs. *Review of International Comparative Management, 15*(3), 360–379. http://www.rmci.ase.ro/no15vol3/09.pdf.

Vătămănescu, E.-M., Pînzaru, F., Andrei, A.G., & Zbuchea, A. (2016). Investigating SMEs sustainability with partial least squares structural equation modeling. *Transformations in Business & Economics (TIBE), 15*(3), 259–273. http://www.transformations.knf.vu.lt/39/article/inve

Vătămănescu, E.-M., Andrei, A.G., Nicolescu, L., Pînzaru, F., & Zbuchea, A. (2017a). The influence of competitiveness on SMEs internationalization effectiveness. Online versus offline business networking. *Information Systems Management, 34*(3), 205–219. https://doi.org/10.1080/10580530.2017.1329997

Vătămănescu E.-M., & Alexandru, V.-A. (2018). Beyond Innovation: The crazy new world of industrial mash-ups. In E.-M. Vătămănescu & F. Pînzaru (Eds.), *Knowledge Management in the Sharing Economy – Cross-sectoral Insights into the Future of Competitive Advantage*, 271–285. Springer International Publishing.

Vătămănescu E.-M., Gorgos, E.-A., & Alexandru, V.-A. (2018). Preliminary insights into SMEs opportunities and vulnerabilities in the European context. A qualitative approach. *Management Dynamics in the Knowledge Economy, 6*(3), 385–404. https://doi.org/10.25019/MDKE/6.3.03.

Vătămănescu, E.-M., Gorgos, E.-A., Ghigiu, A.M., & Pătruţ, M. (2019). Bridging intellectual capital and SMEs internationalization through the lens of sustainable competitive advantage: A systematic literature review. *Sustainability, 11*(9), 2510. https://doi.org/10.3390/su11092510

Vertovec, S. (2009). *Transnationalism*. Routledge.

Vissak, T. (2010). Internationalization: A neglected topic in international business research. *The Past, Present and Future of International Business & Management Advances in International Management, 23*, 559–580. https://doi.org/10.1108/S1571-5027(2010)00000230029

Vrontis, D., Thrassou, A., Santoro, G., & Papa, A. (2017). Ambidexterity, external knowledge and performance in knowledge-intensive firms. *The Journal of Technology Transfer, 42*(2), 374–388. https://doi.org/10.1007/s10961-016-9502-7

Wang, Y., & Lin, J. (2013). An empirical research on knowledge management orientation and organizational performance: The mediating role of organizational innovation. *African Journal of Business Management, 7*(8), 604–612. https://doi.org/10.5897/AJBM11.2072

Welch, L.S., & Luostarinen, R. (1988). Internationalization: Evolution of a concept. *Journal of General Management, 14*(2), 34–55. https://doi.org/10.1177/030630708801400203

Wild, J.J., Wild, K.L., & Han, J.C.Y. (2003). *International Business*. 2nd edition. Pearson Education, Prentice Hall.

Wyer, P., & Smallbone, D. (1999). Export activity in SMEs: A framework for strategic analysis. *Journal of Academy of Business Administration, 4*(2), 9–24.

Zahra S.A., Ireland R.D., & Hitt, M.A. (2000). International expansion by new venture firms: International diversity mode of market entry technological learning and performance. *Academy of Management Journal, 43*(5), 925–951. https://doi.org/10.5465/1556420

4 A phenomenological overview

The Central and Eastern European region and SMEs internationalization

This chapter advances a series of data concerning the Central and Eastern European (CEE) region and its relevance in the context of international business theory development. Contemporary research in international business and international management (IM) focuses on analyzing new phenomena using existing theories, on advancing alternative theoretical perspectives, and on developing new theories (Jaklič et al., 2020; Ipsmiller & Dikova, 2021). While there are many "living laboratories" in the world, which constitute fertile grounds for inquisitive researchers, the countries of CEE offer a particularly abundant array of research options and have provided "a fascinating research laboratory in which to assess the explanatory and predictive power of different theories" (Meyer & Peng, 2005, p. 600). More precisely, the CEE region comprises not one but an entire set of "learning laboratories" that may provide insights into the dynamics of systemic transition processes, marked both by the integration and disintegration of structures and relationships (Rašković, Dikova, & McDougall-Covin, 2020).

It is well known that challenges and opportunities arise for countries that face deep political, economic, social, and cultural shifts, so the magnitude of the transition from a socialist system to a capitalist system leads authors to name it the "great transformation" of the countries in CEE (Kornai, 2008). The acknowledgment of the unique features of this "great transformation" and the particular characteristics of each CEE country raise awareness that a continuous focus on CEE is compelling (Meyer & Peng, 2016; Ipsmiller & Dikova, 2021), that region-oriented research is relevant (Jaklič, Rašković, & Schuch, 2018; Jaklič et al., 2020), and that a good understanding of the CEE and other non-Western countries may come only as a result of exploring the rich contexts they provide, where presumably globally applicable theories can be tested and perhaps improved (Jaklič et al., 2018). To unravel the multiple facets of economic developments and correlative occurrences present in the CEE countries, researchers obviously need to exercise a particular type of sensitivity, and operate with a deep knowledge of history, identity, politics, socio-cultural evolutions, and understand institutional and relationships-driven changes (Rašković et al., 2020).

DOI: 10.4324/9781003432326-5

The SMEs sector of the European Union's economy

Approximately 90% of the businesses that exist nowadays on Earth are SMEs, and they employ around 50% of the global active population, according to an estimation of the World Bank (2022). Consequently, competitivity and performance are considered key topics not only by the people who are directly involved in the existence of these businesses, and concerned with their own level of income, but also to states and to super state entities, as long as the welfare of the citizens, social cohesion, even political stability, are impacted by the health and the level of performance of the economic actors.

SMEs are a vital part of the economy of the European Union (EU), being deeply ingrained in its fabric. The EU considers SME growth a priority and started to focus in 2008 on improving the approach to entrepreneurship, and proceeded to simplifying regulations, to facilitating access to and to consolidating the Single Market, to supporting SMEs' access to financial aid, and to fostering the launching of new businesses. The programmatic document launched in 2008 was called *"Think Small First." A "Small Business Act" for Europe* (European Commission, June 25, 2008), and served as a framework document for all the Member States, leading to many supportive measures to SMEs being implemented on its territory. Consequently, between 2008 and 2017 the SMES from the EU-28 acknowledged the positive impact of the Small Business Act. The value added of EU-28 SMEs increased by 14.3% between 2008 and 2017, the number of employees increased by 2.5%, the exports performed by SMEs increased by 20% between 2012 and 2017, making SMEs account for 88.3% of the exports of all EU-28, even though in 2016 about 80% of those exports were made intra-EU, and by a rather small number of companies (DIW ECON, July 27, 2018).

In March 2020 the European Commission launched a new programmatic report, titled "Unleashing the full potential of European SMEs," which announces that SMEs are the central actors for Europe's competitive transformation, and that SMEs should support in the following years the economic and technological sovereignty of the EU. This desiderate does not come without provocations. A number of challenges are mentioned: 80% of the SMEs in the EU sell their products and services on the Single Market, and only 600.000 SMEs export goods to countries outside of the EU; even the access to the Single Market is considered difficult by 78% of SMEs, who point to complex administrative procedures as a significant obstacle to operating in the Single Market; 40% of SMEs are paid on time, which causes 1/4 of SME bankruptcies; only 1% of SMEs used equity as a financing option; venture capital investments and scale-ups are much less prevalent than in the USA (European Commission, March 2020).

Actions planned to tackle those shortcomings include an ERASMUS program for Young Entrepreneurs Global Scheme to support internationalization, improving access to the Single Market and reducing the barriers within the Single Market, fostering partnerships between border regions, developing an EU Start-up Nations Standard that would push Member States to accelerate growth of high tech SMEs and start-ups in the Single Market, offering support to Member States in implementing the Late Payment Directive (European Commission, March 2020).

During the SARS-CoV-2 pandemic, which started to significantly manifest in Europe in February 2020, a historic drop in the economic activity of the EU-27 was registered, unseen since the Great Depression of the early 1930s. The EU-27 GDP fell by 6.3% in 2020, as a consequence of the lockdowns and multiple governmental sanitary measures, and of the sharp decline of the demand for goods and services yet started to recover in the latter part of 2021 (Hope, 2022, 24). Absorbing the shock of the first pandemic waves and measures taken to limit the virus, many SMEs faced challenges: some had to respond to a steep increase in demand (such was the case for delivery services and e-commerce businesses), while others had difficulties finding customers and even temporarily disappeared (such as tourism agencies, and companies in the hospitality sector) (Hope, 2022, p. 25). A decrease in the added value and a drop in employment were obvious in the case of micro-SMEs in 2020, while medium-sized SMEs were the ones that were most prone to closing their businesses in 2020 (Hope, 2022, p. 30).

In 2021, there were around 22.8 million SMEs in the EU-27 (80–90% of the SMEs in each Member State are micro-enterprises), accounting for 99.8% of the SMEs in the non-financial business sector (NFBS), and more than half of the value-added, meanwhile employing 83.2 billion people, or roughly 64% of the workers in NFBS in the EU-27 (Hope, 2022, p. 16). The sectors that brought about 50% of the value added in the EU-27 economy were "cultural and creative industries (57% of total ecosystem value added), proximity, social economy and civil security (61%), retail (61%), tourism (63%), textiles (65%) and construction (72%)" and only 34% pertained to energy – renewables, and 33% to electronics (Hope, 2022, p. 9). The year 2021 marked a rebound for NFBS SMEs in EU-27, leading to a 2.1% valued added increase compared to 2019, although due to inflation it is still 1.5% below the value it had in 2019, a situation which is identical in what concerns employment (Hope, 2022, p. 31). However, new business registration jumped by 15.5% in 2021, and the annual growth rate of SME employment in 2021 in countries like Romania reached 2.6%, which is above the EU-27 median.

In 2022, after the 2008 economic crisis, after Brexit, after the peak of the COVID-19 pandemic, and with an on-going war between Russia and Ukraine at its borders and many migrants from Ukraine seeking shelter on its territory, the EU faces unprecedented challenges. Following the invasion of Ukraine by Russia, and the sanctions that were imposed by the EU-27 states against Russia and Belarus, it is expected that direct international trade would be affected in a limited way, as "the shares of Russia and Belarus in total EU exports are respectively 1.7% and 0.1% and the shares of Russia and Belarus in total EU imports are respectively 3.0% and 0.1%," with indirect impacts through the higher energy prices and an increase in raw materials prices and commodities impacting both SMEs and larger companies in the following months (Hope, 2022, p. 10).

Supplementary to these conditions, SMEs from the EU-27 face the need to embark on the route towards complying to the European Green Deal, which asks Member States to cut greenhouse emissions with 55% by 2030 compared to 1990 levels, aiming at reaching net-zero emissions by 2050 (European Council, 2022). In the light of the green transition in the EU, the role of SMEs is expected to be critical, as approximately 60% of the greenhouse gas emissions made by companies in the EU come from SMEs (Hope, 2022, p. 11).

Research gaps in the study of CEE SMEs internationalization

A recent article by Koveshnikov et al. (2022) points to the fact that the CEE countries have undergone multiple transformations since the fall of the European communist regimes in the early 1990s, making the region a particularly offering "research laboratory," giving way to the explanatory and forecasting potential of various theories (Meyer & Peng, 2005, p. 600). The 20th and 21st centuries brought about turbulence in the enterprise international macro environment for countries in Europe, and particularly for countries in the CEE region. The factors that lead to turbulence and uncertainty can be coupled with the political environment, the legal environment, the economic environment, the social environment, the cultural environment, the ecological environment, and the technological environment (Drabik, 2022). The changeability and complexity of the environment pose difficulties for companies that aim at developing their international activities, as anticipating the changes that may occur on foreign markets is particularly difficult (Limański et al., 2018).

Western social scientists have long considered the CEE region as an "immense social laboratory" (Whitley & Czaban, 1998, p. 260) that offers great opportunities to investigate radical economic, political, and social changes. Various streams of research have emerged and scholarly cooperation among scientists from multiple countries has flourished, based on their common interest in the empirical characteristics of post-socialism and the variations and specificities of the local systems. Their collaborations lead to exploring and expanding theories that have mostly emerged in North America and other market-oriented economic systems in Europe. Organizational research, in particular, is and has been enriched by the findings and interpretations of data collected from post-socialist countries, as the "polar cases" provided by the post-socialist context are widely different from the "objects" of analysis usually taken into account by Western organization theory developments. Through exploring the structural, historical, cultural, and social specificities of the non-Western settings, a promise of a more culturally sensitive and more globally relevant theory is being made (Soulsby & Clark, 2007).

There have been attempts to collect insights concerning how firms in CEE countries adapt their strategies in resource-constrained business environments that were subjected to profound socio-economic transitions, and an increasing regional focus on the specific CEE context has called IB scholars to re-examine the "CEE research stream" (Jaklič et al., 2018). However, the findings related to CEE internationalization have rarely been (re)tested within the region, so even though special features have been identified, new theories or new takes on the theory able to reshape the research focus of IB have yet to materialize, and very few generalizations were made, leaving place for more exploration and novel understandings of the rich nexus of political, economic, technological, and social developments in the CEE region (Delios, 2017; Jaklič et al., 2020).

The institution-based approach

Business phenomena are studied by scholars worldwide with an acute awareness of the importance of context, which guards against the fallacy of over-generalization, and also gives the particularity of emerging business research through pointing to the everlasting dynamic between what is generalizable and what is unique to a certain context. Meyer and Peng (2016) observed that the institution-based view grew during the 2010s to embrace a more integrative paradigm which explains the interplay of contextual variations, the global megatrends, and micro-behavioral differences across emerging economies and around the world. Coupled with an understanding of the essential role played by institutions for the effective functioning of the market economy this leads to gaining fundamental insight into firm strategies and operations.

Particular to the CEE and other emerging economies, research has highlighted the multifaceted interaction between formal and informal institutions. Informal institutions can take the role of formal institutions which are ineffective or, in other contexts, sap the effectiveness of formal institutions (Estrin & Prevezer, 2011). Many times, however, the changes of laws and regulations do not determine behavioral changes, as norms and values are pervasive and adopted by firms and people alike regardless of the formal shapes. Consequently, companies face various pressures in this divergent environment and studying their strategies is relevant to practice and theory development alike. The cumulative body of knowledge encompassing the economic behaviors of firms and individuals can greatly be expanded through analyzing how institutions operate as mediating factors. Future institution-based research may unravel critical aspects characterizing the emerging economy business field and posit institution-based view as an integrative paradigm, using it to overcome critical shortcomings and disagreements within the paradigm. To an important extent, future research shall look into norms and values and their influence upon how informal institutions work. This would largely help to understand and to manage people issues on institutional level (Meyer & Peng, 2016). Also, the role of institutions in the internationalization of EMFs should be tackled by novel studies, as well as the overall role that institutions have in emerging economies (Jormanainen & Koveshnikov, 2012).

The internationalization approaches of the CEE firms

The review of Ipsmiller and Dikova (2021) has shown that greater reliance on theories and concepts from the field of entrepreneurship and a stronger focus on internationalization decision processes might further enrich our understanding of the internationalization from CEE, and that comparative assessments of international performance of firms originating from various national contexts would further exemplify the idiosyncratic characteristics of countries in the CEE region. A continuous focus on the internationalization strategies of firms from the region will provide the desired new insights into the challenges and opportunities of the transition process. Taking stock of research on CEE firms' internationalization is a first and critical step in this front.

Only recently has the internationalization of CEE firms caught the eye of scientists: Bojnec and Xavier published in 2004 an article on export performance in the region, and the first paper to focus directly on CEE firms' international competitiveness was only published in 2007 by Toming, but the research gained momentum and the internationalization patterns of domestic firms from CEE became the main attraction point during the so-called eclectic period spanning between 2010 and 2016 (Jaklič et al., 2020).

Prevailing internationalization theories have been tested under new conditions and revealed that CEE firms choose a different behavior for doing exports, adopting different entry modes and cross-industry activity, broader product and service portfolios, being less focused and choosing more diverse geographical destinations (Jaklič et al., 2018). With few exceptions, the literature on CEE outward internationalization has neglected the entry mode decision, and while various voices claim different opinions about the need to expand this research area (Hennart & Slangen, 2014; Shaver, 2013), it might prove worthwhile to investigate it, as well as to study the connection between entry mode and performance, the role of perceived distance or asymmetry, and the micro-foundational perspectives on internationalization (Ipsmiller & Dikova, 2021). Other areas that can be subjected to further inquiry regard the orchestration of markets, and the cooperation means with foreign partners that firms have, as well as timing; perhaps studies in this area could also lead to the creation of new typologies/taxonomies of enterprises (Jaklič et al., 2020). Emerging market firms (EMF) and the impact of internationalization on their performance is also to be noted as a potential research stream, and the role that network ties play for an internationalizing EMF shall be investigated, to learn which is the inflection point from which these ties become detrimental to overall performance (Jormanainen & Koveshnikov, 2012). In a similar vein, Bartlett and Ghoshal (2000a, b) and Vătămănescu (2020) speak about a "liability of origin" that firms from CEE countries have to overcome while aiming at conquering international markets, which may affect their entry mode decisions, increase the internationalization costs, and potentially impact their international performance (Ipsmiller & Dikova, 2021).

When assessing the internationalization of CEE firms, several extant studies focused on the antecedents and consequences of local (national) conditions in which the CEE firms operate, such as cultural and geographical proximity, which have been noted as supportive forces to the internationalization strategy (Musteen et al., 2010; Sass, 2012). However, longitudinal, comparative, and mixed research designs can be further employed to delve deeper into the different aspects of the internationalization of EMFs, comparative studies involving more than one country are needed, and the geographical focus may be switched from EMFs in China to other parts of the world, including CEE, but focusing on countries which are underrepresented in the literature (Jormanainen & Koveshnikov, 2012). These studies would help upgrade the extant knowledge on the internationalization of firms, especially at this time, when an increasing corpus of firm-level case studies show that this process is non-linear, hardly predictable, and marked by increased heterogeneity, when the limited databases and short time series data impact research validity and the potential of theoretical generalizations, in a context marked by institutional instability and complexity, encompassing power interplays that impact the firms' behavior (Jaklič et al., 2020).

Local entrepreneurship

The post-socialist context and transition processes are marked by noteworthy features that can only be understood by researchers who take the time to gather abundant knowledge on history, culture (including norms and values), social practices, demographics and ethnicities, economic arrangements and practices, institutional frameworks, and political underpinnings. The Western rationality and theoretical knowledge, created and gathered in fundamentally different human contexts, organized according to different paradigms, are bound to carry bias that is limiting their explanatory force. While similarities do exist, the real patterns, implications, and sensitivities that are particular to the owners, managers, and employees from the CEE only reveal themselves to self-reflexive researchers, who are open to context-sensitive explanations and reject over-generalizations (Soulsby & Clark, 2007). To this end, the research concerning CEE has brought to the fore new questions and puzzles to be solved, while deepening and broadening the literature (Meyer & Peng, 2005), evolving from a macro-level approach to addressing more complex and micro or firm-level topics (Jaklič et al., 2020).

Pursuant to Meyer and Peng (2016) these topics include the on-going managerial challenges regarding resources management and the management of capabilities under institutional peculiarities, shifting from the more traditional approach of studying and trying to explain unfamiliar phenomena. Resource constraints and institutional idiosyncrasies, particular patterns of economic organization, and the local managerial and entrepreneurial approaches – a phenomenon-driven stream of IB research – are understood as context-richness and explored to advance institutional theory (Cantwell, 2016). Future research on emerging markets within IB and management is being supported and enriched by the extant research on CEE as an entity, which offers a sort of a toolkit for further endeavors (Meyer & Peng, 2016; Rašković et al., 2020).

Several factors have been pointed as supportive to the internationalization processes of firms originating from post-socialist countries. Among the propelling factors the founding year of the firm seems to be relevant, companies born after the fall of communism accessing internationalization at a higher speed (Ciszewska-Mlinaric et al., 2018). Proving to have dynamic capabilities or having the capacity to integrate new competencies and rebuild or re-configure the firm to adapt to fast-paced changing environments, as well as being able to mobilize distinctive resources (Vissak, 2007) constitute paramount competitive advantages. The previous experience of the manager, especially their professional activities on foreign markets, coupled with skills development (Sekliuckiene, 2017), and their global orientation or international mindset (Marinova & Marinov, 2017; Vissak, 2007) are prone to offer momentum to the internationalization initiatives. The high education level of the entrepreneur and their completion of management studies are furthermore positively related to an increased export entry (Lafuente et al., 2015), and to an early internationalization (Lamotte & Colovic, 2015). Nonetheless, a relevant and perhaps key asset of a firm that aims at performing internationally is constituted by its specialized marketing capabilities.

In this context of adopting a knowledge-driven approach, the work of Yörük, Öker, and Tafoya (2022) points to the fact that via the combination of internal capabilities, knowledge, and internationalization, early and gradual internationalizers are prone to more rapidly attain product innovation. Furthermore, a proper capitalization of knowledge wells springs as a critical differentiator between high and low-level innovation products whereas internationalization itself pushes local market-oriented companies towards high-level innovation.

Distinctive to the post-socialist environment, the business networks (Peng & Heath, 1996) and strategic flexibility (Uhlenbruck, Meyer & Hitt, 2003) are uniquely important and markedly context-bound (Vătămănescu et al., 2020a, 2020b, 2021). The peculiarities are many, and one of the obvious ones relates to the development and change processes, which are more often interdependent and gradual, continuous, and only rarely radical (Meyer & Peng, 2005). This comes in line with the special connection that businesspersons in the region have to the local resources. Managers and entrepreneurs in this context were described as being attached to the local resources and capabilities when they are faced with novel circumstances, strongly relying on local knowledge and experiences (Soulsby & Clark, 2007).

The local or indigenous resources are nonetheless powerful instruments for value creation in these challenging environments, as research on organizational change in CEE illustrates (Meyer & Peng, 2005). Nonetheless, the scarcity of resources and knowledge that characterizes some entrepreneurial firms in the CEE region is known and liable of particular internationalization processes. Studying the adventurous international activities of entrepreneurial firms in the region, and learning more about how small multinationals grow, at the interplay of political instability, social unrest, and economic developments, would lead IB scientists towards achieving excellence and building original theoretical contributions (Jaklič et al., 2020).

The differences between the countries that belong to the CEE are numerous and deep, ranging from political to social and economic levels, owing to their unique history and heritage and only briefly having in common the communist regime, which, truth be told, was adopted through differing models in these countries (Jaklič et al., 2018). Despite these differences, the CEE has been often treated as a uniform bloc. This practice must be reduced and insights on how each of these differences model the business environment, the internationalization strategies, and the orchestration and network capacities shall be searched for, ideally in a comparative manner and in a context-sensitive key (Jaklič et al., 2020). There is also potential in what concerns the research of individual-level characteristics that influence decision-making in managers and entrepreneurs, including biases and heuristics (Guercini & Milanesi, 2020), and interactions (Foss & Pedersen, 2019).

The non-CEE context is perhaps bound to profoundly differing biases and heuristics and uses alternate reference points, which may impact decisions, learning, opportunities recognition, and attitudes to risk-taking in certain manners (Ipsmiller & Dikova, 2021). While EMF studies are heterogeneous, the stream would be enhanced by incorporating novel conceptual ideas from other fields, including internationalization (Manolova et al., 2010; Musteen et al., 2010), knowledge transfer, human resources management, post-acquisition integration processes, or the dynamics between headquarters and subsidiaries (Jormanainen & Koveshnikov, 2012).

Business relationships and networks in CEE

In recent times, the focus on studying the role of networks in connection to the CEE is prevalent (Nowiński & Rialp, 2016), offering grounds for theory testing and refinement. A solid stream emerged based on the extensive work of Klaus Meyer, who researched into the internationalization of SMEs and the growth paths taken by firms operating in transitioning environments (Jaklič et al., 2020), and one of the most attractive topics under this umbrella regards the power of networks to become a source of competitive advantage. The impact that networks have on the success of SMEs in emerging markets has been found to be especially strong (Manolova et al., 2010; Musteen et al., 2010), mostly as a consequence of the valuable knowledge which is required for international success that SMEs get from other network members (Elango & Pattnaik, 2007; Kotabe et al., 2010; Thomas et al., 2007). Research also shows that SMEs with weak ties tend to internationalize faster than the ones with strong ties and that SMEs from emerging markets are more reliant on networks than large EMFs (Jormanainen & Koveshnikov, 2012).

Networks are relevant to the IB field as they constitute paramount linkages between firms that operate across national borders and may help regulate the relationships between companies in global industries (Musteen, Datta, & Francis, 2014a; Meyer & Peng, 2016; Sun et al., 2012). The knowledge that firms have access to through networks is an essential antecedent for their internationalization, and this is why the process of knowledge acquisition through network cooperation, with the purpose of identifying and measuring various international opportunities, has caught the attention of numerous researchers (Ipsmiller & Dikova, 2021; Vătămănescu et al., 2020a, 2020b, 2021).

Different levels of impact have been acknowledged, including the degree of internationalization, the pace at which the process evolves, and the performance achieved on international markets. Studies point to the fact that networks support internationalization and foster performance, the intensity to which the benefits manifest being moderated by factors such as the firm's size and age (Manolova et al., 2010 2014), or the environmental hostility on the domestic market and technological intensity (Musteen et al., 2014b). Early internationalization is nonetheless linked to firms having access to ICT infrastructure, to originating from an EU members state, to being led by managers who are highly educated and connected to networks, and to operating in highly competitive fields (Musteen et al., 2010, 2014b; Cunningham et al., 2012; Gittins et al., 2015; Lamotte & Colovic, 2015).

Pursuant to various authors (Dymitrowski et al., 2019; Vătămănescu et al., 2020a, 2020b, 2021), the influence of networks on SME internationalization varies across industries, firms from different fields necessitating particular network configurations to succeed on foreign markets, and requiring support from these networks at specific times, some only at the beginning of their international adventure, others at later dates too. Srivastava (2020) additionally explains that internationalization performance depends upon the adoption of the ideal network behavior of the firm. More so, embracing an alliance-based internationalization strategy and selling low-cost but high-quality products propel SME growth on external markets (Malo & Norus, 2009).

Specific to the CEE context, the literature can be enriched by exploring the network-based strategies adopted during the transition. Cultural insights from the CEE countries reveal that historically personal relationships and belonging to a certain informal network of individuals were vital in the shortage economy, with people relying even more on these informal connections than on institutions, or perhaps relying on these networks to access goods and knowledge that the formal networks and institutions did not allow to spread or be accessed by the commoners. These habitudes are long spanning and still mark the behavior of individuals who further today the businesses from these countries.

CEE managers tend to rely on their personal connections to solve the issues they encounter, and to reach their goals, to a significant extent. Peng and Heath (1996) argued that this prevalence of network-based strategies constitutes a reaction to the institutional conditions in transition economies, emphasizing the significance that the ties created by the manager at micro, interpersonal level, as well as firm level represent an intangible asset, a "micro-macro link" working as a safety net for the company. Especially in markets where governing rules are only vaguely defined business networks and personal relationships are needed for firms to operate (Meyer & Peng, 2016).

In transition economies, it is thus expected that entrepreneurial networking would intensely support business internationalization (Peng & Stanislav, 2001) and act as a backing power for smaller SMEs that compete with larger and more powerful companies on markets that are marked by imperfection (McMillan & Woodruff, 2002). While networks may become rigid and institutionalized too, generating inertia and arm's length transactions at times, this is considered to take place only after a longer while. Clear empirical evidence on the role that institutions play with regards to networking and networks, and on which institutions have the more significant impact is still to be found. The connection between institutional change and networking intensity is yet another area that shall be explored (Meyer & Peng, 2005).

While emerging economies display commonalities in what regards the roles played by networks to business internationalization, there are also remarkable country-level idiosyncrasies which need to be explored separately and comparatively. Some of these peculiarities account for how network relationships are being built, maintained, and utilized by managers from various places (Batjargal, 2007). Other unique characteristics that are specific to each country concern the significance of the network partners: in Africa a firm which is connected to tribal leaders or to ruling party incumbents has valuable advantages (Acquaah, 2007), while in China and Russia, it seems more important for the success of a firm to be managed by a person who has connections to the officials (Okhmatovskiy, 2010; Peng, Sun, & Markóczy, 2014; Puffer et al., 2013).

***

In this chapter, we argued that the literature in the International Business field could and should be enriched through the advancement of context-driven perspectives on extant theories, and through eventually proposing new concepts, as descriptors of realities which are specific to certain regions and economies, especially regarding the SMEs sector and the managerial mindset. We underlined that the CEE region offers a particularly relevant environment for novel theoretical underpinnings, due to the profound changes that took place in this area in the last 30 years, touching the political, the economic, the technologic, the social, the cultural, and the demographical levels. Other transitional economies and emerging economies should be studied as well, in more depth, to potentially unravel specific managerial and entrepreneurial behaviors, unwritten norms, public-private sector dynamics, and other phenomena that would enrich the IB knowledge field.

References

Acquaah, M. (2007). Managerial social capital, strategic orientation, and organizational performance in an emerging economy. *Strategic Management Journal*, *20*(12), 1235–1255. 10.1002/smj.632

Bartlett, C.A., & Ghoshal, S. (2000a). Going global: lessons from late movers. *Harvard Business Review*, *78*(2), 132–141. https://hbr.org/2000/03/going-global-lessons-from-late-movers

Bartlett, C.A., & Ghoshal, S., (2000b). *Transition management: Text, cases, and readings in cross-border management* (third edition). Irwin McGraw-Hill.

Batjargal, B. (2007). Network triads: Transitivity, referral and venture capital decisions in China and Russia. *Journal of International Business Studies*, *38*(6), 998–1012. 10.1057/palgrave.jibs8400302

Bojnec, Š., & Xavier, A. (2004). Entry and exit in transition economies: the Slovenian manufacturing sector. *Post-Communist Economies*, *16*(2), 191–214. 10.1080/146313 7042000223886

Cantwell, J. (2016). The *JIBS* 2015 Decade Award: Probing theoretically into Central and Eastern Europe: Transactions, resources, and institutions. *Journal of International Business Studies*, *47*, 1–2. 10.1057/jibs.2015.31

Ciszewska-Mlinaric, M., Obloj, K., & Wasowska, A. (2018). Internationalisation choices of Polish firms during the post-socialism transition period: The role of institutional conditions at firm's foundation. *Business History*, *60*(4), 562–600. 10.1080/00076791.2017.1332045

Cunningham, I., Loane, S., & Ibbotson, P. (2012). The internationalisation of small games development firms: evidence from Poland and Hungary. *Journal of Small Business and Enterprise Development*, *19*(2), 246–262. 10.1108/14626001211223883.

Delios, A. (2017). The death and rebirth (?) of international business research. *Journal of Management Studies*, *54*(3), 391–397. 10.1111/joms.12222

DIW ECON. (July 27, 2018). SMEs Performance Review 2017/2018. Methodological Note on WP 3. www.diw-econ.com.

Drabik, D. (2022). Applied welfare economics, trade, and agricultural policy analysis. *European Review of Agricultural Economics*, *49*(3), 720–722. 10.1093/erae/jbac005

Dymitrowski, A., Fonfara, K., & Deszczyński, B. (2019). Informal relationships in a company's internationalization process. *Journal of Business & Industrial Marketing*, *34*(5), 1054–1065. 10.1108/JBIM-11-2018-0363

Elango, B., & Pattnaik, C. (2007). Building capabilities for international operations through networks: A study of Indian firms. *Journal of International Business Studies*, *38*(4), 541–555. 10.1057/palgrave.jibs.8400280

Estrin, S., & Prevezer, M. (2011).The role of informal institutions in corporate gov-
ernance: Brazil, Russia, India, and China compared. *Asia Pacific Journal of
Management, 28*(1), 41–67. 10.1007/s10490-010-9229-1
European Commission. (June 25, 2008). Think Small First. A Small Business Act for
Europe. COM (2008) 394 final. https://eur-lex.europa.eu/legal-content/EN/TXT/?
uri=CELEX:52008DC0394
European Commission (March 2020). Unleashing the full potential of European
SMEs, https://ec.europa.eu/commission/presscorner/detail/en/fs_20_426----pdf. doi:10.
2775/296379
European Council. (2022). Green Deal. https://www.consilium.europa.eu/en/policies/
green-deal/
Foss, N.J., & Pedersen, T. (2019). Microfoundations in international management research: The case of knowledge sharing in multinational corporations.
Journal of International Business Studies, 50(9), 1594–1621. 10.1057/s41267-019-
00270-4
Gittins, T., Lang, R., & Sass, M. (2015). The effect of return migration driven
social capital on SME internationalization: a comparative case study of IT sector
entrepreneurs in Central and Eastern Europe. *Review of Managerial Science, 9*(2),
385–409. 10.1007/s11846-014-0161-5
Guercini, S., & Milanesi, M. (2020). Heuristics in international business: A systematic
literature review and directions for future research. *Journal of International
Management, 26*(4), 100782. 10.1016/j.intman.2020.100782
Hennart, J.F., & Slangen, A.H. (2014). Yes, we really do need more entry mode
studies! A commentary on Shaver. *Journal of International Business Studies, 46*(1),
114–122. 10.1057/jibs.2014.39
Hope, K. (Ed.) (2022). Annual Report on European SMEs 2021/2022 SMEs and
environmental sustainability. https://single-market-economy.ec.europa.eu/smes/sme-
strategy/sme-performance-review_en
Ipsmiller, E., & Dikova, D. (2021). Internationalization from central and Eastern
Europe: a systematic literature review. *Journal of International Management, 27*(4),
100862. 10.1016/j.intman.2021.100862
Jaklič, A., Obloj, K., Svetličič, M., & Kronegger, L. (2020). Evolution of Central and
Eastern Europe related international business research. *Journal of Business Research,
108*(C), 421–434. 10.1016/j.jbusres.2019.06.046
Jaklič, A., Rašković, M., & Schuch, A. (2018). Examining the contextual richness of
Central and Eastern Europe. *AIB Insights, 18*(1), 3–6. 10.46697/001c.16843
Jormanainen, I., & Koveshnikov, A. (2012). International activities of emerging
market firms a critical assessment of research in top international management
journals. *Management International Review, 52*, 691–725. 10.1007/s11575-011-
0115-y
Kornai, J. (2008). The great transformation of Central Eastern Europe: Success
and disappointment. In J. Kornai, L. Mátyás & G. Roland (Eds.), *Institutional
Change and Economic Behavior. International Economic Association Series*, 1–37.
Palgrave Macmillan. https://doi.org/10.1057/9780230583429_1
Kotabe, M., Jiang, C.X., & Murray, J.Y. (2010). Managerial ties, knowledge acquisition, realized absorptive capacity and new product market performance of
emerging multinational companies: A case of China. *Journal of World Business,
46*(2), 166–176. https://doi.org/10.1016/j.jwb.2010.05.005

Koveshnikov, A., Dabija, D.-C., Inkpen, A., & Vătămănescu, E.-M. (2022). Not running out of steam after 30 years: The enduring relevance of Central and Eastern Europe for international management scholarship. *Journal of International Management*, *28*(3), 10097310.1016/j.intman.2022.100973.

Lafuente, E., Stoian, M.C., & Rialp, J. (2015). From export entry to de-internationalization through entrepreneurial attributes. *Journal of Small Business and Enterprise Development*, *22*(1), 21–37. https://doi.org/10.1108/JSBED-09-2012-0101

Lamotte, O., & Colovic, A. (2015). Early internationalization of new ventures from emerging countries: The case of transition economies. *Management*, *18*(1), 8–30. https://doi.org/10.3917/mana.181.0008

Limański, A., Poplavska, Z., & Drabik, I. (2018). Marketing information system and risk reduction in managing a company on foreign markets. *Ekonomia i Prawo*, *17* (43). https://doi.org/10.12775/EiP.2018.004.

Malo, S., & Norus, J. (2009). Growth dynamics of dedicated biotechnology firms in transition economies. Evidence from the Baltic countries and Poland. *Entrepreneurship & Regional Development*, *21*(5-6), 481–502. https://doi.org/10.1080/08985620802332749

Manolova, T.S., Manev, I.M., & Gyoshev, B.S. (2014). Friends with money? Owner's financial network and new venture internationalization in a transition economy. *International Small Business Journal*, *32*(8), 944–966. https://doi.org/10.1177/0266242613482482

Manolova, T.S., Manev, I.M., & Gyoshev, B.S. (2010). In good company: The role of personal and inter-firm networks for new-venture internationalization in a transition economy. *Journal of World Business*, *45*(3), 257–265. https://doi.org/10.1016/j.jwb.2009.09.004

Marinova, S., & Marinov, M. (2017). Inducing the internationalization of family manufacturing firms from a transition context. *European Business Review*, *29*(2), 181–204. https://doi.org/10.1108/EBR-07-2016-0085

McMillan, J., & Woodruff, C. (2002). The central role of entrepreneurs in transition economies. *Journal of Economic Perspectives*, *16*(3), 153–170. https://doi.org/10.1257/089533002760278767

Meyer, K.E., & Peng, M.W. (2005). Probing theoretically into Central and Eastern Europe: Transactions, resources, and institutions. *Journal of International Business Studies*, *36*(6), 600–621. https://doi.org/10.1057/palgrave.jibs.8400167

Meyer, K.E., & Peng, M.W. (2016). Theoretical foundations of emerging economy business research. *Journal of International Business Studies*, *47*(1), 3–22. https://doi.org/10.1057/jibs.2015.34

Musteen, M., Datta, D.K., & Butts, M.M. (2014a). Do international networks and foreign market knowledge facilitate SME internationalization? evidence from the Czech Republic. *Entrepreneurship Theory and Practice*, *38*(4), 749–774. https://doi.org/10.1111/etap.12025

Musteen, M., Datta, D.K., & Francis, J. (2014b). Early internationalization by firms in transition economies into developed markets: The role of international networks. *Global Strategy Journal*, *4*(3), 221–237. https://doi.org/10.1002/gsj.1077

Musteen, M., Francis, J., & Datta, D.K. (2010). The influence of international networks on internationalization speed and performance: A study of Czech SMEs. *Journal of World Business*, *45*(3), 197–205. https://doi.org/10.1016/j.jwb.2009.12.003

Nowiński, W., & Rialp, A. (2016). The impact of social networks on perceptions of international opportunities. *Journal of Small Business Management*, *54*(2), 445–461. https://doi.org/10.1111/jsbm.12149

Okhmatovskiy, I. (2010). Performance implications of ties to the government and SOEs: A political embeddedness perspective. *Journal of Management Studies*, *47*(6), 1020–1047. https://doi.org/10.1111/j.1467-6486.2009.00881.x

Peng, M.W., & Heath, P. (1996). The growth of the firm in planned economies in transition: Institutions, organizations, and strategic choices. *Academy of Management Review*, *21*(2), 492–528. https://doi.org/10.2307/258670

Peng, M.W., & Stanislav V.S. (2001). How entrepreneurs create wealth in transition economies and executive commentary]. *The Academy of Management Executive (1993-2005)*, *15*(1), 95–110. http://www.jstor.org/stable/4165713

Peng, M.W., Sun, S., & Markóczy, L. (2014). Human capital and CEO compensation during institutional transitions. *Journal of Management Studies*, *52*. https://doi.org/10.1111/joms.12106.

Puffer, S.M., McCarthy, D.J., Jaeger, A.M. (2013). The use of favors by emerging market managers: Facilitator or inhibitor of international expansion? *Asia Pacific Journal of Management*, *30*, 327–349. https://doi.org/10.1007/s10490-012-9299-3

Rašković, M., Dikova, D., & McDougall-Covin, T.P. (2020). International business with Central and Eastern Europe: From tyranny of history to revisited laboratories of learning. *Journal of Business Research*, *108*(1), 417–420. https://doi.org/10.26686/wgtn.12612773.v3

Sass, M. (2012). Internationalization of innovative SMEs in the Hungarian medical precision instruments industry. *Post-Communist Economies*, *24*(3), 365–382. https://doi.org/10.1080/14631377.2012.705470

Sekliuckiene, J. (2017). Factors leading to early internationalization in emerging Central and Eastern European economies. *European Business Review*, *29*(2), 219–242. https://doi.org/10.1108/EBR-12-2015-0158

Shaver, J.M. (2013). Do we really need more entry mode studies? *Journal of International Business Studies*, *44*(1), 23–27. http://www.jstor.org/stable/43653747

Soulsby, A., & Clark, E. (2007). Organization theory and the post-socialist transformation: Contributions to organizational knowledge. *Human Relations*, *60*(10), 1419–1442. https://doi.org/10.1177/0018726707083470

Srivastava, M. (2020). The effect of industry-specific networking behavior on the internationalization performance of Czech SMEs. *Journal of Business & Industrial Marketing*, *36*(3), 436–453. https://doi.org/10.1108/JBIM-09-2019-0405

Sun, P., Mellahi, K., & Wright, M. (2012). The contingent value of corporate political ties. *Academy of Management Perspectives*, *26*(3), 68–82. https://doi.org/10.5465/amp.2011.0164

Thomas, D.E., Eden, L., Hitt., M.A., & Miller, S.R. (2007). Experience of emerging market firms: The role of cognitive bias in developed market entry and survival. *Management International Review*, *47*(6), 845–867. https://doi.org/10.1007/s11575-007-0055-8

Toming, K. (2007). The impact of EU accession on the export competitiveness of the Estonian food processing industry. *Post-Communist Economies*, *19*(2), 187–207. https://doi.org/10.1080/14631370701312170

Uhlenbruck, K., Meyer, K.E., & Hitt, M.A. (2003). Organisational Transformation in Transition Economies: Resource-based and Organizational Learning Perspectives. https://citeseerx.ist.psu.edu/document?repid=rep1&type=pdf&doi=8e8f1772def-c8ad84de71574d1815957b010aa22

Vătămănescu, E.-M. (2020). *Internaționalizarea IMM-urilor și Marketingul Relațional: între Convergență și conectivitate [The internationalization of SMEs and relationship marketing: between convergence and connectivity]*. Pro Universitaria.

Vătămănescu, E.-M., Alexandru, V.-A., Mitan, A., & Dabija, D.-C. (2020a). From the deliberate managerial strategy towards international business performance: A psychic distance vs. global mindset approach. *Systems Research and Behavioral Science, 37*(2), 374–387. https://doi.org/10.1002/sres.2658

Vătămănescu, E.-M., Cegarra-Navarro, J.-G., Andrei, A.G., Dincă, V.-M., & Alexandru, V.-A. (2020b). SMEs strategic networks and innovative performance: A relational design and methodology for knowledge sharing. *Journal of Knowledge Management, 24*(6), 1369–1392. https://doi.org/10.1108/JKM-01-2020-0010

Vătămănescu, E.-M., Mitan, A., Andrei, A.G., & Ghigiu, A.M. (2021). Linking coopetition benefits and innovative performance within small and medium-sized enterprises networks: A strategic approach on knowledge sharing and direct collaboration. *Kybernetes, 51*(7), 2193–2214. https://doi.org/10.1108/K-11-2020-0731

Vissak, T. (2007). The emergence and success factors of fast internationalizers: Four cases from Estonia. *Journal of East-West Business, 13*(1), 11–33. https://doi.org/10.1300/J097v13n01_02

Whitley, R., & Czaban, L. (1998). Institutional transformation and enterprise change in Hungary. *Organization Studies, 19*(2), 259–280. https://doi.org/10.1177/017084069801900205

World Bank (2022). Small and medium enterprises (SMEs) finance. https://www.worldbank.org/en/topic/smefinance

Yörük, E., Öker, İ., & Tafoya, G.R. (2022). The four global worlds of welfare capitalism: Institutional, neoliberal, populist and residual welfare state regimes. *Journal of European Social Policy, 32*(2), 119–134. https://doi.org/10.1177/09589287211050520

Part II

Relationships and SMEs internationalization

A zoom-in perspective

5 Relationship marketing and SMEs internationalization

This chapter aims to bring to the fore the peculiarities of relationship marketing, the reference context being the emergence and development of international business. While the first chapters set out to approach the overarching context, factors, forms, and models of SME internationalization from a process perspective, the fourth chapter focuses on the importance and role of the human component in the dynamics of internationalization, completing the overview with general research models and directions of relationship marketing. The literature review highlights not only the nodal points of research in the field, but also areas of vulnerability, i.e., topics of study that still remain at an embryonic stage.

Once the research guidelines in the field of relationship marketing in general are outlined, the focus shifts to two exponential models for the B2B approach: the interaction-based B2B relationship marketing model and the network-based B2B relationship marketing model. The two conceptual models are specific to the interaction between SMEs in industry, an area of activity explored in the empirical section of the paper. International relationship marketing is a pillar of the development of industrial SME activity in international markets, with a focus on interlinking and establishing business relationships at management level.

Consequently, the last two sections of this chapter mark and set the angle of investigation of international business, focusing on the effect of culture and country-of-origin on international B2B relationship marketing. Processual highlights are given of the enablers and inhibitors that act as moderators in the initiation, creation, development, and maintenance of international partnerships. The study of cultural variables and country-of-origin variables is intended to add value to the conceptual model advanced in the third theoretical chapter which assumes the current environment – intercultural, cross-cultural, highly interconnected – and the fact that profitable businesses and successful organizations show a propensity to seek international, even global, markets for competitive advantage.

Thus, the main theoretical considerations in these sections represent the argumentative background for the vision brought by the following chapter, inculcating the thematic lines of reference in the economy of the whole work.

DOI: 10.4324/9781003432326-7

Relationship marketing in an international context: Models and general research directions

Relationship marketing has been defined in different ways depending on the scientific background of each researcher, and building a comprehensive definition is still a work-in-progress due to the rapid pace of change globally. However, Palmatier (2008, pp. 4–5), synthesizing several previous theoretical perspectives, arrived at the following definition: "Relationship marketing is the process of identifying, developing, maintaining and completing relational exchanges with the aim of increasing performance."

The propensity toward a relational approach to marketing has been driven by the transition to service-based economies, the evolution of communication, logistics and information technologies, increasing global competitiveness, and the growing adaptation of products and services, all of which have concurred to impose a relationship based on loyalty, reciprocity, and respect between transacting parties (Gupta & Sahu, 2012; Sweeney & Webb, 2007). Moreover, these challenges and trends have increased the need and desire for SMEs to benefit from tailored relational exchanges in order to reduce perceived risk, rely on trusting and cooperative relationships, and have greater flexibility in managing transactions internationally (Palmatier, 2008, p. 9). Awareness and assuming that relationship marketing can also have significant benefits in international partnerships, both sellers and buyers have shown interest in managing business relationships based on constant and trusting interactions, the implementation of which is likely to lead to a long-term competitive advantage for both parties (Samy et al., 2015).

The importance of relationships in business exchanges can be traced as far back as Homer's Greece, but substantive interpersonal relationships have continued to be targeted in an incremental fashion throughout history (Palmatier, 2008). However, relationship marketing has emerged as a research priority among marketing experts and members of academia over the past 30 years. The relatively recent emergence of research papers, popular business books, and managerial initiatives based on relationship marketing has materialized later, as business effectiveness and strong long-term relationships could no longer be dissociated (Chai & Dibb, 2014; Danaher et al., 2008; Dibb et al., 2014; Gupta & Sahu, 2012; Vătămănescu 2020, 2020b, 2022).

The establishment of relationship marketing as a separate academic field occurred in the 1980s and 1990s, with researchers such as Grönroos (1994) and Sheth and Parvatiyar (1995, 2000) calling relationship marketing a "paradigm shift" in the broader context of marketing. The authors point out that this shift is marked by moving away from a focus on transactions and the 4 P's model toward effective management of all relational variables. Studies have shown that relationship-based exchanges have been the norm since ancient times. Therefore, relationship marketing can be said to represent "a genuine revival of pre-industrial era marketing practices" (Sheth & Parvatiyar, 1995, p. 399).

Before the industrial age, most trade took place in local markets, where farmers and producers sold their products directly to end users. From that point on, producers (manufacturers) formed and developed relationships with consumers based on mutual trust and respect for business rules, especially as there were no institutionalized forms of protection. From this perspective, although the terminology and academic terms specific to relationship marketing are relatively new, best practices and the importance of relationships on successful exchanges date back hundreds of years (Dibb & Meadows, 2004; Kotler & Keller, 2006; Palmatier, 2008).

The rules of the game changed when mass production and consumption during the industrial revolution significantly influenced the relationship between producers and consumers. Producers took advantage of economies of scale and exploited the production of large volumes of goods at low prices that required transport, storage, and sale over wide geographical areas to be as close as possible to the consumer. Alongside mass production came aggressive sales promotion designed to increase demand sufficiently for a growing volume of goods. Industrialization led to the emergence of inter-mediaries who took on the activities of transport, storage, resale, or retailing, with the new channels interposed emphasizing the transactional nature of exchanges and the distance between the main links in the system (producer-consumer) (Grönroos, 1994; Kotler, 1991; Lages et al., 2008).

Palmatier et al. (2007) consider that the return and reorientation toward the importance of business relationships on organizational effectiveness has been stimulated by the shift from a product-based to a service-based economy, in which the role of the intermediary has been considerably diminished. In addition, technological developments and advances in communication and logistics have catalyzed direct transactions between producers and consumers across spatial constraints. In this sense, one can speak of "a duplication of pre-industrial local bazaars at the global or at least national level" (Palmatier, 2008, p. 10). Sheth and Parvatiyar (1995) found that more and more consumers demand relational exchanges based on trust and loyalty when transacting in the new "global bazaar." Also, the exacerbation of global competition has led many manufacturers to develop strategies that do not put price at the forefront but aim to increase customer loyalty and attachment over the long term (Lages et al., 2008). Confirmation of this is provided by analyzes that identify higher costs associated with retaining customers than those associated with attracting customers. Consequently, strengthening loyalty-building strategies and lending credit to relationship marketing is a critical catalyst. The approach is all the more relevant in the B2B context, where maintaining long-lasting relationships with partners translates into long-term benefits (Samy et al., 2015).

The literature on relationship marketing has over the years dealt with models that have covered various relationship hypostases. Dwyer et al. (1987) and Levitt (1983) spoke of relationship marketing as a gradual process of estab-lishing interpersonal bonds, indicating the existence of five major components: awareness, exploration, expansion, commitment, and dissolution. Hallen and

Weidshiem-Paul (1984) noted the presence of four stages that define the evolution of relationships – precontact, initial interaction, development, and maturation of ties.

Although the forerunners of relationship marketing theory can be traced back to the 1950s, the main theoretical models underpinning this field of research have been crystallizing since the 1990s. Thus, between 1990 and 2000, commitment-trust theory (Morgan & Hunt, 1994) emerges, extrapolating the meaning of relationship marketing beyond seller-buyer interactions. The vision is eminently sociological and psychological, marking the next decade of research on relationship marketing. Commitment-trust theory argues that "the presence of commitment and trust in a relationship is definitive of relationship marketing success, not relationship strength" (Morgan & Hunt, 1994, p. 22). At this level, commitment implies an ongoing desire to maintain an appropriately valued relationship, while trust represents belief in the integrity and trustworthiness of the partner, both of which are key elements of overall performance. Partners who invest trust in the relationship and proof ongoing commitment to the relationship work together to maintain and strengthen ties, consequently influencing the viability of cooperation, financial outcomes and overall positive impact (Brennan et al., 2011; Palmatier et al., 2006a, 2006b).

Another model was proposed by Payne (1995) who highlighted that the phases of relationship marketing depend on the different roles of the actors, starting with potential buyers and buyers, continuing with loyal customers and supporters and ending with members and partners. Additionally, Kotler (1997) points out that there are eight stages of relationship building depending on the attitude and behavior of the parties, namely: 1. The curious person stage; 2. The stage of potential buyers; 3. Stage of first-time buyers; 4. Stage of repeat buyers; 5. Stage of customers; 6. Stage of advocates; 7. Status of members; 8. Status of partners. More recently, Sin et al. (2005a, 2005b) discussed the existence of six main dimensions specific to relationship marketing – empathy, interrelatedness, communication, shared value, reciprocity and trust, while Murphy et al. (2007) concluded that three phases are defining – establishing, maintaining and strengthening relationships. In the same vein, Palmatier (2008, pp. 18–19), speaking of an inter-organizational relationship marketing model, emphasizes "interactions between several individuals and, more precisely, a network of relationships." The author considers that several fundamental characteristics of the relationship-building process can be profiled and here he notes the strength of the relationship (derived from the quality of the relationship – trust and commitment – and the extent or density of the relationship) and the effectiveness of the relationship (derived from the quality of the relationship and its composition – the diversity or attractiveness of the network).

By comparing the models presented above, it is possible to identify certain key concepts that each model brings to the fore: the influence of commitment and trust in a relationship on the effectiveness of relationship marketing;

developing and strengthening links that lead to better economic and financial results; the importance of sustained interaction and communication between parties in crystallizing sustainable partnerships; the processuality of relationship development over time, from the exploration stage to the partnership stage (explicitly highlighted in the work of Kotler, 1997 and Payne, 1995); strengthening the relationship between the parties based on integrity, commitment, loyalty and mutual trust in the medium and long term.

It should be noted that the main elements of these theories are the pillars of the models that emerged after 2000, which focus on three complementary perspectives, namely the resource-based inter-organizational perspective, the B2B relationship marketing based on social exchange, and the network and micro-theories of interpersonal relationships (Palmatier, 2008).

The resource-based inter-organizational perspective integrates multiple theoretical strands into a unified framework of inter-organizational (resource-based) exchanges, demonstrating that the impact of relationship marketing on performance is determined by substantive relationships (commitment, trust), but also by investments in training, communication, which enhance the effectiveness or efficiency of relationship "assets." Palmatier et al. (2007) and O'Cass et al. (2015) point out that both relational constructs and actual investments in relationship building are important for successful collaboration between different partners, the latter playing a defining role in generating sustainable competitive advantage. While commitment and trust enhance the quality of the relationships necessary for effective interchange, additional investments in the relationship solidify and enhance other aspects of a successful relationship.

Recent research in the field of relationship marketing has also focused on discriminating between *business-to-business* (B2B) and *business-to-consumer* (B2C) relationships, with an equal emphasis on areas of convergence and divergence (Palmatier et al., 2007). This concern has resulted in B2B and B2C marketing and the customization of activities according to the two irradiation cores, as exemplified in Table 5.1.

The influence of relationship marketing on the building of international partnerships between SMEs has been addressed primarily through one-dimensional models, with concepts such as "psychic distance," "trust," "commitment," "loyalty," "cross-cultural learning," "sustainability" being treated in separate research contexts. In this sense, the development of an integrative framework is a research priority.

Collaborative relationships and interactions between individuals are a constant in human society in general and an inherent practice in business since the beginning of economic flows. The realization by contemporary organizations that being competitive in the long term depends to a large extent on the effective management of relationships with key partners has led to consistent moves to strengthen links at all levels (Chirica, 2013; Pop et al., 2012). At this level, relationship marketing emerges as an action imperative given its intrinsic nature – "identifying, establishing, maintaining, developing, adjusting and terminating customer relationships to create value for

Table 5.1 Main differences between B2B and B2C marketing (adapted from Kolis & Jirinova, 2013)

No.	Criterion	B2B Marketing	B2C Marketing
1.	Coverage area	It is more concentrated, focused on specialized target markets, with one-to-one communication being the preferred communication	It is broader, targeting more general target markets, with mass communication predominating
2.	Focus	It involves offering complex solutions based on sustained consultation between the parties to enhance the value of the partnership	It is more product-oriented without a developed interrelation component to maximize transaction value
3.	Notoriety	The brands of products traded are not well known and the budgets allocated to promotional activities are lower	Traded product brands are better known, with much larger budgets allocated to promotional activities
4.	Sales cycle	It is longer, based on a multi-stage process, involving a higher level of price and risk	It is shorter, based on a single-stage process, involving a lower level of price and risk
5.	Type of relations between	Aim for strong and long-lasting interpersonal relationships with existing partners	Relationships are product-oriented, not people-oriented
6.	Type of decision	It focuses on rational criteria, on the value of the business itself	It focuses on emotional criteria such as status, image and social comparison

customers and profit for the organization through a series of relational exchanges that have both a past and a future" (Kanagal, 2009, p. 1). In other words, relationship marketing encompasses a broad spectrum of relationship types and strategies, reflecting the status quo of marketing practices in different industries, of which the *business-to-business* sectors stand out.

From a sustainability perspective, relationship marketing brings to the forefront the emergence and development of long-term relationships between SMEs and their stakeholders, with the aim of generating benefits for all those involved in the value co-creation process (Halinen et al., 2012; Pop et al., 2012). In this regard, many theorists and researchers have emphasized that long-term relationships with key stakeholders should be seen as a key strategy for organizations to maintain their competitive advantage in the current market (Arnett et al., 2003; Brito, 2011; Gronroos, 2007; Palmatier, 2008; Palmer et al., 2005; Reinartz et al., 2008). Pragmatically speaking, long-term business relationships between SMEs facilitate cost containment, based on the premise that the operational costs incurred by "an old customer are much lower than those incurred by a new customer" (Maxim, 2009, p. 289).

Similarly, as Anderson and Weitz (1989, p. 310) point out, long-term business relationships between SMEs combine the advantages of vertically integrated distribution systems (control and coordination) with the advantages of systems using independent channels (flexibility, economies of scale, efficiency and low overheads). In order to make these processes explicit, the authors point out that organizations relying only on transactional relationships, i.e., episodic collaborators, risk being treated as "one of many" and are likely to face multiple obstacles due to a lack of prior shared experience. As a result, the crystallization of sustainable and specialized relationships between parties (producers and distributors) has some major benefits for both producing and distributing SMEs (Anderson & Weitz, 1989, p. 311): there is a higher likelihood of collaborating to develop new products tailored to market requirements; there is a higher likelihood that they will jointly or separately conduct formal and informal market research on the products and services traded; they are more likely to agree longer payment terms, support each other in managing sales and associated expenses; there is a higher likelihood that one party will find better and faster solutions to the other party's requests; there is a greater likelihood that parties will demonstrate flexibility and goodwill when unforeseen circumstances arise.

While cost and price incentives are very important, sustainable competitive advantage relies on the social ties between business partners, which require appropriate personalization of relationships. In other words, achieving long-term financial performance by SMEs is dependent on increasing profitability through sustainable relationship marketing strategies rather than through separate transactions that are inherently profitable in the short term (Kanagal, 2009; Kotler & Keller, 2006; Miller, 2005; Tan & Sousa, 2015).

At a general level, interaction-based relationship marketing focuses on face-to-face interaction between potential partners, with both parties expressing an interest in developing mutually beneficial, mutually valuable and sustainable relationships. In addition, network-based relationship marketing is interrelationship-oriented, with an inter- and trans-organizational focus. Partner SMEs will become nodes of a specialized network, between which various collaborative links develop over time.

B2B relationship marketing model based on interaction

Interaction-based relationship marketing considers face-to-face interaction between potential partners, with both parties interested in investing the resources necessary to create an interpersonal relationship seen as mutually beneficial (Brodie et al., 2008, p. 85). Over time, marketing definitions have identified interpersonal relationships as a key factor in the success of any transaction, analogous to elements of the traditional marketing mix. The explicit focus, however, on relationships and relationship marketing itself has been attributed to Berry (1983).

The most prominent definitions of interaction-based relationship marketing (as outlined by Bouzdine-Chameeva et al., 2014; Gronroos, 1997;

Mandják & Durrieu, 2000; Palmatier, 2008; Sheth & Parvatiyar, 2000) have at their core three key elements.

A The first element refers to the level of commitment of the potential or existing partner and the activities subsumed by the phases of the relationship life cycle. It is recognized that the dynamic nature of the interrelationship configuration and the fact that the activities related to marketing and relationship exchanges differ significantly in relation to the specificity of each stage of SME interaction (Ivanova & Torkkeli, 2013).

B The second key issue concerns the target or reach of relationship marketing activities. While some definitions focus strictly on customer relationships, others extend to relationships with any type of constituent, such as internal departments, competitors, suppliers, etc. On this point, Morgan and Hunt (1994) point out that relationship marketing tactics vary for different types of partners, but the theories, conceptual frameworks and models on which they are based do not change substantially. Moreover, authors such as Rindfleisch and Moorman (2003), Palmatier (2007, 2008), Leek and Mason (2010) believe that recent research has placed a premium on building strong relationships with all stakeholders in a business, with customers themselves being only one link in a dynamic social network. Also, from the perspective of the scope of relationship marketing, the unit of analysis or reference level of the relationship must be taken into account. Relationships can be assessed at the interpersonal level, as well as at the person-organization level (B2C or vice-versa, organization-person) or at the inter-organizational level (B2B). On this level, Palmatier et al. (2007) highlight the fact that relationships with multiple stakeholders often run concurrently, with different effects on performance. Even from a B2B relationship marketing perspective, the focus falls on inter-individual interrelationships, on the cultural meanings that stakeholders attribute to interactions, experiences, events, and concepts (Ellis & Hopkinson, 2010; Tähtinen & Blois, 2011).

C The third key element is the type of benefits derived from relationship marketing activities. In this context, individuals are the only entities that can significantly influence the social world, and, by implication, business relationships viewed as social constructs created by interacting parties (Peters et al., 2013). Interactions between key individuals are thus the main catalyst for inter-individual orientation, co-creation of value and gaining mutual benefits. The focus falls on analyzing the success of relationships between parties from the perspective of mutual benefits of sustaining a long-term collaboration (Rakic & Rakic, 2015). Beyond theoretical considerations, the viability of business relationships (created on the foundation of consistent B2B relationship marketing) depends on the existence and perception of benefits by both parties, whether these are expressed through social rewards, achieving long-term performance goals, consistently earning considerable profits, etc. (O'Cass et al., 2015;

Tan & Sousa, 2015). In line with the latter idea, Egan (2004) insists that relationship marketing should not be perceived as an altruistic or eminently benevolent endeavor as long as its fundamental rationale is to achieve profitable outcomes that support the smooth running of the business. The "win-win" rationale recognizes *in nuce the* profit logic assumed by both parties, which is paramount to managers being oriented toward investing in relationships that can generate optimal benefits.

The integration of the above three elements into a unified conceptual framework can be captured in the definition of relationship marketing provided by Palmatier (2008, p. 3): "the process of identifying, developing, maintaining and terminating relational exchanges with the aim of increasing business performance." The driving force of the interrelationship in business is the perception by both parties of the existence of a relationship and its assumption as a relationship that goes beyond casual contact and is mutually invested with a special status (Barnes & Howlett, 1998). Similarly, businesspeople (managers, entrepreneurs) are defined as partners or parties irrespective of their status in a transaction: seller or buyer, supplier or customer, producer or trader, etc. They are approached in the sense of "relational managers" who engage in dyadic (interpersonal and inter-organizational) relationships in order to achieve personal, professional and organizational goals. The perspective drawn reflects Kanagal's (2009, p. 10) conception that relationship managers are value creators – "they have the knowledge, talent and skills to do their jobs well (...) Some of the strengths that relationship managers draw on include creative problem solving, innovation capability, multi-functional interaction, conflict management, trust building, planning and project management and team leadership." In addition, the angle of analysis is given by one-to-one marketing, which calls for the establishment of long-term relationships and a sustainable dialog between parties based on adaptation and mutual understanding. Through the filter of one-to-one marketing, relationships are underpinned by in-depth customization, leading to strong partnerships, and strong partnerships to profitable exchanges (Kanagal, 2009).

According to Brennan et al. (2011), behind every purchase in the context of the modern economy is a network of B2B transactions, with the authors pointing out that even a simple supermarket transaction is made possible by the existence of a B2B network. On this level, the terms B2B marketing and business marketing are interchangeable, both describing a dynamic and complex environment that actualizes both opportunities and constraints from the perspective of inter-organizational partnerships.

The focus of B2B marketing is the bilateral (or multilateral, in some contexts) assumption of co-creation and value interchange. At this level, the joint creation of added value for each of the partners involved in a deal involves the consideration of several variables with direct influence on the effectiveness of the collaboration (Chai & Dibb, 2014; Dibb & Meadows, 2004). B2B marketing involves the constant evaluation of relationships both in terms of their stability and in terms of their evolution and transformation over time. It involves the analysis of relationships from the particular to the general, from unity to complexity and diversity, from dyads to multipolar networks (Bouzdine-Chameeva et al., 2014; Brennan et al., 2011; Mandják & Durrieu, 2000).

The essential role of a business relationship is the optimal management of an economic exchange. The general assumption is that the parties involved in an exchange regard collaboration as a necessity, each of them intending to exercise control over the effectiveness of the relationship. As social constructs, relationships become a fundamental component of the social system, characterized by a well-defined social structure. This is seconded by economic value when – through cooperation – both parties achieve their business goals (Ford & McDowell, 1999; Samy et al., 2015).

Interaction-based relationship marketing from the perspective of the Industrial Marketing and Purchasing Group

From an interactionist perspective, relationships unfold through a long series of actions and reactions between the parties involved. The Industrial Marketing and Purchasing Group (IMP) provides a comprehensive explanatory framework of the relational strand as follows (Anderson & Narus, 1999; Brennan et al., 2011; Walter et al., 2000):

a the exchange is more than a simple transaction resulting in occasional financial benefits;
b integrates all types of interaction between parties – financial, product, informational and social;
c the exchange revolves around a dyad in the sense that both parties involved in an exchange can act convergently or divergently in relation to the other entity;
d exchange implies an ambivalent perspective – political-economic – in terms of the latent power structures attached to the exchange relationship and in terms of the subsequent processes.

In B2B markets, the buyer may be even more active than the seller, leading many authors (Sin et al., 2005a, 2005b; Sweeney & Webb, 2007; Turnbull & Valla, 1986) to talk only about interaction, not action and reaction. In this type of market, customers are of different sizes, have widely varying demands for products and services, and the interactive process needs to follow the guidelines of personalization of offers and interrelation approaches. The vision proposed by the IMP Group is all the more complex as it differentiates between spontaneous or one-off economic and financial transactions and solid business relationships resulting from the combination and substance of individual interactions.

Sporadic, one-off interactions are referred to as episodes or events (Schurr, 2007; Brennan et al., 2011) and are seen as "engines that generate the energy of the relationship" (Schurr, 2007, p. 161), but not the consistency of the relationship. On this level, interaction is influenced by several variables that also impact on the nature of relationships: there are product/service-based relationships, with the links between the parties built around these elements and directly determined by the intrinsic specifications and advantages of the goods and services; there are financial relationships that are dependent on the level and volume of money transacted by virtue of interchange, directly affecting the coherence of the relationship itself; there are informational relationships, such as making technical and/or commercial details explicit, effective two-way information management investing the relationship with added value; social exchanges play a defining role in maintaining and strengthening the relationship between economic transactions themselves, managing to reduce the overall level of uncertainty caused by cultural or geographical distance (Brennan et al., 2011). As a result of social exchanges, partners get to know each other better and develop clear correlative expectations in line with assumed or assigned responsibilities. On this level, B2B marketing requires the inclusion of a minimum of two organizations in the equation, and thus a minimum of two interacting individuals (Tidström & Hagberg-Andersson, 2012).

The interaction model advocated by the IMP Group does not, however, elide the importance of organizational factors, namely the physical characteristics of organizations: size, structure and technological resources (Mandják & Durrieu, 2000; Payne & Frow, 2005; Gupta & Sahu, 2012). Organizational size has a direct effect on the relative power within a relationship and often determines the level of pre-eminence versus subservience at the interaction level. It is a form of social organization whereby the dominant party (who has the size advantage) has a superior ability to influence the relationship. Organizational structure refers to the level of centralization of authority, organizational formalization and standardization, the degree of specialization of functions within partner firms, all of which reverberate in the configuration of inter-organizational relations. These characteristics are reflected through the types of interaction allowed between different organizational actors, i.e., between individuals at different hierarchical levels.

Shifting the angle of investigation to technological resources, inter-organizational relationships and, by implication, B2B marketing are conducted on the basis of the resources that the parties have and are interested in exploiting in the context of the business relationship. Technology systems extend beyond equipment or infrastructure-based resources. They also encompass fewer tangible factors such as organizational strategy and firms' prior experience (Payne & Frow, 2005; Gupta & Sahu, 2012; Al-Hawari et al., 2013). In the IMP Group's approach, this type of resource also integrates objectified intellectual capital in the form of organizational members' knowledge, personalities, experiences, motivations, all of which impact on the B2B interaction.

For example, what each party seeks to achieve through the business relationship is reflected – through different indicators – in the collaboration as a whole. Further, organizations' previous relational experiences lead to varying degrees of engagement with their partners. The relational substance is conferred by the interaction between the organizational members themselves who initiate, create and sustain the business relationship. The personalities of these individuals and their individual experiences project unconditionally onto the nature of the relationship, mapping the coordinates of the interaction and the actors' motivation to interact (Brennan et al., 2011).

It should be noted that the external environment that contextualizes dyadic relationships also emerges as a relevant predictor of firms' relational behavior. The effects of the external environment are targeted in: the current market structure – this marks the business relationship in terms of the availability and attractiveness of collaboration alternatives with other partners; the location of the relationship within the collaboration chain – this is influenced by and influences the characteristics of the wider social system, with strategies and changes in a particular area of the network also affecting the relational behavior of a dyad through a multiplier effect.

Over time, interactions lead to a relationship that is more than the sum of individual episodes. The relationship is dynamic, being shaped by the co-ordinates of each unfolding episode. Over time, the relationship is invested with a higher degree of stability, generating an atmosphere conducive to sustained interaction (Lambert et al., 1998; Sin et al., 2005a, 2005b; Sweeney & Webb, 2007). By virtue of the model proposed by the IMP Group, the relationship climate can be described through bipolar variables such as: power-dependence, cooperation-conflict, closeness-departure, with the mutual expectations of the parties being the catalyst of business relationships.

The model under discussion integrates different elements in an organic conceptual framework with the potential to influence the evolution of the B2B business relationship both in the short and long term, demonstrating that the relationship itself can affect the parties involved through the overall relational climate (Lenney & Easton, 2009; Ramos et al., 2013). From the perspective of optimal managerial relationships (carried out at the inter-organizational level), several aspects need to be highlighted. Firstly, relationships should always be seen as two-way, which requires managers to consider the aspirations, potential and expectations of all parties involved in the interchange if they are to ensure the clarity and coherence that are essential for a strong relationship. Secondly, managers need to take on board the complexity of relationships that can be described by a multiple system of variables with different effects and different potential for updating depending on the reference context. The situational diversity and the broad spectrum of variables likely to explain a given relationship indicate that there are no universally valid recipes for optimal partnership management. Third, whether a relationship is short or long term, at a given point in time, the basic characteristics of the interaction up to that point can be traced. The history of the relationship gives its intrinsic nature and simultaneously sets the premises for the future evolution of the relationship. A proper understanding of the history of the interaction is an essential milestone in prescribing the indefinite business relationship.

B2B network-based relationship marketing model

Unlike interaction-based relationship marketing, network-based relationship marketing is interrelationship-oriented, but its focus is inter-organizational and trans-organizational. Representative for this marketing practice is the assumption by SMEs of a certain position in a network with various relationships between similar firms (Coviello et al., 2001, p. 26, as cited in Brodie et al., 2008).

The literature review (Brennan et al., 2011; Brito, 2011; Corăbieru et al., 2015; Henneberg et al., 2010) brings to the fore that the B2B relationship between SMEs cannot be accurately conceptualized in individual, uni-directional or even exclusively bidirectional terms as a network of relationships frames any singular relationship considered as a reference point. Thus, the strategic understanding of the business relationship derives from an under-standing of the network within which it originates, a network that influences it either directly or indirectly (Brennan et al., 2011). In this framework, the premise is that the emergence and development of SME relationships can only be objectified in the context of a business network, a chain of collaboration (between a producer's customers, supplier and producer, end-user and inter-mediary, stockists, and customers, etc.), the catalyst being commitment and mutual interdependence to create financial value and competitive advantage in terms of profit (Mandják & Durrieu, 2000). Addressing the issue of the non-economic value of business relationships, Mandják and Durrieu (2000) sys-tematize in a unified framework the meaning of the network, highlighting both strengths and vulnerabilities. Thus, the constructive and integrative value of the network is seen in terms of transferability of resources, complementary activi-ties, generalizability of the advantages derived from the interaction of actors, close collaboration, and operational efficiency. At the antipodal level, mar-ginalization or inappropriate positioning within the network can lead to inaccessibility of resources, irreconcilability of activities or incompatibility between the actors involved.

Assuming these lines, B2B marketing from the perspective of network analysis and management postulates that SMEs can only achieve their goals through business relationships. However, managerial decisions about re-lationships and the intrinsic motivations to initiate and strengthen certain partnerships are not limited to the relationship itself (Ford & McDowell, 1999). The arguments that enter the decision-making equation extend beyond the unit of analysis of a relationship and cover the relational portfolio of all partnerships in which organizations are involved. Moreover, the nature and evolution of a relationship between parties is directly or indirectly conditioned by the flows between them and other organizational actors in a given system (other firms, agencies, governments, banks, associations, etc.). All of these have a high potential to influence a particular business relationship because of their interconnectivity and interdependence – all relationships are interconnected in a network. Thus, B2B relationships between SMEs involve multiple interactions between several actors or, more precisely, in a network of relationships.

Network theory provides a valuable insight into the impact that structural features of the interaction between multiple entities (individuals, firms) have on the network as a whole (Borgatti & Foster, 2003; Granovetter, 1985; Van Den Bulte & Wuyts, 2007). This network perspective has recently been operationalized in the B2B context to show that not only relationship quality (commitment, trust), but also relationship focus (relationship density) and relationship nature (network diversity/attractiveness) significantly influence the effectiveness of interchanges (Palmatier, 2008). Thus, Palmatier (2008) talks about three major areas and influencing factors related to the effectiveness of network-based relationship marketing: quality, concentration and nature, each dimension marking an important aspect of B2B relationships between SMEs. In addition, achieving the desired effect is based on the synergistic and correlative functioning of the relationship components.

The quality of relations with a given partner represents the quality of the relationship, with the corresponding concepts of strength of ties in network theory and closeness and degree of reciprocity in social ties theory (Palmatier, 2008, p. 20). Studies (Andersen & Kumar, 2006; Mouzas et al., 2007; Vesel & Zabkar, 2010) have supported the composite nature of relationship quality, including here the fundamental characteristics of a high performing relationship: commitment, trust, reciprocity, and exchange efficiency. Thus, although all the concepts listed are integrated in the understanding of relationship quality, each of them captures a unique aspect of collaboration, defining the holistic nature of the interrelationship.

On the one hand, commitment is the desire of the partners to preserve valuable relationships and implies the motivation to continue the relationship indefinitely. Further, as a result of the assessment of the partner's integrity and reliability, trust in the partner's future actions and in a mutually beneficial cooperation crystallizes. Reciprocity denotes the beliefs and expectations assumed by an organization about the balance of outcomes from an ambivalent perspective, while inter-exchange efficiency refers to the assessment of time, effort and resources required to maintain a relationship and responds to the imperative to boost relationship performance through better management of total costs. In sum, by corroborating all components, relationship quality will positively affect the long-term relationship performance (Palmatier, 2008; O'Cass et al., 2015; Vesel & Zabkar, 2010).

Relationship focus, the second most effective factor in relationship marketing, is the number of connections with a partner. Inter-organizational relationships that include multiple interpersonal links can provide additional information, profit maximization opportunities and relationship feasibility over time (in the context of localized disruptions occurring in particular relationships). For example, extended inter-organizational relationships can be more easily reconfigured if a particular contact person leaves the partner organization (Bendapudi & Leone, 2002). In the context of reasonable concentration, the new entrant can more readily conform to pre-existing relational norms, preserving social relationships at the inter-organizational level.

Relationship concentration is adjacent to the concept of network density (which refers to the interconnectivity between network members) and the concept of degree of centrality (the number of direct links between a given member and other network members) (Houston et al., 2004). Interconnections within the network positively influence cooperation, knowledge transfer, communication efficiency and progressive relationship development. Two partner organizations, united by more interpersonal links, and therefore with greater concentration, ensure better access to information and to the exploitation of common opportunities, more stability in the event of the departure of certain members from the organization.

The nature of the relationship refers to the ability of the interacting actors to make important decisions – the greater the degree of authority an actor has, the more powerful a decision-making and informational node it can become in relation to the partner organization. The nature of the relationship is an important variable depending on different contextual parameters, in the sense that despite strong relationships with several members of the partner organization (despite concentration of relationships), often the type of relationship prevails. Typically, the nature of the relationship is underpinned by the links established between decision-makers or between similar positions, but by linking with higher (horizontal and vertical) density, the yield of interchanges can be significantly increased (Palmatier, 2008). At this level, the type of relationship with strong effects on success at the inter-organizational level can be shifted away from the area of relationships between the most influential members to become more pragmatic and efficient, as members with lower overall influence are substituted by members with higher influence on specific segments. The concept of relationship nature is matched by the terms of diversity and attractiveness in network theory (Anderson et al., 1994; Wasserman & Faust, 1994), terms that refer to the level of knowledge, information, skills and competencies held by network actors. At this point, the diversity of partners is a source of added value and complementarity, boosting network performance and efficiency.

In summary, the three determinants of B2B exchanges (quality, focus and nature of relationships) are likely to second and reinforce each other to create the conditions for optimal relationship value. Their interaction results in two other aggregate components, namely relationship strength and relationship effectiveness (Palmatier, 2008).

Relationship strength results from the interplay between relationship quality and relationship focus, defining the ability of inter-organizational relationships to withstand stress and conflict so that quality relationship constructs develop into strong, enduring relationships. Quality contacts organized on multiple levels (both horizontal and vertical) are coupled with considerable relational motivation (commitment and norms of reciprocity) and trust (sustaining over time), which directly reflects on the performance of partner organizations in the wider network.

The second outcome, relationship effectiveness, derives from the interplay of the quality and nature of the relationship, and is defined as the effectiveness of the relationship and describes the ability of the inter-organizational relationship to lead to the achievement of pre-determined objectives. High-quality relationships between partners in positions of power enable the implementation of effective inter-organizational strategies that strengthen the competitive advantage of partner organizations within the overall sector. Focusing on analogies with network theory it is imperative to understand that the most desirable relationships are both strong and diverse (Li, 2007), with performance resulting from the interplay of the two components.

The components outlined up to this point place the framework of relationship marketing in the broader context of social network theories that both systematize and clarify the main relational factors underpinning B2B relationships. Moreover, the conceptual framework described reveals the importance of corroborating and correlating the dimensions addressed in order to exert a substantial impact on performance at the inter-organizational, and even network level (O'Cass et al., 2015).

In conclusion, network-based B2B marketing highlights the imperative for firms to accept that they are interdependent and embedded in a system of interactions that limits their ability to think and act independently. It is therefore the duty of each manager to analyze the network in which he or she operates in order to determine the position he or she has taken and to assume the relational leadership that will enhance his or her position. According to Håkansson and Snehota (1995, 2000), there are three defining components brought to the fore by networks and, by extension, by the underlying organizations: the actors who engage in inter-relational behavior (the links between actors), the resources created or exploited within the business relationships (the links between resources) and the activities carried out within the relationships (the links between activities).

The analysis of the position of an organization within the network is, in this context, essential for its level of influence on other actors. Changes and positional evolution in the network are gradually operationalised by exploring and exploiting existing relationships to generate new links between actors, resources and activities that can strengthen the parties involved. A relevant example of networks in the industrial environment is the strategic partnerships established between raw material suppliers, producers, distributors, and final customers (all organizations). Each link depends on the other to operate coherently and efficiently. The emergence of a malfunction in any actor (e.g., failure to make payments on time) has a multiplier effect within the network and can even lead to the chain insolvency of closely collaborating organizations.

The effect of the national culture on B2B international relationship marketing

The acceptance of culture from the perspective of international relationship marketing at the SME level brings to the fore patterns related to values, norms, beliefs, perceptions, behaviors that influence how individuals evaluate different situations and lead to different processing and management of data from the environment (Hofstede, 1991; Palmatier et al., 2006a, 2006b; Samaha et al., 2014; Yaprak, 2008). According to Hofstede (1991, p. 4), culture is "the entrainment or refinement of the individual's mind due to the social environments in which the individual has grown up." Given that B2B relationship marketing is founded on social interchange, it goes without saying that the impact of culture will be felt in all components of the interaction, marking the dynamics of norms, roles and expectations associated with the development of partnerships between organizations in different countries.

Culture is thus a moderator of business relationships, reflected in the way relationship marketing strategies are interpreted and responded to, especially in B2B interactions between SMEs internationally. Culture will determine different types of engagement (social and emotional) on the part of potential partners belonging to different countries, constituting a catalyst versus a braking factor in the context of international collaborations (Palmatier et al., 2006a; Samaha et al., 2014; Weck & Ivanova, 2013). Cultural and national filters guide social judgment and condition to some extent the way in which information that arises throughout the phases of an international collaboration is encoded and used. At this level, the impact of cross-cultural business relationships on organizational performance has been intensively theorized and operationalized empirically in numerous current studies (Ghemawat, 2001; O'Cass et al., 2015; Samaha et al., 2014; Swaminathan & Moorman, 2009), with the emphasis falling on the assumption of a multiple system of cultural variables influencing actual business relationships and leading to a new imperative, namely "avoiding cross-cultural generalizations" (Steenkamp, 2005, p. 6).

Drawing on Hofstede's (1980) taxonomy, Samaha et al. (2014, p. 80) examine the moderating effect of cultural dimensions on the effectiveness of international relationship marketing. In doing so, the authors develop a synthesis of classic and recent literature on the role of culture in the context of international relationship marketing, concluding that there are major differences between individualistic and collectivistic cultures, between feminine and masculine cultures, between cultures with varying distances from power and with distinct degrees of uncertainty avoidance. Some examples of this are reflected in Table 5.2.

Table 5.2 Cross-cultural differences based on Hofstede dimensions (adapted from Cheung & Chann, 2008)

No.	Dyads	Size	Features	Examples from an SME perspective	Reference countries
1.	Individualism versus collectivism	Individualism	The individual is most important Independence in decision-making Individual achievements must be rewarded Individual uniqueness is valued	Association decisions are taken relatively quickly The prevailing vision is an interpersonal one New partnerships are concluded by the negotiator without additional consultation	Australia, USA, UK, Canada
		Collectivism	Vision, aspirations, and group goals are most important The rule is very important The individual defines himself in relation to others The focus is on cooperation, not competition	Managers feel responsible for their community The prevailing vision is an intergroup one The experience and competence of the parties matters Decision-making is slow as managers consult with other decision-makers in the organization	Singapore, Korea, Italy, Mexico
2.	High versus low level of uncertainty avoidance	High level of uncertainty avoidance	Avoiding ambiguity Strict codes of conduct Confidence in absolute truths	Managers are more calculating and skeptical about new collaborations They want to be in control of important aspects of partnerships	Greece, Japan, France, Korea
		Low level of uncertainty avoidance	Acceptance of ambiguity and flexible structures Risk-oriented and non-conformist approach Rules are avoided or ignored	Managers are open and flexible to new proposals They are interested in starting the business as soon as possible Easily establish new agreements with new partners	Singapore, Denmark, United Kingdom, India

3.	High versus low distance to power	High distance to power	Power is a resource characteristic only of leadership Power is centralised Power is natural and inevitable	Managers appreciate meeting deadlines Gives clear indications of what they expect from others They are authoritarian and seemingly intransigent	Mexico, Italy, France, India
		Reduced distance to power	Power differences are minimal The hierarchy is not rigid Power can be gained through work	Managers are open about concessions Discusses and argues when supporting a particular position	Austria, Denmark, USA, Germany
4.	Masculinity versus femininity	Masculinity	Clear differentiation of roles Men are assertive, ambitious and competitive Women are supportive, deferential and	Managers will be tempted to discuss business even at social gatherings Not open to talking about personal issues in business contexts Not interested in developing friendships Communicate directly and concisely Make value judgments about the other party's professional identity	Japan, Mexico, Germany, UK
		Femininity	Role flexibility Women and men are equal Interpersonal relationships are important	Managers are open to developing close relationships and discussing personal issues even in business contexts Use social contexts to get to know the partner better from a human perspective	Sweden, Denmark, Portugal
5.	Long-term versus short-term orientation	Long-term orientation	Reserves are important Action is directed toward achieving a goal	Managers invest in long-term relationships with potential or existing partners	China, Japan, Hong Kong

(Continued)

Table 5.2 (Continued)

No.	Dyads	Size	Features	Examples from an SME perspective	Reference countries
			The long-term impact of action is important	They are persistent and try to create strong links at all levels Adapts to new contexts if this has long-term beneficial implications	UK, USA, Germany, France
		Short-term orientation	Immediate reward is sought Short-term investments are favoured No concessions that bring long-term results	Managers are anchored in their own traditions and customs Opportunistic behavior prevails Does not allocate substantial funds for investment Are interested in knowing all the details of a problem	
6.	Indulgence versus restriction	Indulgence	Indulgence is a characteristic of a society open to the satisfaction of basic human needs related to the pleasure of living, having fun	Managers are open to combining business with pleasure when negotiating a collaboration They also like to discuss issues not directly related to the subject of the transaction	Mexico, Nigeria, Australia, Sweden
		Restriction	Restriction is characteristic of a society that limits the satisfaction of human needs and creates strict rules for managing them	Managers focus on the professional aspects and avoid personal discussions or colloquial contexts when seeking to conclude a partnership	France, Japan, Italy, Germany

Managerial effectiveness from an international B2B relationship marketing perspective relies on understanding the local climate, infrastructure, and expectations, but also on the manager's motivation and willingness to adapt appropriately to new cultural contexts. Recent studies postulate that differences in terms of culture, economy, regulatory environments call for continuous adaptation of international marketing strategies (Chua et al., 2012; Griffith & Hoppner, 2013; Navarro et al., 2010).

In Mooij and Hofstede's (2010) view, the six cultural dimensions are particularly important in the context of international relationship marketing because they illustrate national values not only in business contexts, but in general. The authors thus studied the application of Hofstede's dimensions in the field of global branding, marketing strategies and consumer behavior at the international level, inculcating the idea that internationalizing organizations, including SMEs, need to adapt their products and services to local customs and preferences and a prerequisite in this endeavor is a pertinent understanding of the specificity of the foreign market. For example, if the organization intends to market street surveillance systems in a country where uncertainty avoidance is high, then the marketing strategy will need to focus on safety in the public space.

Another example is the marketing strategy for selling mobile phones. If the target market is China, then the marketing strategy will address the concept of collective experience, while positioning in the United States will enhance the idea of efficient use of time and money. Mooij and Hofstede (2010) insist that Hofstede's cultural model can be operationalised in many cross-cultural contexts and can even be applicable to web design, designed to respond to the national preferences and reference values of the target population.

Based on the above considerations, the understanding and the relevant representation of the social and cultural changes brought about by the internationalization of SMEs requires a careful analysis of the patterns of cross-cultural interaction and communication at managerial level. On this point, the Communication Accommodation Theory developed by Howard Giles in 1973, a professor at the University of California, Santa Barbara, focused on face-to-face interaction to explain the main cognitive rationales behind code-switching and other changes in speech, as individuals try to potentiate or minimize socio-cultural differences between themselves and their interlocutors. In other words, the theory targets "linguistic variation determined by the particularities of who a particular speaker is addressing" (Jaworski & Coupland, 2006, p. 229) and has a strong negotiating nature in that managers intend to achieve a winning position through the communicative and relational attitudes assumed (Giles & Baker, 2008).

Giles and Baker (2008) insist that when interlocutors intend to gain approval in a social situation, it is very likely that the access will converge toward the communication type of their interlocutors – the strategy includes the behavioral adjustments that individuals aim for during communication in order to express certain values, attitudes or intentions – choice of language, accent, dialect, paralinguistic elements used in the interaction, etc.

Although individuals systematically seek to value homogeneity in order to preserve social identity (Yzerbyt & Schadron, 2002), the absence of negotiation-oriented behavioral skills can create barriers to communication.

From a B2B relationship marketing perspective, language is a "social diagnostic," relational adaptation is seen as a set of plural alternatives with a particular conjunctural complexity, serving to achieve solidarity or dissociation with a potential partner in a reciprocal and dynamic way (Glasford et al., 2009). In a cross-cultural context, B2B relationship marketing is influenced by different variables, of which the socio-historical context, the adaptive orientation of the parties, the data of the immediate situation, evaluation and future intentions are significant benchmarks (Gudykunst, 2003, p. 172).

The socio-historical context is the general foundation for any potential relationship. Influencing factors may be cultural variability, horizon of expectations, political-economic or historical relations between two countries, regions or the ideological or religious perspectives of groups interacting or negotiating a possible agreement.

In terms of adaptive orientation, there are three essential factors that need to be considered: intrapersonal factors (e.g., personal identity, social identity, personality of the parties), intergroup factors (e.g., feelings of the parties toward other groups) and initial perceptions (e.g., perceived conflict potential, long-term motivation to adapt in relations with the other party) (Gudykunst, 2003, p. 172).

Shifting the focus to the data of the immediate situation, the actual communication, five key issues emerge: *socio-psychological states* (e.g., interpersonal and intergroup perceptions in a given situation), the *party's purpose and goals* (e.g., motivations related to the interaction, communication and relationship needs), *socio-linguistic strategies* (e.g., convergence vs. divergence, approximation, discourse management), *behavior and tactics* (e.g., topic of discussion, paralanguage) and *labeling and attributions*. All these elements need to be understood in an interrelated manner.

Through evaluation and future intentions, the question arises as to how each partner perceives the behavior of the other, anticipating the future consequences of a certain relational conduct. Convergent behavior perceived to be based on a benevolent intention is positively evaluated and will most likely lead to further interactions between the parties (Gudykunst, 2003, p. 16).

As a whole, the Communication Accommodation Theory integrates aspects related to communication and negotiation strategies, participants' motivation, aspects that can explain the dynamics of intercultural interactions. Based on the premise that B2B relationship marketing aims to personalize the interaction between parties, there is a presupposition that business partners will try to converse with their communication partners, i.e., shape their language to become as similar as possible to others as a means of identifying with them or as a means of gaining their approval (Ward et al., 2003). "Approximation strategies" aimed at enhancing similarity between partners are called adaptive strategies and involve effective discourse management, interest in rationality or sensitivity, etc., depending on the situation (Giles & Gasiorek, 2012).

Convergence describes the process in which individuals shape their communication styles to become increasingly similar to those with whom they interact (Sand, 2012). In other words, convergence refers to the ways in which a business partner adjusts their communication style in different interactions so that they can move closer to the interlocutor's reference system. Convergence indicators can be located on multiple levels, such as sentence length, speaking pace, information density, frequency and length of pauses, response time, degree of transparency and communicative openness, humor, expression of solidarity, opinions, preferences, gestures, kinetics, proxemics, mimicry, posture, etc. When deciding what to say and how to say it, individuals in most cases choose the course that will lead to a positive outcome rather than a negative one – engaging in convergent communication should involve potentially more advantages than disadvantages (Giles & Marlow, 2011). For example, based on Hofstede's taxonomy, a manager in Portugal – if he wants to be convergent with a manager in Germany, knowing his cultural particularities – will insist on aspects that define masculine culture: he will discuss business even in social gatherings, communicate directly and concisely, emphasize professionalism rather than making personal connections.

At this point, Magnusson et al. (2013) address the concept of "cultural intelligence," pioneered by Earley and Ang (2003) and operationalised by Ang et al. (2007) in the context of international business relations. It involves adjusting in relation to other cultures and thus generating optimal outcomes in international negotiations (Imai & Gelfand, 2010; Wu & Ang, 2011). Managers are, in this context, the key actors of international partnerships, as optimal management of the versatile and conjunctural global environment depends on managerial ability to constantly develop, implement, and recalibrate international marketing strategies. A relevant example in this framework is the anticipatory study of the specific cultural characteristics of a potential business partner, especially those from very different cultures: American versus Japanese, European versus Indian, or Chinese, etc.

Griffith (2010) and Griffith and Hoppner (2013) point out that SME managers need to possess a particular cultural intelligence that enables them to actively respond to the realities and challenges of the external environment – international and/or global – and to identify the optimal formula for positioning themselves in the equation of strategic partnerships. Although cultural intelligence does not in itself influence performance at international level, it is a central moderator of the adaptation of relationship marketing activities to extra-organizational signals. This is possible given its main components, namely the motivational, behavioral, cognitive, and metacognitive dimensions (Ang et al., 2007, p. 338). *The motivational dimension* reflects the ability to direct attention and energy toward intercultural learning and operating in situations characterized by cultural differences, while the *behavioral dimension* is concerned with the ability to manifest appropriate verbal and non-verbal actions when individuals interact with people from different cultures.

Further, the *cognitive dimension* involves knowledge of norms, practices, and conventions across cultures, including knowledge of economic, legal, and social systems specific to other cultures. *The metacognitive dimension* concludes the set of components of cultural intelligence as understood by Ang et al. (2007) and reflects the mental processes that individuals access and use to acquire and understand cultural differences, and the skills relevant to this are planning, monitoring and revising mental models about cultural norms specific to countries or groups of individuals from other cultures. In the view of Chua et al. (2012), the metacognitive dimension is the most important component of cultural intelligence as it creates a bridge between cognition and behavior. Concluding, Ang et al. (2007) consider that the metacognitive dimension is directly related to cross-cultural reasoning and decision-making, while the motivational dimension is mostly related to adjustments within cross-cultural interactions.

Other authors (Imai & Gelfand, 2010; Chua et al., 2012) have taken the analysis further, pointing out that cultural intelligence itself correlates positively with the effectiveness of cross-cultural negotiations, the density of social networks, and the optimization of international business relationship outcomes. Accessing cultural intelligence across episodes of interaction between parties simultaneously engages intercultural adaptation. According to Weck and Ivanova (2013), the latter is a result of acquiring primary and secondary knowledge about the partner's cultural specificities. Secondary knowledge circumscribes the reputation of a company, an individual or the general business climate in a particular country and is acquired from external sources, from the experiences of third parties. Positive reputations are likely to strengthen trust and catalyze prolific interactions, however, sourcing information from external sources may be affected by national stereotypes, standard generalizations about a particular society and may imply negative associations that are difficult to notice in the first instance (Ailon-Souday & Kunda, 2003). This case is recurrent for countries with a negative image in the international public space.

Not infrequently, Romanian managers have to fight against wrong stereotypes about their professionalism and seriousness in doing business, stereotypes assumed by foreign managers as a result of defamatory reports and documentaries broadcast by the international media about Romania in general. In my opinion, the ideas conveyed about the level of corruption, imposture, the Roma population, and the crimes committed by many of its members create prejudices about a particular country or culture over time, beyond the truth value or generality of the information conveyed.

The prevalence of this type of knowledge is characteristic only for the early phases of the relationship when the parties do not interact directly with each other. At the antipode, primary knowledge is assimilated in the later stages of the business relationship through direct interaction between the partners. They allow the accumulation of relevant information about the partner's cultural system, facilitating adaptation to cultural differences as a result of reduced cultural distance and increased mutual trust (Ivanova & Torkkeli, 2013; Weck & Ivanova, 2013).

The country-of-origin effect on B2B international relationship marketing

From a B2B relationship marketing perspective, country image is an important influencing factor, encompassing both a material dimension and a non-productive dimension, such as people (Heslop, Lu & Cry, 2008). Most of the time, the expansion of an SME into a foreign market is done after management considers all the elements that might be relevant to the success or failure of the internationalization effort. The external "assessors" of the country in question need to focus on multiple dimensions to design effective market entry and positioning strategies. Country image dimensions have been defined and operationalised by various authors, including Brymer (2003); Daye and van Auken (2008); Morgan et al. (2004); Nicolescu et al. (2008); Zeugner-Roth and Diamantopoulos (2009).

Thus, Morgan et al. (2004, p. 40) defined country image as "the sum of the beliefs and impressions that people have about places, these representing a simplification of the large number of associations and information attributed to a particular place." The country picture is a product of the mind that has to process and select essential information from a large amount of data and is influenced by its historical background, geographical location, cultural activity, political situations, art, music, sporting activities, lifestyle and many other features (Morgan et al., 2004).

Nicolescu et al. (2008) consider country image a special type of mental representation that encompasses products, brands, companies and many other elements. It is formed on the basis of experiences and opinions about a nation or country and on the basis of information received through various channels. The channels through which information about a country is communicated are politics (domestic affairs and foreign policies), tele-communications, entertainment (films) and rumors. Country image includes multiple elements such as national symbols, colors, clothing, types of buildings, objects, works of art, specificity of the political system, tradi-tions, historical and cultural heritage, etc. (Jenes, 2005, 2007; Nicolescu et al., 2008). Papadopoulos and Heslop (2002) consider that country images are also influenced by factors such as: culture, media, sports, economy, and political and social environments. Like any other type of mental repre-sentation country image is multidimensional, with researchers investigating essentially distinct but sometimes overlapping dimensions (Zeugner-Roth & Diamantopoulos, 2009).

Addressing the issue of country image, Fakeye and Crompton (1991) developed a model that can describe the relationship between *organic images* (determined by traditions, media, books, education, etc.), *induced images* (resulting from exposure to promotional campaigns) and *complex images* (formed by the blending of organic and induced images). The authors point out that, depending on the motivations and perceptions already formed, individuals will actively seek information about countries of interest. The typology and intensity of organic images will directly influence an individuals' efforts to find out detailed information about these countries, with the evaluation of new data depending on the characteristics of the organic and formally induced images, as well as the direct experience of the subjects. The more consolidated a particular country's complex image, the more favorable the reporting of interested individuals will be.

In turn, Baloglu and McCleary (1999) consider that country image, as a multidimensional construct, is based on both perceptual/cognitive (beliefs and knowledge) and affective (feelings) evaluations, and that the overall image of a country is formed by the interaction between the two components. According to O'Regan (2000, p. 347), the image consists of "what remains in people's minds as a result of everything they know about the physical characteristics of a product or service and all the assumptions, associations, ideas and experiences they have had in relation to a product, service or country over the years."

At this level, a country's name can act in a similar way to a brand name. Hsieh et al. (2004) focus the definition of country image into three distinct categories: general country image; aggregated product-country image; product-specific country image. The authors consider that the overall country image totals the descriptive, inferential, and informational opinions that a given consumer holds about a particular country, the reference products associated with that country and the specific brands promoted. Orbaiz and Papadopoulos (2003) developed a measure of general country image based on five key elements, such as standard of living, well-being, technological level, education, and stability, and concluded that there is a positive relationship between a country's image and the relationship with its products.

Adjacently, Laroche et al. (2005) operationalized the overall country image as an exhaustive factor comprising three essential components – individuals' views of the country's industrial development and technological progress, affective response to a country's inhabitants, and desirability of interacting with a particular country. In other words, Laroche et al. (2005) consider that the country image should comprise: *a cognitive component* that includes individuals' beliefs about a particular country, *an affective component* that describes the emotional value of a country to interested audiences, and a *conative component* concerning individuals' intentions toward that country.

Like brand image, country image is a set of associations in relation to the country-of-origin, organized into distinct clusters in a meaningful way (Gallarza et al., 2002; Keller, 1993). In this context, two different conceptualizations of country image exist in the international marketing literature – *the macro-level country image conceptualization* (Martin & Eroglu, 1993) and the *micro-level conceptualization* (Agarwal & Sikri, 1996).

Among the indicators of country image at the macro level, the following can be listed (Martin & Eroglu, 1993, pp. 204–206): the level of technological research; production of high-quality goods; high standard of living; expensive labor; the welfare of the system; high level of industrialization; effective government policy; high economic development; level of knowledge and research; open market system; political system – democracy.

Among the indicators used for the country image at the micro level are (Nagashima, 1977, pp. 95–100): exceptional quality of work; advanced technique; innovation, openness to new and change; advertising development; recognizable brand name; the credibility of key public and private actors; cost level.

Further, Pappu et al. (2007) categorize country image into two dimensions: macro (including economic, technological, and political components) and micro (including innovation, design, professional skill and reputation). Zeugner-Roth and Diamantopoulos (2009) also review existing studies on country image and classify definitions according to *macro* and *micro factors*. Macro-factors refer to the level of economic and political maturity, culture, technological development, conflict with other countries, working conditions and environmental issues, all of which converge toward the generic country image. On this level, the term "image" includes concepts such as perceptions, knowledge, mental representations, impressions, beliefs, and associations. The second, *micro-factor* perspective looks at the association between country image and products originating in the reference country, based on existing stereotypes – customers associate the quality of a particular product with the image of that country. For example, the image of France is often associated with good quality wine (Bordeaux), the image of India with spices, the image of the UK with 5 o'clock tea, the image of Italy with spaghetti, etc.

From an international relationship marketing perspective, country image is a defining criterion in SME expansion into a foreign market (Bhaskaran & Sukumaran, 2007; Fan, 2008; Hsieh et al., 2004; Petison, 2010; Verlegh & Steenkamp, 1999). The country-of-origin effect is reflected in management's decision to choose one market over another, with subjective images of the environment and climate in a particular location often mattering more than objective reality (Brymer, 2003; Daye & van Auken, 2008; Shimp et al., 2001). The view is also shared by other authors who consider the country-of-origin effect to be an important determinant of perceptions and action by potential partners (Chu et al., 2010; Lotz & Hu, 2001; Pappu et al., 2006; Tse & Lee, 1993).

Yasin et al. (2007) and Chu et al. (2010) mention that managers consider the country-of-origin effect when thinking about B2B marketing strategies internationally. In most situations, a positive image of the home country leads to an initial decision to invest, to expand business activity in that area (Cervino et al., 2005; Tam, 2008; Zeugner-Roth & Diamantopoulos, 2009; Kabadayi & Lerman, 2011). Further, in the context of international B2B relationship marketing, managers design their initial strategies according to the imagological landmarks of the country and, by implication, the reference culture. On this level, decisions are made based on perceptions of values and customs in the target country, as managers develop interpersonal sensitivity skills, assimilate flexible business practices and socially validated protocols. The cultural filter proposed by Hofstede is a first step in this respect.

In the absence of direct experience and unmediated knowledge, SME managers are forced to adjust their actions based on the experience of others, information available in different media or existing studies about the country, culture and target market (Barnes et al., 2010; Hampton & Rowell, 2010, 2013). This information provides a first relational framework against which to build the behavioral pattern of management toward potential foreign market partners. For example, if an SME in a country with an individualistic culture (e.g., the US) is going to expand into a market in a country perceived to have a collectivistic culture (e.g., Italy), then the SME's management will adopt relationship marketing strategies that include assumptions such as: Italian managers are very community-oriented; their vision is predominantly group-oriented, they pursue significant benefits for the whole organization; for them, the experience and competence of the other party matters; they make decisions rather slowly as they consult with other decision-makers in the organization, etc.

Focusing on international B2B relationship marketing, Quester et al. (2000) and Srinivasan et al. (2004) conclude that SMEs in the industrial sector are influenced by the country-of-origin effect which in many cases is stronger than the image of the partner company or the traded goods. The authors' research demonstrates that major business decisions are still determined by non-rational influences, which relate to perceptions, representations, and attitudes toward a particular country.

The 2000s, however, brought complex realities and networks of interdependencies between different regions and countries of the world to the global stage, with a vast amount of goods and brands interacting in foreign markets. At this level, 21st century researchers have begun to question whether the country-of-origin effect is still an important factor for individual or organizational actors (SMEs in particular) in a globalized world where many brands are considered global (Pharr, 2005; Nicolescu, 2012). Recent literature has shown that the level of interest in country-of-origin has become much less important on the evaluation of acquisitions and internationalization decisions (Balbanis & Diamantopoulos, 2008; Josiassen & Harzing, 2008; Samiee et al., 2005; Usunier & Cestre, 2008). These studies point to problems in conceptualizing the country-of-origin effect and to the gap between the research designs used to test it and the actual situations in which the effect might become relevant in market games (Zeugner-Roth & Diamantopoulos, 2009; Samiee, 2010).

Conceptual problems start from the very definition of the terms "country" and "origin" which nowadays do not only refer to certain entities states but can be applicable to regions and equally to cities and communities (Lentz et al., 2006). Also, the very concept of "origin" is questionable insofar as it raises the issue of where the product or service is created, assembled or designed (Pharr, 2005). Many studies that problematize the conceptualization and measurement of the country-of-origin effect start from the reconfiguration of the origin of products given the freedom of production flows, insofar as the outsourcing of production becomes a truism in the contemporary world. Some scientific articles address the moderating effects of staged production of the same good in several countries. Thus, hybrid products resulting from a design-create-assemble process undertaken by several countries confirm the difficulty of conceptualizing country-of-origin effects in the context of current technological interdependencies and interconnectivity (Samiee et al., 2005; Nicolescu, 2012; Kornberger, 2010).

Limits of relationship marketing models in the international context

Although relationship marketing in its various forms (interaction-based, network-based) has been treated sporadically in the literature and from the perspective of culture and country-of-origin effect, recent studies focused on relationship marketing and business internationalization have found that "there is no unified theoretical framework" and that the correlative analysis of the two processes needs to be a priority for future research (Khojastehpour & Jones, 2014). On this level, internationalization is seen as a gradual groping and approaching of foreign markets with the aim of adding value to the business by accessing new resources, collaborating with other companies and stakeholders, and exploiting other opportunities (Khojastehpour & Jones, 2014). All these stakes can be achieved through the prism of a well-managed international relationship marketing that starts from the challenges of a dynamic global environment and stakeholder-specific socio-cultural diversity (Leonidou et al., 2011).

Setting the focus on a correlative approach to relationship marketing and the internationalization process, Khojastehpour and Jones (2014) associate the elements of relationship marketing (communication, trust, commitment, and satisfaction) with two phases of business internationalization – pre-internationalization (focused on overcoming psychological distance) and post-internationalization (focused on market and positioning). In the authors' view, communication is the essence of any relationship strategy in an international context. Without communication, trust cannot be built, and relationships cannot evolve further with internationalization. At this point, the researchers (Khojastehpour & Jones, 2014, p. 245) insist that their proposed model is the first to articulate "a conceptual framework likely to describe relationship marketing in an internationalized context."

Adjacently, Malhotra et al. (2003, pp. 2–3) have attempted to develop a multi-theoretical model to analyze the emergence of international business from the perspective of both relationship marketing and foreign stakeholder relationship management. Assuming that a one-sided approach is eminently limited, the authors pointed to the need to advance new frameworks to understand the processes and interactions that take place globally. The challenge is to analyze different factors simultaneously so as to result in integrative, holistic and viable research that responds to a changing and re-defining environment. The same perspective is embraced by Danciu (2012, pp. 29–30) who confirms that none of the existing models of international-ization fails to cover and clarify the specificity of the phenomenon, empha-sizing the importance of relational capital within dynamic social networks.

An adjacent account is also present in recent studies by Hampton and Rowell (2013, p. 161), with the authors suggesting that a comprehensive view of the challenges characterizing international business relations still remains in the crystallization stage. Hampton and Rowell (2013) consider that the literature has clarified only a narrow range of factors between which the interdependencies are still uncertain. The development of linear models fails to describe the complexity of transnational business relationships. Therefore, international business success needs to be approached in a broader context, through the lens of business models implemented by proactive managers who do not wait for results to come by themselves but are aware of the defining role of personal and social relationships in complementing established international economic relationships (Denicolai Zucchella, & Strange, 2014).

At this point, the sustainability of international relationship marketing strategies should be examined in terms of the long-term competitiveness of the business. Business internationalization is one of the core projects that define the sustainable growth and progress of the organization, and therefore, the development of international relationships should be seen as a condition for organizational competitiveness, regardless of the size of the firm or the field in which it operates (Sousa & Novello, 2014; Sandberg, 2014; Suh & Kim, 2014).

In this respect, the global economy has been strongly encouraging eco-nomic relationships through cross-border cooperation – lowering customs duties, increasing operational and financial flows, reducing transport costs, multiplying communication channels, boosting the global vocation of citi-zens, etc. In order to achieve superior economic performance, become more competitive, adapt intelligently to market conditions, and be proactive and dynamic in a highly competitive environment, SMEs often have to find new markets, new stakes, and especially new business networks (Hilmersson, 2014; Sandberg, 2014); thus, businesspeople have to effectively manage the challenges of intercultural interactions, of forming, developing, adjusting and strengthening relationships beyond the domestic environment (Cannone & Ughetto, 2014; Villar et al., 2014).

***

Corroborating the main theoretical issues explored in this chapter, two types of relationship marketing specific to the industrial domain – interaction-based marketing and network-based marketing – have been highlighted and operationalised. The focus was on the internationalization process of SMEs, the role and influence of cultural and home country dimensions on international business relationships.

Summarizing the directions outlined above, a close examination of international relationship marketing is a relevant and useful research topic for understanding relationship dynamics. Therefore, building an integrative model that reflects the conditions, contexts, catalysts, consequences, and connections inherent in the construction of international relationships is a necessity. The model should reflect both manifest and latent causes, processes, and effects of relationship marketing in the pre-internationalization, internationalization, and post-internationalization phases.

References

Agarwal, S., & Sikri, S. (1996). Country image: Consumer evaluation of product category extensions. *International Marketing Review, 13*(4), 23–39.

Ailon-Souday, G., & Kunda, G. (2003). The local selves of global workers: The social construction of national identity in the face of organizational globalization. *Organization Studies, 24*(7), 1073–1096.

Al-Hawari, M., Hartley, N., & Ward, T. (2013). Measuring banks' automated service quality: A confirmatory factor analysis approach. *Marketing Bulletin*, 16, Article 1. http://marketing-bulletin.massey.ac.nz/V16/MB_V16_A1_AlHawari.pdf.

Andersen, P.H., & Kumar, R. (2006). Emotions, trust and relationship development in business relationships: A conceptual model for buyer–seller dyads. *Industrial Marketing Management, 35*(4), 522–553.

Anderson, E., & Weitz, B. (1989). Determinants of continuity in conventional industrial channel dyads. *Marketing Science, 8*(4), 310–323.

Anderson, J.C., & Narus, J.A. (1999). *Business Market Management, Understanding, Creating and Delivering Value*. Prentice Hall.

Anderson, J.C., Håkansson, H., & Johanson, J. (1994). Dyadic business relationships within a business network context. *Journal of Marketing, 58*(4), 1–15.

Ang, S., Van Dyne, L., Koh, C., Ng, K.-Y., Templer, K.J., Tay, C., & Chandrasekar, N.A. (2007). Cultural intelligence: Its measurement and effects on cultural judgment and decision making, cultural adaptation and task performance. *Management and Organization Review, 3*(3), 335–371. doi:10.1111/j.1740-8784.2007.00082.x

Arnett, D.B., German, S.D., & Hunt, S.D. (2003). The identity salience model of relationship marketing success: The case of nonprofit marketing. *Journal of Marketing, 67*(2), 89–105.

Balbanis, G., & Diamantopoulos, A. (2008). Brand origin identification by consumers: A classification perspective. *Journal of International Marketing, 16*(1), 39–71.

Baloglu, S., & McCleary, K. (1999). A model of destination image formation. *Annals of Tourism Research, 26*, 868–897.

Barnes J.G., & Howlett D.M. (1998). Predictors of equity in relationships between service providers and retail customers. *International Journal of Bank Marketing, 16*(1), 5–23.

Barnes, B.R., Leonidou, L.C., Siu, N.Y.M., & Leonidou, C. (2010). Opportunism as the inhibiting trigger for developing long-term-oriented western exporter-Hong Kong importer relationships. *Journal of International Marketing, 18*(2), 35–63.

Bendapudi, N., & Leone, R.P. (2002). Managing business-to business customer relationships following key contact employee turnover in a vendor firm. *Journal of Marketing, 66*(April), 83–101.

Berry, L.L. (1983). Relationship Marketing. In L.L. Berry, G.L. Shostack, & G.D. Upah (Eds.), *Emerging Perspectives in Services Marketing* (pp. 25–28). Chicago: American Marketing Association.

Bhaskaran, S., & Sukumaran, N. (2007). Contextual and methodological issues in COO studies. *Marketing Intelligence & Planning, 25*(1), 66–81.

Borgatti, S.P., & Foster, P.C. (2003). The network paradigm in organizational research: A review and topology. *Journal of Management, 29*(6), 991–1013.

Bouzdine-Chameeva, T., Durrieu, F., & Mandjak, T. (2014). Understanding relationship value applying a cognitive mapping approach: A customer perspective. In H.E. Spotts (Ed.), *Assessing the Different Roles of Marketing Theory and Practice in the Jaws of Economic Uncertainty. Developments in Marketing Science: Proceedings of the Academy of Marketing Science*, 145–150. Springer International Publishing.

Brennan, R., Canning, L., & McDowell, R. (2011). *Fundamentals of Business-to-Business Marketing*, 2nd ed. Sage Publications.

Brito, C. (2011). Relationship marketing: Old wine in a new bottle? *Innovative Marketing, 7*(1), 66–77.

Brodie, R.J., Coviello, N.E., & Winklhofer, H. (2008). Contemporary marketing practices research program: A review of the first decade. *Journal of Business & Industrial Marketing, 23*(2), 84–94.

Brymer, C. (2003). Branding a country. 1-4. http://www.brandchannel.com/images/papers/Country_Branding.pdf.

Cannone, G., & Ughetto, E. (2014). Born globals: A cross-country survey on high-tech start-ups. *International Business Review, 23*, 272–283.

Cerviño, J., Sánchez, J., & Cubillo, J.M. (2005). Made in effect, competitive marketing strategy and brand performance: An empirical analysis for spanish Brands. *Journal of American Academy of Business, 6*(2), 237–243.

Chai, J., & Dibb, S. (2014). How consumer acculturation influences interpersonal trust. *Journal of Marketing Management, 30*(1-2), 60–89.

Cheung, H.Y., & Chann, A.W.H. (2008). Relationships among cultural dimensions, educational expendure and class size of different nations. *International Journal of Educational Development, 28*(6), 698–707.

Chirica, C. (2013). Relationship marketing – Best practice in the banking sector. *Amfiteatru Economic, XV*(33), 288–300.

Chu, P.-Y., Chang, C.-C., Chen, C.-Y., & Wang, T.-Y. (2010). Countering negative country-of-origin effects: The role of evaluation mode. *European Journal of Marketing, 44*(7/8), 1055–1076.

Chua, R.Y.J., Morris, M.W., & Mor, S. (2012). Collaborating across cultures: Cultural metacognition and affect-based trust in creative collaboration. *Organizational Behavior and Human Decision Processes, 118*(2), 116–131.

Corăbieru, P., Corăbieru, A., & Vasilescu, D.D. (2015). Research and trends in product life cycle management in the context of sustainable development. *Environmental Engineering and Management Journal*, *14*, 205–212.

Danaher, P.J., Conroy, D.M., & McColl-Kennedy, J.R. (2008). Who wants a relationship anyway? Conditions when consumers expect a relationship with their service provider. *Journal of Service Research*, *11*(1), 43–62.

Danciu, V. (2012). Models for the internationalization of the business: A diversity-based approach. *Management & Marketing Challenges for the Knowledge Society*, *7*(1), 29–42.

Daye, D., & Van Auken, B. (2008). Branding: The country-of-origin effect. http://www.brandingstrategyinsider.com.

Denicolai, S., Zucchella, A., & Strange, R. (2014). Knowledge assets and firm international performance. *International Business Review*, *23*, 55–62.

Dibb, S., & Meadows, M. (2004). Relationship marketing and CRM: A financial services case study. *Journal of Strategic Marketing*, *12*(2), 111–125.

Dibb, S., Simoes, C., & Wensley, R. (2014). Establishing the scope of marketing practice: insights from practitioners. *European Journal of Marketing*, *48*(1-2), 380–404.

Dwyer, F., Schurr, P., & Oh, S. (1987). Developing buyer-seller relationships. *Journal of Marketing*, *51*(2), 11–27.

Earley, P.C., & Ang, S. (2003). *Cultural Intelligence: Individual Interactions Across Cultures*. Stanford University Press.

Egan, J. (2004). *Relationship Marketing: Exploring Relational Strategies in Marketing*, 2nd ed. Financial Times/Prentice Hall.

Ellis, N., & Hopkinson, G. (2010). The construction of managerial knowledge in business networks: Managers' theories about communication. *Industrial Marketing Management*, *39*(3), 413–424.

Fakeye, P., & Crompton, J. (1991). Image differences between prospective, first-time, and repeat visitors to the lower Rio Grande valley. *Journal of Travel Research*, *30*(10), 9–16.

Fan, Y. (2008). Country of origin, Branding strategy and internationalization: the case of Chinese piano companies. *Journal of Chinese Economic and Business Studies*, *6*(3), 303–319.

Ford, D., & McDowell, R. (1999). Managing business relationships by analysing the effects and value of different actions. *Industrial Marketing Management*, *28*(3), 429–442.

Gallarza, M., Gil Saura, I., & Garcia Calderon, H. (2002). Destination image: Towards a conceptual frame work. *Annals of Tourism Research*, *29*(1), 56–78.

Ghemawat, P. (2001). Distance still matters. The hard reality of global expansion. *Harvard Business Review*. https://hbr.org/2001/09/distance-still-matters-the-hard-reality-of-global-expansion

Giles, H., & Baker, S.C. (2008). Communication accommodation theory. In W. Donsbach, (Ed.). *The International Encyclopedia of Communication*. Blackwell Publishing.

Giles, H., & Gasiorek, J. (2012). *Parameters of Non Accommodation: Refining and Elaborating Communication Accommodation Theory*. Santa Barbara: University of California. http://www.sydneysymposium.unsw.edu.au/2012/chapters/GilesEASP2012.pdf.

Giles, H., & Marlow, M.L. (2011). Theorizing language attitudes: Existing frameworks, an integrative model, and new directions. In C. Salmon (Ed.), *Communication Yearbook*, *35*, 161–197. Erlbaum.

Glasford, D.E., Dovidio, J.F., & Pratto, F. (2009). I continue to feel so good about us: In-group identification and the use of social identity-enhancing strategies to reduce intragroup dissonance. *Personality and Social Psychology Bulletin*, *35*, 415–427. http://psp.sagepub.com/content/35/4/415.

Granovetter, M. (1985). Economic action and social structure: The problem of embeddness. *American Journal of Sociology*, *91*(3), 481–510.

Griffith, D.A. (2010). Understanding multi-level institutional convergence effects on international market segments and global marketing strategy. *Journal of World Business*, *45*(1), 59–67.

Griffith, D.A., & Hoppner, J. (2013). Global marketing managers: Improving global strategy through soft skill development. *International Marketing Review*, *30*(1), 21–51.

Grönroos, C. (1994). From marketing mix to relationship marketing: Towards a paradigm shift in marketing. *Management Decision*, *32*(2), 4–20.

Grönroos, C. (2007). *Service Management and Marketing: Customer Management in Service Competition*. 3rd edition. Chichester: John Wiley and Sons.

Grönroos, C. (1997). Value-driven relational marketing: From products to resources and competencies. *Journal of Marketing Management*, *13*(4), 407–419.

Gudykunst, W.B. (Ed.) (2003). *Cross-cultural and Intercultural Communication*. Sage Publications.

Gupta, A., & Sahu, G.P. (2012). A literature review and classification of relationship marketing research. *International Journal of Customer Relationship Marketing and Management*, *3*(1), 56–81.

Håkansson, H., & Snehota, I.J. (2000). The IMP Perspective: Assets and liabilities of business relationships. In J.N. Sheth, & A. Parvatiyar (Eds.), *The Handbook of Relationship Marketing*, 69–94. Sage Publications.

Håkansson, H., & Snehota, I.J. (Eds.) (1995). *Developing Relationships in Business Networks*. Routledge.

Halinen, A., Medlin, C.J., & Törnroos, J-Å. (2012). Time and process in business network research. *Industrial Marketing Management*, *41*(2), 215–223.

Hallen, L., & Weidershiem-Paul, F. (1984). *The evolution of psychic distance in international business relationships in Haag, Between Market and Hierarchy*. University of Uppsala, Department of Business Administration.

Hampton, A., & Rowell, J. (2010). Leveraging integrated partnerships as a means of developing international capability: An SME case study. *International Journal of Knowledge, Culture and Change Management*, *10*(6), 19–30.

Hampton, A., & Rowell, J. (2013). An evolution in research practice for investigating international business relationships. *Management Dynamics in the Knowledge Economy*, *1*(2), 161–178.

Henneberg, S.C., Naudé, P., & Mouzas, S. (2010). Sense-making and management in business networks—some observations, considerations, and a research agenda. *Industrial Marketing Management*, *39*(3), 355–360.

Heslop, L.A., Lu, I.R.R., & Cray, D. (2008). Modeling country image effects through an international crisis. *International Marketing Review*, *25*(4), 354–378.

Hilmersson, M. (2014). Small and medium-sized enterprise internationalization strategy and performance in times of market turbulence. *International Small Business Journal, 32*(4), 386–400.

Hofstede, G.H. (1980). *Culture's Consequences: International Differences in Work-Related Values.* SAGE Publications.

Hofstede, G.H. (1991). *Cultures and Organizations: Software of the Mind.* McGraw-Hill.

Houston, M.B., Hutt, M.D., Moorman, C., Reingen, P.H., Rindfleisch, A., Swaminathan, V., & Walker, B.A. (2004). A network perspective on marketing strategy. In C. Moorman & D.R. Lehman (Eds.), *Assessing Marketing Strategy Performance*, 247–268. Cambridge Marketing Science Institute.

Hsieh, M., Pan, S., & Setiona, R. (2004). Product-, corporate-, and country-image dimensions and purchase behavior: a multicountry analysis. *Academy of Marketing Science, 32*(3), 251–270.

Imai, L., & Gelfand, M.J. (2010). The culturally intelligent negotiator: The impact of cultural intelligence (cq) on negotiation sequences and outcomes. *Organizational Behavior and Human Decision Processes, 112*(2), 83–98.

Ivanova, M.N., & Torkkeli, L. (2013). Managerial sensemaking of interaction within business relationships: A cultural perspective. *European Management Journal, 31*(6), 717–727.

Jaworski, A., & Coupland, N. (Eds.) (2006). *The Discourse Reader*, 2nd edition. Routledge.

Jenes, B. (2007). Connection between the ecologically oriented consumer behavior and country image. *Marketing and Management, 6*(1), 34–43.

Jenes, B. (2005). Possibilities of shaping country image. *Marketing and Management, 2*(1), 18–29.

Josiassen, A., & Harzing, A-W. (2008). Descending from the ivory tower: reflections on the relevance and future of country-of-origin-research. *European Management Review*, 5, 264–270.

Kabadayi, S., & Lerman, D. (2011). Made in China but sold at FAO Schwarz: Country-oforigin effect and trusting beliefs. *International Marketing Review, 28*(1), 102–126.

Kanagal, N. (2009). Role of relationship marketing in competitive marketing strategy. *Journal of Management and Marketing Research, 2*(1), 1–17.

Keller, K.L. (1993). Conceptualizing, measuring and managing customer-based brand equity. *Journal of Marketing, 57*(1), 1–22.

Khojastehpour, M., & Johns, R. (2014). Internationalization and relationship marketing: an introduction. *European Business Review, 26*(3), 238 – 253.

Kornberger, M. (2010). *Brand Society – How brands transform management and lifestyle.* Cambridge University Press.

Kolis, K., & Jirinova, K. (2013). Differences between B2B and B2C customer relationship management. Findings from the Czech Republic. *European Scientific Journal*, 4(SI), 22–27.

Kotler, P. (1991). Philip Kotler explores the new marketing paradigm. *MSI Review*, 4–5.

Kotler, P. (1997). *Marketing Management: Analysis, Planning, Implementation, and Control*, 9th edition. Pearson Prentice Hall.

Kotler, P., & Keller, K.L. (2006). *Marketing Management*, 12th edition. Pearson Prentice Hall.

Lages, L.F., Lancastre, A., & Lages, C. (2008). The B2B-RELPERF scale and scorecard: Bringing relationship marketing theory into business-to-business practice. *Industrial Marketing Management, 37*(2008), 686–697.

Lambert, D.M., Cooper, M.C., & Pagh, J.D. (1998). Supply chain management: Implementation issues and research opportunities. *International Journal of Logistics Management, 9*(2), 1–18.

Laroche, M., Papadopoulos, N., Heslop, L.A., & Mourali, M. (2005). The influence of country image structure on consumer evaluations of foreign products. *International Marketing Review, 22*(1), 96–115.

Leek, S., & Mason, K. (2010). The utilisation of network pictures to examine a company's employees' perceptions of a supplier relationship. *Industrial Marketing Management, 39*(3), 400–412.

Lenney, P., & Easton, G. (2009). Actors, resources, activities and commitments. *Industrial Marketing Management, 38*(5), 553–561.

Lentz, P., Holzmuller, H.H., & Schirrmann, E. (2006). City-of-origin effects in the german beer market: Transferring an international construct to a local context. *Advances in international Marketing, 17*(17), 251–274.

Leonidou, L.C., Palihawadana, D., Chari, S., & Leonidou, C.N. (2011). Drivers and outcomes of importer adaptation in international buyer – seller Relationships. *Journal of World Business, 46*, 527–543.

Levitt, T. (1983). *The Marketing Imagination*. The Free Press.

Li, P.P. (2007). Social Tie, social capital, and social behavior: Toward an integrative model ofinformal exchange. *Asia Pacific Journal of Management, 24*(2), 227–246.

Lotz, S., & Hu, M. (2001). Diluting negative country of origin stereotypes: A social stereotype approach. *Journal of Marketing Management, 17*(1), 105–135.

Magnusson, P., Westjohn, S.A., Semenov, A.V., Randrianasolo, A.A., & Zdravkovic, S. (2013). The role of cultural intelligence in marketing adaptation and export performance. *Journal of International Marketing, 21*(4), 44–61.

Malhotra, N.K., Aggarwal, J., & Ulgado, F.M. (2003). Internationalization and entry modes: A multitheoretical framework and research propositions. *Journal of International Marketing, 11*(1), 1–31.

Mandják, T., & Durrieu, F. (2000). Understanding the non-economic value of business relationships. Accesat la adresa http://www.impgroup.org/uploads/papers/89.pdf.

Martin, I.M., & Eroglu, S. (1993). Measuring a multi-dimensional construct: country image. *Journal of Business Research, 28*(3), 191–210.

Maxim, A. (2009). Relationship marketing – a new paradigm in marketing theory and practice. *Analele ştiinţifice ale universităţii "Alexandru Ioan Cuza" din Iaşi Tomul LVI Ştiinţe Economice.*

Miller, V.L. (2005). An Examination of Contemporary Marketing Practices Used by Organization with Different Culture Types: A Test of the Convergence Theory in the US and Cote d'Ivoire. Disertaţie, Georgia State University. http://scholarworks.gsu.edu/marketing_diss/2

Mooij, M., & Hofstede, G. (2010). The Hofstede model – Applications to global branding and advertising strategy and research. *International Journal of Advertising, 29*(1), 85–110.

Morgan, N., Pride, R., & Pritchard, A. (2004). *Destination branding: creating the unique destination proposition*, 4th edition. Oxford.

Morgan, R., & Hunt, S. (1994). The commitment-trust theory of relationship marketing. *Journal of Marketing, 58*(3), 20–38.

Mouzas, S., Henneberg, S., & Naudé, P. (2007). Trust and reliance in business relationships. *European Journal of Marketing, 41*(9/10), 1016–1032.

Murphy, P.E., Laczniak, G.R., & Wood, G. (2007). An ethical basis for Relationship Marketing: a virtue ethics perspective. *European Journal of Marketing, 41*(1/2), 37–57.

Nagashima, A. (1977). A comparative "made in" product image survey among Japanese businessmen. *Journal of Marketing, 41*(2), 95–100.

Navarro, A., Losada, F., Ruzo, E., & Díez, J.A. (2010). Implications of perceived competitive advantages, adaptation of marketing tactics and export commitment on export performance. *Journal of World Business, 45*(1), 49–58.

Nicolescu, L. (2012). The analysis of conceptual tools for the study of country-of-origin effect for hybrid offerings. *Management & Marketing Challenges for the Knowledge Society, 7*(1), 3–14.

Nicolescu, L., Păun, C., Popescu, I.A., & Drăghici, A. (2008). *Romania trying to be a European brand. Management & Marketing Challenges for the Knowledge Society, 3*(1), 61–72. Disponibil la adresa: http://www.managementmarketing.ro/pdf/articole/93.pdf.

O'Cass, A., Ngo, L.V., & Siahtiri, V. (2015). Marketing resource-capability complementarity and firm performance in B2B firms. *Journal of Business & Industrial Marketing, 30*(2), 194–207.

O'Regan, M. (2000). The use of image in tourism destination marketing. In J. Ruddy & S. Flanagan (Eds.), *Tourism Destination Marketing; Gaining the Competitive Edge*. Tourism Research Centre, Dublin Institute of Technology.

Orbaiz, L.V., & Papadopoulos, N. (2003). Toward a model of consumer receptivity of foreign and domestic products. *Journal of International Consumer Marketing, 15*(3), 101–126.

Papadopoulos, N., & Heslop, L. A. (2002). Country equity and country branding – Problems and prospects. *Journal of Brand Management, 9*(4-5), 294–314.

Palmatier, R.W. (2007). *What Drives Customer Relationship Value in Business-to-Business Exchanges*. Cambridge, Mass.: Marketing Science Institute, Report No. 07-118.

Palmatier, R.W. (2008). *Relationship Marketing*. Marketing Science Institute.

Palmatier, R.W., Dant, R.P., & Grewal, D. (2007). A comparative longitudinal analysis of theoretical perspectives of interorganizational relationship performance. *Journal of Marketing, 71*(October), 172–194.

Palmatier, R.W., Dant, R.P., Grewal, D., & Evans, K.R. (2006a). Factors influencing the effectiveness of relationship marketing: A meta-analysis. *Journal of Marketing, 70*(October), 136–153.

Palmatier, R.W., Gopalakrishna, S., & Houston, M.B. (2006b). Returns on business-to-business relationship marketing investments: Strategies for leveraging profits. *Marketing Science, 25*(September-October), 477–493.

Palmatier, R.W., Scheer, L.K., & Steenkamp, J.B. (2007). Customer loyalty to whom? Managing the benefits and risks of salesperson-owned loyalty. *Journal of Marketing Research, 44*(May), 185–199.

Palmer, R., Lindgreen, A., & Vanhamme, J. (2005). Relationship marketing: Schools of thought and future research directions. *Marketing Intelligence and Planning*, *23*(3), 313–330.

Pappu, R., Quester, P.G., & Cooksey, R.W. (2006). Consumer-based brand equity and country-of-origin relationships: Some empirical evidence. *European Journal of Marketing*, *40*(5/6), 696–717.

Pappu, R., Quester, P.G., & Cooksey, R.W. (2007). Country image and consumer-based brand equity: Relationships and implications for international marketing. *Journal of International Business Studies*, *38*(4), 726–745.

Payne, A. (1995). *Advances in Relationship Marketing*. Kogan Page.

Payne, A., & Frow, P. (2005). A strategic framework for customer relationship management. *Journal of Marketing*, *69*(4), 167–176.

Peters, L.D., Pressey, A.D., Vanharanta, M., & Johnston, W.J. (2013). Constructivism and critical realism as alternative approaches to the study of business networks: Convergences and divergences in theory and in research practice. *Industrial Marketing Management*, *42*(3), 336–346.

Petison, P. (2010). Cross cultural relationship marketing in the Thai context: The Japanese buyer's perspective. International Journal of Trade. *Economics and Finance*, *1*(1), 17–23.

Pharr, J.M. (2005). Synthesizing country-of-origin research from the last decade: Is the concept still salient in an era of global brands. *Journal of Marketing*, *13*(4), 34–45.

Pop, N.A., Roman, M., Săniuţă, A., & Petrişoaia, C. (2012). Relationship marketing, engine of sustainable development and organizational change in the Romanian business environment. *Amfiteatru Economic*, *XIV*(32), 349–364.

Quester, P.G., Dzever, S., & Chetty, S. (2000). Country-of-origin effects on purchasing agents' product perceptions: An international perspective. *Journal of Business & Industrial Marketing*, *15*(7), 479–490.

Rakic, B., & Rakic, M. (2015). Holistic management of marketing sustainability in the process of sustainable development. *Environmental Engineering and Management Journal*, *14*, 887–900.

Ramos, C., Roseira, C., Brito, C., Henneberg, S.C., & Naude, P. (2013). Business service networks and their process of emergence: The case of the Health Cluster Portugal. *Industrial Marketing Management*, *42*(6), 950–968.

Reinartz, W., Thomas, J., & Bascoul, G. (2008). Investigating cross-buying and customer loyalty. *Journal of Interactive Marketing*, *22*(1), 5–20.

Rindfleisch, A., & Moorman, C. (2003). Interfirm cooperation and customer orientation. *Journal of Marketing Research*, *40*(11), 421–436.

Samaha, S.A., Beck, J.T., & Palmatier, R.W. (2014). The role of culture in international relationship marketing. *Journal of Marketing*, *78*(Septembrie), 78–98.

Samiee, S. (2010). Advancing the country image construct – a commentary essay. *Journal of Business Research*, *63*(4), 442–445.

Samiee, S., Shimp, T.A., & Sharma, S. (2005). Brand origin recognition accuracy: Its antecedents and consumers' cognitive limitations. *Journal of International Business Studies*, *36*(4), 379–397.

Samy, G.M., Samy, C.P., & Ammasaiappan, M. (2015). Integrated management systems for better environmental performance and sustainable development – A review. *Environmental Engineering and Management Journal*, *14*, 985–1000.

Sand, N.T. (2012). Communication accommodation in context: an analysis of convergence and divergence in action. A Paper Submitted to the Graduate Faculty of the North Dakota State University of Agriculture and Applied Science. Fargo, North Dakota.

Sandberg, S. (2014). Experiential knowledge antecedents of the SME network node configuration in emerging market business networks. *International Business Review*, 23(1), 20–29. 10.1016/j.ibusrev.2013.08.001

Schurr, P.H. (2007). Buyer-seller relationship development episodes: theories and methods. *Journal of Business & Industrial Marketing*, 22(3), 161–170.

Sheth, J.N., & Parvatiyar, A. (1995). The evolution of relationship marketing. *International Business Review*, 4(4), 397–418.

Sheth, J.N., & Parvatiyar, A. (2000). *Handbook of Relationship Marketing*. SAGE Publications.

Shimp, T., Samiee, S., & Sharma, S. (2001). The country-of-origin effect and brand origin knowledge: How little consumers know and how important knowledge is. *European Advances in Consumer Research*, 5(1), 325–326.

Sin, L.Y.M., Tse, A., & Yim, F. (2005a). CRM: conceptualization and scale development. *European Journal of Marketing*, 39(11-12), 1264–1290.

Sin, L., Tse, A., Yau, O., Chow, R., Lee, J., & Lau, L. (2005b). Relationship Marketing orientation: scale development and cross-cultural validation. *Journal of Business Research*, 58, 185–194.

Sousa, C.M.P., & Novello, S. (2014). The influence of distributor support and price adaptation on the export performance of small and medium-sized enterprises. *International Small Business Journal*, 32(4), 359–385.

Srinivasan, N., Jain, S.C., & Sikand, K. (2004). An experimental study of two dimensions of country-of-origin (manufacturing country and branding country) using intrinsic and extrinsic cues. *International Business Review*, 13(1), 65–82.

Steenkamp, J.-B.E.M. (2005). Moving out of the U.S. Silo: A call to arms for conducting international marketing research. *Journal of Marketing*, 69(October), 6–8.

Suh, Y., & Kim, M.-S. (2014). Internationally leading SMEs vs. internationalized SMEs: Evidence of success factors from South Korea. *International Business Review*, 23, 115–129.

Swaminathan, V., & Moorman, C. (2009). Marketing Alliances, Firm Networks, and Firm Value Creation. *Journal of Marketing*, 73(Septembrie), 52–69.

Sweeney, J.C., & Webb, D.A. (2007). How functional, psychological, and social relationship benefits influence individual and firm commitment to the relationship. *Journal of Business & Industrial Marketing*, 22(7), 474–488.

Tähtinen, J., & Blois, K. (2011). The involvement and influence of emotions in problematic business relationships. *Industrial Marketing Management*, 40(6), 907–918.

Tam, J.L.M. (2008). Brand familiarity: Its effects on satisfaction evaluations. *Journal of Service Marketing*, 22(1), 3–12.

Tan, Q., & Sousa, C.M.P. (2015). Leveraging marketing capabilities into competitive advantage and export performance. *International Marketing Review*, 32(1), 78–102.

Tidström, A., & Hagberg-Anderson, Å. (2012). Critical events in time and space when cooperation turns into competition in business relationships. *Industrial Marketing Management*, 41(2), 333–343.

Tse, D.K., & Lee, W. (1993). Removing negative country images: Effects of decomposition, branding, and product experience. *Journal of International Marketing*, *1*(4), 25–48.

Turnbull, P., & Valla, J.P. (Eds.) (1986). *Strategies for international industrial marketing*. Croom Helm.

Usunier, J-C., & Cestre, G. (2008). Further considerations on the relevance of country-of-origin research. *European Management Review*, *5*, 271–274.

Van den Bulte, C., & Wuyts, S. (2007). *Social Networks and Marketing*. Marketing Science Institute.

Vătămănescu, E.-M., Alexandru, V.-A., Mitan, A., & Dabija, D.-C. (2020a). From the deliberate managerial strategy towards international business performance: A psychic distance vs. global mindset approach. *Systems Research and Behavioral Science*, *37*(2), 374–387. 10.1002/sres.2658

Vătămănescu, E.-M., Cegarra-Navarro, J.-G., Andrei, A.G., Dincă, V.-M., & Alexandru, V.-A. (2020b). SMEs strategic networks and innovative performance: a relational design and methodology for knowledge sharing. *Journal of Knowledge Management*, *24*(6), 1369–1392. 10.1108/JKM-01-2020-0010

Vătămănescu, E.-M., Cegarra-Navarro, J.-G., Martínez-Martínez, A., Dincă, V.-M., & Dabija, D.-C. (2022). Revisiting online academic networks within the COVID-19 pandemic – From the intellectual capital of knowledge networks towards institutional knowledge capitalization. Journal of Intellectual Capital, Vol. ahead-of-print No. ahead-of-print. 10.1108/JIC-01-2022-0027.

Verlegh, P.W.J., & Steenkamp, J.-B. E.M. (1999). A review and meta-analysis of country-of-origin research. *Journal of Economic Psychology*, *20*(5), 521–546.

Vesel, P., & Zabkar, V. (2010). Comprehension of relationship quality in the retail environment. *Managing Service Quality*, *20*(3), 213 – 235.

Villar, C., Alegre, J., & Pla-Barber, J. (2014). Exploring the role of knowledge management practices on exports: A dynamic capabilities view. *International Business Review*, *23*(1), 38–44.

Walter, A., Ritter, T., & Gemünden, H.G. (2000). Value creation in buyer–seller relationships: Theoretical considerations and empirical results from a supplier's perspective. *Industrial Marketing Management*, *30*(4), 365–377.

Ward, C., Bochner, S., & Furnham, A. (2003). *The Psychology of Culture Shock*, 2nd edition. Routledge.

Wasserman, S., & Faust, K. (1994). *Social Network Analysis*. Cambridge University Press.

Weck, M., & Ivanova, M. (2013). The Importance of cultural adaptation for the trust development within business relationships. *Journal of Business and Industrial Marketing*, *28*(3), 210 – 220.

Wu, P.-C., & Ang, S.H. (2011). The impact of expatriate supporting practices and cultural intelligence on cross-cultural adjustment and performance of expatriates in Singapore. *International Journal of Human Resource Management*, *22*(13), 2683–2702.

Yaprak, A. (2008). Culture study in international marketing: A critical review and suggestions for future research. *International Marketing Review*, *25*(2), 215–229.

Yasin, N.M., Noor, M.N., & Mohamad, O. (2007). Does image of country-of-origin matter to brand equity? *Journal of Product & Brand Management, 16*(1), 38–48.

Yzerbyt, V., & Schadron, G. (2002). *Cunoașterea și judecarea celuilalt, o introducere în cogniția social [Knowing and judging the other, an introduction into the social cognition].* Polirom.

Zeugner-Roth, K.P., & Diamantopoulos, A. (2009). Advancing the country image construct. *Journal of Business Research, 62*(1), 726–740.

6 Leveraging the managerial global mindset for SMEs internationalization

In the previous chapter, we focused on relationship marketing as a prerequisite for the success of small- and medium-sized enterprises (SMEs) that nowadays undergo internationalization processes. As relationships are established between people, regardless of the organizations that they represent, a further step needs to be made, and a deeper analysis of the factors that support relationship building in a business context must be unraveled. Thus, this chapter highlights the roles that managers, entrepreneurs, and even employees play with regard to relationship marketing.

The first part of the chapter argues that internationalization cannot be conceptualized today without taking into consideration the mental models that a manager may have, that allow for business growth in the knowledge economy. The second part of the chapter recognizes the significance that the human capital, as embodied by managers, entrepreneurs, and employees, specifically has on a company's development. As the manager is the person in charge, who imprints the company's strategy, and network development, and as his relationship portfolio works as an asset to the company's internationalization, the last part of the chapter focuses on the manager's psychological makeup, namely on the managerial global mindset, on the psychic distance, on the personal values, and on the cultural intelligence – all being concepts that allow a better understanding of the manager's capacity to establish and leverage relationships with the aim of propelling the business on foreign markets.

The role of the manager's mental models in the knowledge economy

Internationalization has also gradually led to a change in the management model. Managers can no longer limit themselves to the organization's day-to-day problems and the usual local demands. They are increasingly forced to keep up with innovations in their field of interest, global market trends and the development trends of competitors operating internationally or even globally. In transnational companies, managers are trained in line with the company's strategic objectives through long-term training programs designed to stimulate international management. On this level, globalization is taken

DOI: 10.4324/9781003432326-8

on board through multidisciplinary solutions adopted by managers, who take into account the implications of their decisions in line with the extra-organizational environment.

Studying the constraints of SMEs relative to those of multinational or transnational organizations, Hutchinson and Quintas (2008) pointed out that corporate managers have superior resources for professional and entrepreneurial development, a situation quite distinct from that of managers in SMEs. A similar approach was taken by Gabrielsson et al. (2008a, 2008b) who focused their attention on the resource differences between SMEs and large firms in terms of developing business management skills. They consider that small- and medium-sized businesses can become international due to the emergence and growth of international networks of managers from different countries.

Frazier et al. (2009) have also highlighted the undeniable reality that there are major costs involved in developing international relations, but the results of establishing such links between managers and, by extension, businesses, are likely to bring considerable benefits. The international openness of managers and their willingness to pool resources, to participate in events of common interest, to share expertise with colleagues can be seen as a long-term investment in the well-being of the firm. In this vein, Frazier et al. (2009) note the importance attributed to social activities within the business, as they are prerequisites for the effective internationalization of the business and the organization.

The concept of "global mindset" describes the quality of managers to look at their business from a global perspective, even when it comes to small firms. This is supported by Cohen (2010)) who proposes a key to interpreting global mindedness – "the ability to influence individuals, groups, organizations and systems that have a different type of intellectual, social and psychological knowledge and intelligence from one's own" (p. 6). In other words, a new paradigm of international business is emerging with the process of organizational change that requires businesspeople to become aware of the dynamic environment in which they operate and respond accordingly.

In the mid-1960s, Peter Drucker (2006) wrote the emblematic book *The Effective Executive,* opening the discussion on knowledge economy and on the role that the intellectual capital embodied by the managers and other employees play in the modern organization's success. He argued that after the Second World War a shift of the center of gravity has happened in modern organizations, making knowledge workers more relevant for the firms' development and current activities than manual workers. Focusing on the central role that knowledge workers, be they managers or not, play in the organizational context, Drucker (2006) advocated for novel means of measuring the effectiveness of workers and for a novel perspective on management, focusing more on understanding the workers, their values, and their needs, instead of considering them as replaceable parts of a mechanism.

Knowledge economy is an economic system describing the modern take on organizational productivity, which relies now more on the intellectual capabilities of people, and less on traditional inputs, such as raw or natural resources (Carlaw et al., 2006; Peters, 2009). The use of technology, of automation, and of data analytics, is vital to firms in the knowledge economy (as these are their primary resource of production), leading to a dependency on perpetual innovation at the level of technology, procedures, and products (Mangabeira Unger, 2019). Peters (2010) believes that the discourse on knowledge economy presents itself under multiple intricacies, the main correlates that we should delineate it from being the learning economy, the creative economy, and the open knowledge economy.

The World Bank (2013) described knowledge economy as being influenced by the level of education and training of the people, that enables them to create, use and share knowledge, on the information infrastructure, which ranges from radio to Internet services, that is required to process information and to disseminate knowledge and data, on economic incentives and on the existence of a robust regulatory environment that supports investments in Information and Communications Technology (ICT) and stimulates entrepreneurs to engage in creating and developing business centered around knowledge, and on innovation systems, such as universities, think tanks, research networks, clusters, and other groups, where knowledge can be shared and enriched, so that it leads to the emergence of new knowledge.

Recently, Sánchez Ramírez (2021) underlined that the extent to which the knowledge economy developed has led to the flourishing of a novel type of system – the Knowledge Capitalism – which emerged in the 1980s and currently replaces the Fordist-Keynesian Welfare State narrative, as that collapsed in 2008, pursuant to the global financial crisis. In this new developmental stage, the economic activities are dependent on knowledge and on technology (microprocessors, software). This dependency of the economy on knowledge paves the pathway for further theoretical and empirical studies on the knowledge workers, and on the intellectual capital as strategic intangible resources of the firm.

In order to better understand how people operate as knowledge workers, and to set the stage for the discussion on the managerial global mindset that we introduce in Chapter 4, it is necessary for us to refer to the concept of mental models. Mental models or mental images are reflections of the reality, which connect concepts (Forrester, 1971). These models are used to represent reality in a simplified manner; they are not synonyms of the realities they represent. The social system in which people live is a multi-loop nonlinear feedback system, and people use these fuzzy mental models to estimate the behavior of the system, even though these estimations often times prove to be faulty (Forrester, 1971).

Although Plato already wrote about this idea in his work the *Republic*, introducing it through the Cave allegory, and Wittgenstein's *Tractatus Logico-Philosophicus* described the picture theory of language in the early 1920s, Forrester's take on the topic and his explanations fostered an arduous debate and lead to an increased interest in understanding how the human mind operates with these models, in relation to work and the economy. The concept of mental model was extensively promoted to the members of the business and management community by Senge (1990), who explained in his seminal book *The Fifth Discipline: The Art and Practice of the Learning Organization* that mental models are based on estimations, suppositions, generalizations, and images that are deeply set in the Man's mind, which influence the way people understand the world.

Bratianu (2015) identified several mental models that highly impact the Man's capacity to develop strategic thinking, and the manager's ability to lead the company. By using time as the angular stone, mental models can be described by inertial thinking, dynamic thinking, and entropic thinking:

1 *Inertial thinking* is a static thinking pattern that eliminates time as a landmark. Stability, predictability, and habit are specific to this pattern. Managers who adopt this model find comfort in doing things in the same way, in allowing for inertia to lead, and in resisting change. Conservatism, the desire to maintain the status quo as it, is specific to this mental model.
2 *Dynamic thinking* is the thinking pattern that incorporates time as referential. Managers who adopt this mental model embrace transformations and understand that change is an intrinsic part of life. They are able to identify and operate with the parameters of change and anticipate how the processes unfold. The amount of knowledge they use in order to make these evaluations is significantly higher than in the case of the managers operating with an inertial mental model.
3 *Entropic thinking* is a higher order thinking pattern, the most complex with respect to the use of time as referential. It implies that the manager has the capacity to understand that some processes are irreversible, while others are reversible, and to project a change program for the organization in the light of their vision for the future of the firm. Entropic thinking operates with the idea of risk and uses time as a scale to place on the present, the desirable future, the probable future, and the possible future. Understanding that there is not one single future but that there is a multitude of options, and that these options are modeled through the action of multiple variables, paves the way for strategic thinking to emerge.

Complexity is another criterion that Bratianu (2015) uses to explain the different mental models that influence the managerial capabilities of people. *Causal thinking* is the first model that can be used by Man to operate with complexity. It is a rather oversimplifying way of operating with reality, as often one event may be the cause of multiple effects, and many effects are the result of the action of multiple causes, over time. *Linear thinking* is another simple model, based on the ideal of linearity and on the assumption that complex phenomena can be approximated through linear processes.

Nonlinear thinking is a more complex model, based on the acknowledgment of nonlinearity, of phenomena that develop following logarithmic progression, exponential equations and so on. *Systemic thinking* reveals itself as most significant to managers, who need to be able to make correlations between high numbers of variables that evolve over time, in order to be able to make decisions in a complex system.

Operating with uncertainty is another major request that managers need to comply with, in the knowledge economy (Bratianu, 2015). *Determinism* describes a simple mental model that is characterized by the absence of uncertainty and of risk. *Probabilistic thinking* is a mental model that enables the person who works with it to estimate the probability of an event to take place and to act accordingly. Forecasts are made based on what is known, but some phenomena, such as economic turbulence, are highly chaotic and can hardly allow for probabilities to be extracted. Thus, *chaotic thinking* emerges as a superior mental model, embraced by the people who are able to operate in environments that are described by a certain degree of turbulence.

Further, emotionality shall also be considered when discussing about the mental models relevant to managers (Bratianu, 2015). *Emotional thinking* operates with emotional knowledge and reflects the emotional intelligence of the person. Self-knowledge and self-mastery appear as prerequisites of a successful integration of emotional thinking into the managerial approach to leading. Supplementary, *positive thinking* uses optimism as a philter to measure perceptions and knowledge and stimulates strategic thinking through integrating the broader landscape and through identifying opportunities and solutions instead of drawbacks. All of the mental models introduced above represent options concerning the cognitive approach to reality that are expected to impact a manager's capacity to evaluate the circumstances in which the firm finds itself, to assess risks, to draw the strategy, and to lead the firm (Bratianu, 2015).

Nevertheless, the dynamic managerial capabilities (i.e., the capabilities of managers to exert change in organizations), have been shown to underlie the managerial resources – the managerial cognition or the models and beliefs that managers operate with, their mental processes and emotions, the managerial social capital, or the goodwill that derives from the good formal and informal relationships that the manager has with various people, that can enable them to draw in resources, and the managerial human capital, or the knowledge and skills of the manager, as derived from their education and experience (Helfat & Martin, 2014). These managerial resources are thought to impact the firm performance as well as strategic changes (Helfat & Martin, 2014), and are joined, in the growth equation of any firm, by the skills, mental models and capabilities of employees, who are highly significant for the positive evolution of any firm, talent management being a core preoccupation for multinational companies especially in relation to foreign subsidiaries and international expansion (Collings et al., 2018).

Mental models, such as the ones introduced in this section, are used by managers as lenses for looking at the reality of the environment they and the firm pertains to and may act as barriers or facilitators of the firm's success in local and international endeavors. The next sections describe some of the main macro-factors that mold the environment in which companies operate today and point to some of the major macro-shifts that have been noted by recent analysts, on multiple levels.

Studies on internationalization have started to mention in the 1970s psychological factors pertaining to the entrepreneur and manager as significant influences on firm performance and international activity. Over the years, Bilkey and Tesar (1977), Wiedersheim-Paul et al. (1978) and Eisenhardt and Schoonhoven (1990) wrote about the fact that people with different mental characteristics make different choices in similar circumstances.

In this chapter, we focus on the role that human capital, as embodied by the entrepreneur, manager, and employees of an SME, plays in relation to SME internationalization. The section introduces multiple perspectives on studying the manager/entrepreneur and their features, which may influence on many levels the internationalization of the company they lead. Among the concepts that will be addressed we mention psychic distance, cultural intelligence, personal values, and the global mindset.

The role of the human capital in supporting SMEs internationalization

The organizational structure of SMEs, the scale of operations, the way in which they engage in competition with other companies, the capacity to respond to changes in the environment, the managerial capacities and styles specific to SMEs are different to the ones of MNEs, posing particular barriers to internationalization (Coviello & Martin, 1999). Above all, managerial skills and experience are essential to internationalization (Ibeh, 2003), but SMEs many times lack or have insufficient managerial competence and know-how regarding international markets, one of the issues being that they have difficulties hiring specialized managers (Ortiz et al., 2008). A proactive attitude of the manager may act as a door-opener for the SME seeking to improve their presence on foreign markets, yet the issues with human capital are prone to limit the international expansion of SMEs (Vătămănescu et al., 2018). To diminish the potential harming effects of the abovementioned factors, Ruzzier and Konecnik Ruzzier (2015) advise the entrepreneurs and managers of SMEs to plan for their international expansion at the very moment when they start the company. This translates into designing a specific organizational structure, opting for a specific resource allocation strategy, and to adopting a foreseeing human capital strategy, in order to increase their chances to succeed abroad.

The information presented above hints to the fact that knowledge and people are extremely important for SME development. Over the years, the various types of knowledge that a company operates with, have been linked to the existence of a specific type of capital – the organizational intellectual capital – which is an intangible asset of the firm, including three areas (human capital, relational capital, structural capital). The organizational intellectual capital may lead a company toward superior performance in the future, but it is rather provocative to measure it (Jianu & Bratianu, 2006). Various models of the organizational intellectual capital have been presented in the literature. While the Skandia model and the Svaiby model are perhaps the most popular approaches to theorizing intellectual capital, although static, newer approaches, such as the one introduced by Bratianu (2006) underline the fact that intellectual capital is the result of the dynamic process through which individual contributions of the human capital of the employees of the firm become integrated. The individual human capital of the employees is followed, in the model of Bratianu, by the organizational capital, and the consumer capital, the latter being the result of a dynamic differentiation process with regard to the demands and the expectations of the consumers.

For Bratianu (2008), human capital is split into knowledge, intelligence, and values, and these components might also be considered the *building blocks* of the organizational intellectual capital, as they are discrete categories, that can be measured. Combined using the power of an integrator, the individual knowledge, intelligence, and values merge to create the organizational intellectual capital, which is then reflected as organizational knowledge (tacit ot explicit), organizational intelligence (cognitive and emotional), and organizational values (regarding business and social aspects). An intelligent team management, for instance, is able to create the force field that leads to a synergy effect, which aligns the components/intangible resources in the company; other factors that support this type of fields are the organizational culture, the mission and vision of the company, the leadership, and the technology (Bratianu et al., 2011, 2013).

Organizational capital is a complex adaptative system, which results from the interactions between the cognitive knowledge field, the emotional knowledge field, and the spiritual knowledge field, is best described by entropy or disorder, and is conceived both as potential and as having operational capacity, incapsulating a vision for the probable future and a desire to reach the goal of attaining a competitive advantage (Bratianu & Orzea, 2013). This is a complex system, which points to the significance of studying and understanding the building blocks of the organizational intellectual capital. In the following pages we address in more depth only the concept of human capital – as a reflection of those building blocks – and introduce various theoretical approaches that may connect human capital to SME performance and SME internationalization.

Going back to the origins of the concept of human capital, we learn it has been introduced by Becker in the 1960s, while he was searching for a method to measure the yield/ performance of the investment in education (Becker, 1962). The most important characteristic of human capital is that it is embodied by people (Becker, 1993). Human capital refers to the knowledge, abilities, habits, expertise (task-specific human capital, see Waldman & Gibbons, 2003), and the social and psychological qualities that define a person, that help a person conduct activities that lead to economic value creation (Goldin, 2014). Human capital is seen to include two components: educational capital, which is developed through education and refers to those abilities and knowledge that a person develops or gains while they study in school or in other places dedicated to teaching/learning, and the biologic capital, which refers to the innate physical characteristics that a person has (Voicu, 2004), most often presented as *health level.*

A bibliometric analysis performed by Dabić et al. (2020) shows that, beginning with the 2000s, there is an increasing interest in studying the role of knowledge management and human capital in connection to the SMEs internationalization, and that many papers focus on businesses from developed countries, that are in urban areas, and are high-tech, but few addresses low-tech businesses, businesses from the Eastern Europe, or from emergent economies.

Human capital has a significant role to business development (Javalgi & Todd, 2011) and is vital to SME internationalization (Ruzzier et al., 2007). Mubarik et al. (2020) have proven that human capital has a direct and significant influence on exports in the case of SMEs, companies that export more being impacted to a greater extent. They observed that education, experience, attitude, training, and compliance, at managerial level, influence the export performance of the firm, the level of experience (job tenure, similar industry experience, work-related experience) being the strongest predictor for SMEs to scale their operations abroad. The study also mentions that human capital has an indirect effect upon the export performance of the SME, mediated by the absorptive capacity (i.e., capacity to learn, to make use of external market knowledge, in order to integrate with the global market), especially when the company is highly engaged in exporting activities.

Cabrilo and Dahms (2018) concluded that human capital has a significant negative impact on the firm's innovative performance when moderated by strategic knowledge management and explain the results as their study was conducted in SEE countries, from where capable workers immigrated to other countries, however the firms they studied seemed to perform well by mobilizing relational capital and structural capital.

A study on manufacturing SMEs from Belgium showed that there is a significant correlation (reversed U type) between human capital and the intensity of exports, when the company chooses an accelerated internationalization strategy, but that this correlation is not significant in the case of the SMEs who choose a gradual internationalization approach (Onkelinx et al., 2015). This is why investments in human capital are higher in the case of the SMEs who choose to go international at an accelerated pace, and this has a direct impact on improving productivity and on the exports. Productivity does not seem to influence the intensity of internationalization in the case of the SMEs who choose a gradual approach (Onkelinx et al., 2016).

The role of employees in SME internationalization

Kianto et al. (2017) posit that intellectual capital plays the role of a positive mediator between the knowledge-based practices in the human resources management and the innovation performance of the firm, consequently demonstrating that human capital is center fold to firm's performance in innovation-related activities, enhancing both the relational capital and the structural capital.

Employees, through their abilities, knowledge, talent, and experience, create value for the companies (Fletcher, 2004). The formal education of the employees is considered to be a decisive factor for the internationalization, their lack of training being directly linked to issues in export performance (Acs & Armington, 2006; Capelleras & Rabetino, 2008; Littunen, 2003; Mata & Portugal, 2002; Pennings et al., 1998). A company employing skilled workers is better equipped to compete in high-income markets (Brambilla et al., 2011). Companies with teams that have high intrapreneurial and interpersonal skills are more resilient (Teixeira, 2002) and are more often capable to compete on foreign markets (Fernandez-Mesa & Alegre, 2015). The vast previous experience, the compliance of employees to managerial decisions, and their overall stability are also mentioned as factors that shape the export performance of a firm (Bayus & Agarwal, 2007; Khan & Khan, 2012).

Bogers et al. (2018) found that companies that had employees with diverse educational backgrounds were more open to engaging in open innovation. Neffke and Henning (2012) found that firms are likely to diversify their activities into industries where leveraging on the skills that their employees had is possible, suggesting that the human capital is highly relevant for business diversification.

We therefore understand that employees, though their human capital, impact the company's development on various circumstances, but especially when it comes to development, be it on the domestic market, or on foreign markets.

The role of entrepreneurs in SME internationalization

As decision-makers for the SME, entrepreneurs have a fundamental role in SME internationalization (Glancey, 1998; Westhead et al., 2002). The managerial urge is one of the main factors propelling business internationalization (Danciu, 2012; Hollensen, 2008). A study signed by Kunday and Pişkinsüt Şengüler (2015) has shown that the export orientation of the SME is influenced by the business skills of the entrepreneur, as well as by the motivation of the entrepreneur for starting the SME, and by innovation. Rutihinda (2008) previously underlined the fact that SMEs with owner managers who have an international orientation are more likely to proactively undertake international operations and succeed. Rutihinda's research has proven that the international orientation of the owner manager is, in fact, the single most important factor propelling the SME toward international activity.

Studies by Acedo and Jones (2007), Harveston et al. (2000), and Nummela et al. (2005) also point to the importance of the managerial and entrepreneurial desire to internationalize the firm as a determinant of fast internationalization.

Entrepreneurs who manage their businesses have psychological characteristics, which make them unique among the general population: they invest in uncertainty, they prefer simplicity to complexity, they have a tolerance to risk (Gomez-Mejia, 1988), they are solutions-oriented, and they never cease to learn from their previous actions (Gruber & MacMillan, 2017; Gürol & Atsan, 2006; McGrath & MacMillan, 2000). The entrepreneurial propensity toward working in contexts marked by uncertainty or higher risk was also observed by Kulkarni (2001), Milliken (1990) and Wiedersheim-Paul et al. (1978). Other studies underline that, apart from manifesting openness to engaging in risk taking, entrepreneurs are also proactive and have an unmistakable interest in innovation (Dess et al., 1997). Overall, psychological characteristics were mentioned as predictors of the managerial strategic vision, including the envisioning of international success for their company (Allinson et al., 2000; Barr et al., 1992).

Saghebi et al. (2019) indicate that the international orientation of the entrepreneur has a significant correlation with proactivity, tolerance of ambiguity, knowledge intensity and risk perception; and, that there is a significant relation between knowledge intensity, risk perception and the speed of internationalization.

While willing to identify the internal (i.e., firm-related) determinants of international entrepreneurship, Zahra and George (2002) noticed that there are three main sets of factors that have a definitive impact on internationalization: the top management team (experience working abroad, origins of founders, education in foreign countries, having a vision of a global development of the company), the internal resources of the company (expenditure on R&D, the ability to work in a network, firm's reputation), and the specifics of the firm (size, age, location, legal form, financial strength, pro-development orientation, testing business environment). similar results were presented by Johanson and Vahlne (2003), who believe that the level of knowledge of the manager regarding foreign markets is a condition for success in operations performed on those foreign markets, by Wach (2014), who mentioned the unique knowledge possessed by the manager, especially acquired through direct experience overseas, as a determinant of internationalization, and by Knight and Cavusgil (2004), who explain the global vision of the entrepreneur through the influence of education and international experience, and who believe that the entrepreneur shall also possess market expertise, the capacity to identify growth opportunities for the firm, to speak foreign languages, to be properly educated (level and type of education are important), and to choose to employ managers that are able to lead the company to international success.

The manager as the main force behind SMEs internationalization

SME managers play the central part in the process of internationalization by drawing the strategy, selecting the target market, by initiating and maintaining business relationships with foreign partners. These relationships support the cultivation of the competitive advantage and performance (Vătămănescu et al., 2019).

Much of the extant literature regarding managers operating in international business focuses on their technical and operational skills. More and more voices acknowledge though that this perspective needs to be enriched, as the shift from domestic to global business puts a particular pressure on managers: these specialists not only need to possess strategic thinking and strategic leadership abilities, but also need to have a keen understanding of the culturally diverse settings in which the companies they lead operate, which means they need to have an adequate level of cultural intelligence (Mannor, 2008). The work of the manager is also highly influenced by his or her capacity to identify the psychic distance, by their capacity to develop a global mindset, and by their personal values.

SMEs tend to offer fewer opportunities for managers to expand their managerial capabilities than MNEs (Kim & Hemmert, 2016). This acts as a phrenic force for SME internationalization, as having a broader palette of managerial competencies facilitates international success (Cerrato & Piva, 2012; Westhead et al., 2001). Nevertheless, the individual characteristics of managers contribute to the internationalization outcomes to a great extent (Dimitratos et al., 2016). Managers of SMEs from CEE do not usually learn in school the skills necessary to perform on international markets, and need training (Svetličič et al., 2007). This is susceptible of posing difficulties to SMEs from the region succeeding on international markets.

Managers of SMEs that prepare for entering export markets need to have managerial skills which differ from the ones that are employed after the presence on foreign markets is already established (Mubarik et al., 2020; Ruzzier et al., 2007). Managers that lead SMEs to international success are individuals who possess the capacity the ability to innovate, who are willing to accept high levels of risk (also Brustbauer, 2016), who often have a global business vision and previous international experience, and who can assess the environment outside of the home market, in search for growth opportunities (McDougall & Oviat, 2000; Oviatt & McDougall, 2005). These characteristics are even more important in human resource selection, as it is known that the actions that many managers undertake are reactive to events instead of being actions programmed to help mitigate future risks or prepare the company for better handling of future events (Wedawatta et al., 2011).

Managers who graduated college or post-university degrees tend to internationalize faster the SMEs that they lead, regardless of the route that they choose (gradual or accelerated), while the level of expertise of the managers in what concerns internationalization and their fear of failure tend to influence the process based on the culture that they belong to. For example, Spanish managers who were part of a study of Baier-Fuentes et al. (2018) chose to put their hopes on relational capital and human capital, while Chilean managers chose to put their trust on formal education and the development of human capital.

Executive managers play a very important role in SME internationalization, their individual characteristics being uncommonly valuable (Aaby & Slater, 1989; Chiara & Minguzzi, 2002; Miesenbock, 1988). Their impact on exports, for example, is considered crucial (Graves & Thomas, 2006; Hutchinson et al., 2006; Westhead et al., 2001). Board members and executives who have local knowledge, such as returnee entrepreneurs or managers who had previous international experience, are a valuable asset to the company, as they are able to protect the proprietary knowledge of the firm on foreign markets, and to process new knowledge in a manner that is beneficial to the international performance of the company (Schwens et al., 2017). However, companies (MNEs) whose international trade depends upon many executive managers tend to perform worse than companies who rely on fewer managers, this pointing to the fact that perhaps SMEs might not be at a disadvantage in what concerns foreign trade for employing fewer managers (Sadeghi & Biancone, 2018).

SMEs that proceed to addressing foreign markets need to develop coherent strategies. Managers tend to be more often than the entrepreneurs the individuals who decide upon the emergent initiatives, and who mobilize the company's internal resources and attract external resources in order to improve the international performance of the firm, choosing the strategy and drawing the plans (Eden et al., 2011). The managers' deliberate decision-making has a definitive impact upon the success of any international undertaking (Gabler et al., 2016). For the overall success of the company, its relevance is equal to the manager's decision-making upon emerging strategies (Neugebauer et al., 2016).

Managers' role implies the need to conduct rational assessments of the organizational structures, operations, and resources, leading to deliberate decision-making concerning business initiatives and investments (Franco & Haase, 2015; Geyskens et al., 1996). Indeed, managers play a determinant role with regard to observing the environment, to deciding which strategy shall be employed, to setting the targets, and to estimating the impact of each international endeavor at organizational level (Dauber et al., 2012).

The internationalization of SMEs is often a gradual process, and the manager plays the key role in propelling the SME on foreign markets through identifying prospective foreign allies and business partners and through establishing trust-based relationships with the counterparts. His or her characteristics, skills, level of knowledge, personality traits, values, are especially relevant when the SME is supposed to develop strong ties with foreign partners, which would work together in a stable, long term and efficient manner. Long-term collaboration is especially solid when the companies are represented by individuals with culturally compatible views, shared values, and similar objectives (Colombo et al., 2018; Holtbrijgge, 2004). These characteristics emulate trust building, rational engagement (i.e., the managers understand that they need to work with the other to achieve the goals of their company), and affective responses from all parties involved (i.e., the managers start to enjoy working with the other), which emerge via increased social interaction and networking (Franco & Haase, 2015; Geyskens et al., 1996). Both affective and rational reasoning are prerequisites of any fruitful business collaboration.

Building trust between business partners, regardless of whether they are members of a business network or not, is a time consuming, gradual process, which weaves as the representatives/managers of the said companies interact and learn more about each other and about the capabilities, objectives, strategies and needs of the other (Forsgren & Johanson, 1992; Thorgren et al., 2009). Several studies investigated the connection between business internationalization; global mindset and psychic distance, but the literature largely leaves the topic open to further exploration (Colombo et al., 2018; den Dekker, 2016; Vătămănescu et al., 2019).

From the psychic distance toward the managerial global mindset

Psychic distance

The Uppsala model of internationalization may lead the reader to believe that geographical proximity to the target market is a prerequisite of successful internationalization. Korsakienė and Tvaronavičienė, (2012), and, later, Colombo et al. (2018) showed that this is, indeed, a supporting factor: proximity is a influences the choices of SMEs that want to expand their operations on foreign markets; its relevance being connected to the extant relationships with stakeholders in the destination country, and to the already established informal relations with counterparts, as well as to the level of knowledge, broadness of experience and intuition of the manager, and to the perception that the manager has regarding the opportunity to obtaining resources and support in the targeted market. Mabey et al. 2015 highlight that managers tend to believe that physical proximity of the target market increases their sense of control over the foreign market operations and may entail efficacy. Nonetheless, assuming that geographical proximity between two countries/ markets implies cultural, social, institutional, or legislative similarities is no more than a trap. In fact, there are potentially substantial differences between geographically close countries, and fewer differences between countries situated further apart. The concept which measures the cultural and civilizational similarities between countries is the psychic distance, and this explains the paradox we mentioned above (O'Grady & Lane, 1996).

Psychic distance is said to impact decision-making and share characteristics with cultural distance, thus influencing the level of perceived difficulty in conducting business in a different country (Nordström & Vahlne, 1992).

Funny as it may seem, O'Grady and Lane (1996) observed that companies that do business in countries between which psychic distance is small tend to report having more problems adjusting to the extant cultural differences than they were in situations when the psychic distance was large.

Psychic distance pertains to the behavioral ontology perspective on business internationalization (Törnroos, 2002) and embodies a series of cultural and civilizational characteristics of the domestic market and of the destination market, that the manager may have in mind when choosing a progressive approach to internationalization and/ or a fast internationalization (Nordman & Tolstoy, 2014; Sandberg, 2014). To a certain extent a lower psychic distance between the domestic and the foreign market might suggest to a manager that there is a lower risk associated with penetrating that market, as long as there are significant similarities between the two.

The literature offers multiple perspectives on defining psychic distance. Sousa and Lages (2011) identified two dimensions of the concept: the first is country distance, and the second is people distance. Both dimensions are influenced by the cultural distance, which impacts the product, the price that can be used, the way the product is promoted and where it is sold on the foreign market. Griffith and Dimitrova (2014) also tried to break down the concept in parts, and they identified business distance and cultural distance as components of psychic distance. To them, business distance describes the similarity (or rather differences) pertaining to the economic environments of the two countries, the varied legal practices, the political influences, the business practices, the market peculiarities, and the language. The cultural distance embodies the values that offer the structure of the market's environment. Dauber (2011) mentions that, in this context, cultural values might work as barriers that impede the learning process between foreign partners. The potential phrenic effect that competing values or just plainly different values may have on the development of the firm on foreign markets has also been mentioned by Johanson and Vahlne (2009), who show that a lower distance might act as an incentive for expansion. Nevertheless, psychic distance is based on perception, thus a subjective concept, applying to space, social aspects, cultural norms, and might be named foreign distance or perceptual distance (Dow & Karunaratna, 2006; Håkanson & Ambos, 2010; Johanson & Wiedersheim-Paul, 1975; Ojala, 2015).

Having a long-term horizon for the collaboration, cultural compatibility, shared values, similar moral, similar organizational structures that make decisions and identifying common objectives influence the efficacy and the stability of the companies that work in partnership (Colombo et al., 2018). This is why managers need to be aware of the psychic distance, or the sum of the factors that impede the flow of information to the market and from the market, including the language differences, education differences, different business practices, cultural differences and the level of industrial development (Johanson & Vahlne, 1977, p. 24). Managers who have gained extensive international experience are well aware of that and tend to be more open to developing the business on new markets, their overall perception regarding the characteristics of the new country being framed under a lower or shorter psychic distance (Andersen, 1993). Young managers tend to ignore psychic distance (Vătămănescu et al., 2014a, 2014b), even though they work to internationalize the business they lead, but is relevant to more mature managers, who tend to approach internationalization gradually.

Cultural intelligence

Cultural intelligence (CQ) is the "ability to interact effectively" (Thomas et al., 2015, p. 1101) and has been defined as the capacity of the individual to function and lead efficiently in situations that involve cross-cultural interactions (Ang et al., 2007).

Individuals who have a higher level of cultural intelligence are able to establish and to cultivate trust-based relationships with foreigners (Triandis, 2006; Vătămănescu et al., 2017a, 2017b), which may predict the future efficacy of their international business relations. The cultural intelligence dimensions are (Earley & Ang, 2003):

1 metacognitive – it measures the capacity of the person to acknowledge the cultural differences to develop their capacity to interact with people in different cultures;
2 cognitive – it measures the competency based upon the knowledge of practices, conventions and rules that work within foreign cultures, which an individual builds through personal experience and education;
3 motivational – it measures the capacity of a person to concentrate and learn how to operate in situations where different cultures mix, and behavioral;
4 behavioral – which refers to the capacity of a person to behave in an adequate way both verbally and nonverbally during interactions with individuals from foreign culture. This means the person needs to have a wide and flexible repertoire of behaviors that they are able to use depending upon the situation.

Personal values

Personal values are motivational constructs, universally valid, that stand behind the actions that individuals take (Schwartz, 1992; Schwartz & Bardi, 2001). To measure the personal values of individuals, Schwartz and his team created the *Schwartz Value Inventory*, which includes ten umbrella values and 56 subdimensions. The ten measured dimensions are: power, success, hedonism, stimulation, self-determination, universalism, benevolence, conformism, tradition, security. By looking at the scores that an individual has for each dimension, personal profiles can be created, and those profiles show the fundamental filter that the person uses when they look at themselves, the others, and the world at large.

The managerial global mindset

The global mindset is '*a highly complex cognitive structure characterized by an openness to and an articulation of multiple cultural and strategic realities on both global and local levels, and the cognitive ability to mediate and integrate across this multiplicity*' (Levy et al., 2007), a cognitive filter which combines '*an openness and an awareness of diversity across cultures and markets with a propensity and ability to synthesize across this diversity*' (Gupta & Govindarajan, 2002, p. 117).

Back in the 1990s, Srinivas (1995) mentioned that global mindset was a vital business competence for managers to invest in developing. This early conceptualization pointed to global mindset as manifesting through the curiosity of the manager, through their desire to learn more about the context in which the business grows, through their capacity to manage complexity and respond to challenges, through them seeking opportunities when the situations are uncertain or surprising, through them being self-assured and believing that the organization would continue to work, through them focusing on their continuous improvement, to them embracing diversity and to being sensitive, as well as to them having the mental capacities needed to understand how systems work, to understand the cause and effect mechanisms, to anticipate and to manage reactions.

As a structure, the global mindset includes: (1) the capacity of the individual to be open and pay attention to many levels of meaning and action, (2) the individual's complex representation and expression of the dynamics that take place on the cultural and strategic level, (3) the individual's capacity to be moderate and to incorporate ideals and actions oriented toward the global and the local levels at the same time (Javidan et al., 2007).

Beechler and Javidan (2007) identified three components of the global mindset, which were later developed to create the *Global Mindset Inventory* (Javidan et al., 2010). This instrument is widely used for assessment in business settings. According to the authors, the global mindset can be measured across the following lines: (1) intellectual capital, a dimension which incorporates references to being global business savvy, to having cognitive complexity and a cosmopolitan outlook, (2) psychological capital, which refers to having a passion for diversity, a zest for going on a quest for adventure, and being self-assured, and (3) social capital, which comprises of three subdimensions, namely having intercultural empathy, searching for interpersonal impact, and operating with diplomacy.

Dominici (2012) suggests that managers with a global mindset are better equipped to manage complexity and deal with uncertainty, while having a focus on competitiveness. Dealing with nonlinearity, changing market dynamics, increased connectivity, in a society that is marked by intense transformations, is part of what a manager who possesses a global mindset is able to manage (Dominici, 2015). These assumptions were and are backed by other studies too. It is notable that SMEs who are led my managers who have developed a global mindset benefit from competitive advantages in the global arena (Javidan & Bowen, 2013; Javidan et al., 2007), as this is a key factor leading to successful global leadership (den Dekker, 2016). This influences in a positive manner the financial performance of the firm on international markets (Nummela et al., 2009) and even predicts the successful internationalization of SMEs (Torkkeli et al., 2018).

***

As shown in this chapter, the human capital embodied by the managing team, by the entrepreneurs, and by the employees, is a vital resource for the company's development. Particularly, managers and their mental models, global mindset, personal values, level of cultural intelligence, and perception of the psychic distance, impact the capacity to engage in meaningful relationships with partners, consequently supporting or negatively impacting the company's internationalization processes, and overall performance.

Based on this understanding of the managerial mindset and of the forces that mold the manager's approach to relationships in a business context, the next chapter advances an integrative relationship-driven model, based on the resource-based view of the firm.

References

Aaby, N., & Slater, S.F. (1989). Management influences on export performance: A Review of the empirical literature 1978–1988. *International Marketing Review*, *6*(4), p.null. 10.1108/EUM0000000001516

Acedo, F.J., & Jones, M.V. (2007). Speed of internationalization and entrepreneurial cognition: Insights and a comparison between international new ventures, exporters and domestic firms. *Journal of World Business*, *42*(3), 236–252. 10.1016/j.jwb.2007. 04.012

Acs, Z.J., & Armington, C. (2006). New firm survival and human capital. In C. Karlsson, B. Johansson & R. Stough, (Eds.), *Entrepreneurship and Dynamics in the Knowledge Economy*, 125–148. Routledge.

Allinson, C.W., Chell, E., & Hayes, J. (2000). Intuition and entrepreneurial behavior. *European Journal of Work and Organizational Psychology*, *9*(1), 31–43. 10.1080/ 135943200398049

Andersen, O. (1993). On the internationalization process of firms: A critical analysis. *Journal of International Business Studies*, *24*(2), 209–223. 10.1057/palgrave.jibs. 8490230

Ang, S., Van Dyne, L., Koh, C., Ng, K.-Y., Templer, K.J., Tay, C., & Chandrasekar, N.A. (2007). Cultural intelligence: Its measurement and effects on cultural judgment and decision making, cultural adaptation and task performance. *Management and Organization Review*, *3*(3), 335–371. 10.1111/j.1740-8784.2007.00082.x

Baier-Fuentes, H., Hormiga, E., Amorós, J.E., & Urbano, D. (2018). The influence of human and relational capital on the rapid internationalization of firms: A comparative study between Spain and Chile. *Academia Revista Latinoamericana de Administración*, *31*(4), 679–700. 10.1108/ARLA-12-2016-0333

Barr, P.S., Stimpert, J.L., & Huff, A.S. (1992). Cognitive change, strategic action, and organizational renewal. *Strategic Management Journal, 13*(S1), 15–36. 10.1002/smj.4250131004

Bayus, B.L., & Agarwal, R. (2007). The role of pre-entry experience, entry timing, and product technology strategies in explaining firm survival. *Management Science, 53*(12), 1887–1902. https://www.jstor.org/stable/20122346

Becker, G.S. (1962). Investment in human capital: A theoretical analysis. *The Journal of Political Economy, LXX*(5), 9–49.

Becker, G.S. (1993). *The Economic Way of Looking at Life.* https://chicagounbound.uchicago.edu/cgi/viewcontent.cgi?article=1509&context=law_and_economics

Beechler, S., & Javidan, M. (2007). Leading with a global mindset. In M. Javidan, R.M. Steers & M.A. Hitt (Eds.), *The Global Mindset: Advances in International Management,* 131–169. Emerald Publishing. 10.1016/S1571-5027(07)19006-9.

Bilkey, W.J., & Tesar, G. (1977). The export behavior of smaller Wisconsin manufacturing firms. *Journal of International Business Studies, 8*(1), 93–98. 10.1057/palgrave.jibs.8490783

Bogers, M., Foss, N.J., & Lyngsie, J. (2018). The "human side" of open innovation: The role of employee diversity in firm-level openness. *Research Policy, 47*(1), 218–231. 10.1016/j.respol.2017.10.012

Brambilla, I., Dix-Carneiro, R., Lederman, D., & Porto, G. (2011). Skills, exports, and the wages of seven million Latin American workers. *World Bank Economic Review, 26*(1), 34–60. 10.1093/wber/lhr020

Bratianu, C. (2006). Un model de analiză a capitalului intelectual organizational [A model of analyzing intellectual capital]. *Management&Marketing, 1*(3), 17–32. http://www.managementmarketing.ro/pdf/articole/20.pdf

Bratianu, C. (2008). A dynamic structure of the organizational intellectual capital. In M. Naaranoja (Ed.). *Knowledge Management in Organizations,* 233–243. Vaasan Yliopisto.

Bratianu, C. (2013). Nonlinear integrators of the organizational intellectual capital. In M. Fathi (Ed.), *Integration of Practice-oriented Knowledge Technology: Trends and Perspectives,* 3–16. Springer-Verlag.

Bratianu, C. (2015). *Gândirea strategică [Strategic thinking].* ProUniversitaria.

Bratianu, C., & Orzea, I. (2013). The entropic intellectual capital model. *Knowledge Management Research & Practice, 11,* 133–141. 10.1057/kmrp.2013.11

Bratianu, C., Jianu, I., & Vasilache, S. (2011). Integrators for organizational intellectual capital. *International Journal of Learning and Intellectual Capital, 8*(1), 5–17. 10.1504/IJLIC.2011.037355

Brustbauer, J. (2016). Enterprise risk management in SMEs: Towards a structural model. *International Small Business Journal, 34*(1), 70–85. 10.1177/0266242614542853

Cabrilo, S., & Dahms, S. (2018). How strategic knowledge management drives intellectual capital to superior innovation and market performance. *Journal of Knowledge Management, 22*(3), 621–648. 10.1108/jkm-07-2017-0309

Capelleras, J.-L., & Rabetino, R. (2008). Individual, organizational and environmental determinants of new firm employment growth: Evidence from Latin America. *International Entrepreneurship and Management Journal, 4*(1), 79–99. 10.1007/s11365-006-0030-z

Carlaw, K., Oxley, L., Walker, P., Thorns, D., & Nuth, M. (2006). Beyond the hype: Intellectual property and the knowledge society/knowledge economy. *Journal of Economic Surveys, 20*(4), 633–690. 10.1111/j.1467-6419.2006.00262.x

Cavusgil, S.T., & Knight, G. (2015). The born global firm: An entrepreneurial and capabilities perspective on early and rapid internationalization. *Journal of International Business Studies, 46*(1), 3–16. 10.1057/jibs.2014.62

Cerrato, D., & Piva, M. (2012). The internationalization of small and medium-sized enterprises: The effect of family management, human capital and foreign owner-ship. *Journal of Management and Governance, 16*(4), 617–644. 10.1007/s10997-010-9166-x

Chiara, A. de, & Minguzzi, A. (2002). Success factors in SME's internationalization processes: An Italian investigation. *Journal of Small Business Management, 40*(2), 144–153. 10.1111/1540-627X.00046

Cohen, S.L. (2010). Effective global leadership requires a global mindset. *Industrial and Commercial Training, 42*(1), 3–10.

Collings, D.G., Mellahi, K., & Cascio, W.F. (2018). Global talent management and performance in multinational enterprises: A multilevel perspective. *Journal of Management, 45*(2), 540–566. 10.1177/0149206318757018

Colombo, G., Vătămănescu, E.-M., Alexandru, V.-A., & Gazzola, P. (2018). The influence of internationalization process-based factors on international per-formance in the case of SMFEs. Economia Aziendale Online. *Business and Management Science International Quarterly Review, 9*(3), 319–332. 10.13132/2038-5498/9.3.1945

Coviello, N., & Martin, M. (1999). Internationalization of service SMEs: An inte-grated perspective from the engineering consulting sector. *Journal of International Marketing, 7*, 42–66. 10.1177/1069031X9900700404

Dabić, M., Maley, J., Dana, L.-P., Novak, I., Pellegrini, M.M., & Caputo, A. (2020). Pathways of SME internationalization: A bibliometric and systematic review. *Small Business Economics, 55*, 705–725. 10.1007/s11187-019-00181-6

Danciu, V. (2012). Models for the internationalization of the business: A diversity-based approach. *Management & Marketing Challenges for the Knowledge Society, 7*(1), 29–42.

Dauber, D. (2011). *Hybridization in mergers and acquisitions.* Doctoral thesis, Vienna University of Economics and Business, Austria. https://research.wu.ac.at/en/publications/hybridization-in-mergers-and-acquisitions-3

Dauber, D., Fink, G., & Yolles, M. (2012). A configuration model of organizational culture. *Sage Open, 2*(1), 1–16. 10.1177/2158244012441482

den Dekker, W. (2016). *Global Mindset and Cross-Cultural Behavior. Improving Leadership Effectiveness.* Macmillan Publishers Ltd.

Dess, G.G., Lumpkin, G.T., & Covin, J.G. (1997). Entrepreneurial strategy making and firm performance: Tests of contingency and configurational models. *Strategic Management Journal, 18*(9), 677–695. 10.1002/(SICI)1097-0266(199710)18:9<677::AID-SMJ905>3.0.CO;2-Q

Dimitratos, P., Johnson, J.E., Plakoyiannaki, E., & Young, S. (2016). SME Internationalization: How does the opportunity-based international entrepreneurial culture matter? *International Business Review, 25*(6). 10.1016/j.ibusrev.2016.03.006

Dominici, G. (2012). Why does systems thinking matter? *Business Systems Review, 1*(1), 1–2. 0.7350/bsr.a02.2012

Dominici, G. (2015). Systems thinking and sustainability in organizations. *Journal of Organizational Transformation & Social Change, 12*(1), 1–3. 10.1179/1477963314Z.00000000036

Dow, D., & Karunaratna, A. (2006). Developing a multidimensional instrument to measure psychic distance stimuli. *Journal of International Business Studies*, *37*(5), 578–602. 10.1057/palgrave.jibs.8400221

Drucker, P. (1966/ 2006). *The Effective Executive*. HarperCollins Publishers.

Earley, P.C., & Ang, S. (2003). *Cultural Intelligence: Individual Interactions Across Cultures*. Stanford University Press.

Eden, L., Dai, L., & Li, D. (2011). International business, international management, and international strategy. What's in a name? *International Studies of Management and Organization*, *40*(5), 54–68. 10.2753/IMO0020-8825400405

Eisenhardt, K.M., & Schoonhoven, C.B. (1990). Organizational growth: Linking founding team, strategy, environment, and growth among U.S. semiconductor ventures, 1978-1988. *Administrative Science Quarterly*, *35*(3), 504–529. 10.2307/2393315

Fernández-Mesa, A., & Alegre, J. (2015). Entrepreneurial orientation and export intensity: Examining the interplay of organizational learning and innovation. *International Business Review*, *24*(1), 148–156. 10.1016/j.ibusrev.2014.07.004

Fletcher, D. (2004). International entrepreneurship and small business. *Entrepreneurship & Regional Development*, *16*(4), 289–305. 10.1080/0898562042000263267

Forrester, J.V. (1971). *World Dynamics*. Pegassus Communications.

Forsgren, M., & Johanson, J. (Eds.). (1992). *Managing Networks in International Business*. Routledge.

Franco, M., & Haase, H. (2015). Interfirm alliances: A taxonomy for SMEs. *Long Range Planning*, *48*, 168–181. 10.3390/joitmc6040193

Frazier, G., Maltz, E., Antia, K., & Rindflesch, A. (2009). Distributor sharing of strategic information with suppliers. *Journal of Marketing*, *73*(1), 31–43. 10.1509/jmkg.73.4.031

Gabler, C.B., Panagopoulos, N., Vlachos, P.A., & Rapp, A. (2016). Developing an environmentally sustainable business plan: An international B2B case study. *Corporate Social Responsibility and Environmental Management*, *24*(4), 261–272. 10.1002/csr.1409

Gabrielsson, M., Kirpalani, V.H.M., Dimitratos, P., Solberg, C.A., & Zucchella, A. (2008a). Conceptualizations to advance born global definition: A research note. *Global Business Review*, *9*(1), 45–50. 10.1177/097215090700900103

Gabrielsson, M., Kirpalania, V.H.M., Dimitratos, P., Solberg, C.A., & Zucchellag, A. (2008b). Born globals: Propositions to help advance the theory. *International Business Review*, *17*(4), 385–401. 10.1016/j.ibusrev.2008.02.015

Geyskens, I., Steenkamp, J.B.E.M., Scheer, L.K., & Kumar, N. (1996). The effects of trust and interdependence on relationship commitment: A trans-atlantic study. *International Journal of Research in Marketing*, *13*, 303–317. 10.1016/S0167-8116(96)00006-7

Glancey, K. (1998). Determinants of growth and profitability in small entrepreneurial firms. *International Journal of Entrepreneurial Behavior & Research*, *4*(1), 18–27. 10.1108/13552559810203948

Goldin, C. (2014). *Human Capital*. https://scholar.harvard.edu/files/goldin/files/human_capital_handbook_of_cliometrics_0.pdf

Gomez-Mejia, L.R. (1988). The role of human resources strategy in export performance: A longitudinal study. *Strategic Management Journal*, *9*(5), 493–505. https://www.jstor.org/stable/2485958

Graves, C. & Thomas, J., 2006. Internationalization of Australian family businesses: A managerial capabilities perspective. *Family Business Review*, *19*(3), 207–224. 10.1111/j.1741-6248.2006.00066.x

Griffith, D.A., & Dimitrova, B. (2014). Business and cultural aspects of psychic distance and complementarity of capabilities in export relationships. *Journal of International Marketing*, *22*(3), 50–67. 10.1509/jim.14.0019

Gruber, M., & MacMillan, I.C. (2017). Entrepreneurial behavior: A reconceptualization and extension based on identity theory. *Strategic Entrepreneurship Journal*, *11*(3), 271–286. 10.1002/sej.1262

Gupta, A., & Govindarajan, V. (2002). Cultivating a global mindset. *The Academy of Management Perspectives*. *16*(1), 116–126. 10.5465/ame.2002.6640211

Gürol, Y., & Atsan, N. (2006). Entrepreneurial characteristics amongst university students: Some insights for entrepreneurship education and training in Turkey. *Education and Training*, *48*(1), 25–38. 10.1108/00400910610645716

Håkanson, L., & Ambos, B. (2010). The antecedents of psychic distance. *Journal of International Management*, *16*(3), 195–210. 10.1016/j.intman.2010.06.002.

Harveston, P.D., Kedia, B.L., & Davis, P.S. (2000). Internationalization of born global and gradual globalizing firms: The impact of the manager. *Journal of Competitiveness Studies*, *8*(1), 92. https://link.gale.com/apps/doc/A78630769/AONE?u=anon~be3ca03d&sid=googleScholar&xid=1a343992

Helfat, C.E., & Martin, J.A. (2014). Dynamic managerial capabilities. *Journal of Management*, *41*(5), 1281–1312. 10.1177/0149206314561301

Hollensen, S. (2008). *Essential of Global Marketing*. Pearson Education.

Holtbrijgge, D. (2004). Management of international strategic business cooperation: Situational conditions, performance criteria, and success factors. *Thunderbird International Business Review*, *46*(3), 255–274. 10.1002/tie.20008

Hutchinson, K., Quinn, B., & Alexander, N. (2006). The role of management characteristics in the internationalization of SMEs: Evidence from the UK retail sector. *Journal of Small Business and Enterprise Development*, *13*(4), 513–534. 10.1108/14626000610705723.

Hutchinson, V., & Quintas, P. (2008). Do SMEs do knowledge management? Or simply manage what they know? *International Small Business Journal*, *26*(2), 131–154. 10.1177/0266242607086571

Ibeh, K.I.N. (2003). Toward a contingency framework of export entrepreneurship: Conceptualisations and empirical evidence. *Small Business Economics*, *20*(1), 49–68. 10.1023/A:1020244404241

Javalgi, R.G., & Todd, P.R. (2011). Entrepreneurial orientation, management commitment, and human capital: The internationalization of SMEs in India. *Journal of Business Research*, *64*(9), 1004–1010. 10.1016/j.jbusres.2010.11.024

Javidan, M., & Bowen, D. (2013). The 'Global Mindset' of Managers: What it is, why it matters, and how to develop it. *Organizational Dynamics*, *42*(2), 145—155. 10.1016/j.orgdyn.2013.03.008

Javidan, M., Hough, L., & Bullough, A. (2010). Conceptualizing and measuring global mindset: Development of the global mindset inventory. Thunderbird School of Global Management. www.globalmindset.com.

Javidan, M., Steers, R.M., & Hitt, A.M. (Eds). (2007). *The Global Mindset. Advances in International Management*, 19th edition. Emerald Publishing. 10.1016/S1571-5027(2007)19

Jianu, I., & Bratianu, C. (2006). Dinamica semantică a conceptului de capital intelectual [The semantic dynamics of the concept of intellectual capital]. *Management & Marketing, 2*, 15–26. http://www.managementmarketing.ro/pdf/articole/45.pdf

Johanson, J., & Wiedersheim-Paul, F. 1975. The internationalization of the firm-four swedish cases. *Journal of Management Studies, 12*, 305–322. 10.1111/j.1467-6486. 1975.tb00514.x.

Johanson, J., & Vahlne, J.E. (1977). The internationalization process of the firm—A model of knowledge development and increasing foreign market commitments. *Journal of International Business Studies, 8*(1), 23–32. 10.1057/palgrave.jibs.8490676

Johanson, J., & Vahlne, J.E. (2003). Business relationship learning and commitment in the internationalization process. *Journal of International Entrepreneurship, 1*(1), 83–101. 10.1023/A:1023219207042

Johanson, J., & Vahlne, J.E. (2009). The Uppsala internationalization process model revisited: From liability of foreignness to liability of outsidership. *Journal of International Business Studies, 40*(9), 1411–1431. 10.1057/jibs.2009.24

Khan, N.R., & Khan, M.R. (2012). Human resource practices in SME sector: An exploratory case study of Pakistan. *EuroEconomica, 31*(3), 7–19. https://journals. univ-danubius.ro/index.php/euroeconomica/article/view/1396/1309

Kianto, A., Sáenz, J., & Aramburu, N. (2017). Knowledge-based human resource management practices, intellectual capital and innovation. *Journal of Business Research, 81*, 11–20. 10.1016/j.jbusres.2017.07.018

Kim, J.J., & Hemmert, M. (2016). What drives the export performance of small and medium-sized subcontracting firms? A study of Korean manufacturers. *International Business Review, 25*(2), 511–521. 10.1016/j.ibusrev.2015.09.002.

Knight, G.A., & Cavusgil, S.T. (2004). Innovation, organizational capabilities and born global firm. *Journal of International Business Studies, 35*(2), 124–141. 10.1057/ palgrave.jibs.840007

Korsakienė, R., & Tvaronavičienė, M. (2012). The internationalization of SMEs: An integrative approach. *Journal of Business Economics and Management, 13*(2), 294–307. 10.3846/16111699.2011.620138

Kulkarni, S.P. (2001). The influence of the type of uncertainty on the mode of international entry. *American Business Review, 19*(1), 94–101. https://www.econbiz. de/Record/the-influence-of-the-type-of-uncertainty-on-the-mode-of-international-entry-kulkarni-subodh/10001545377

Kunday, Ö., & Pişkinsüt Şengüler, E. (2015). A study on factors affecting the internationalization process of small and medium enterprises (SMEs). *Procedia – Social and Behavioral Sciences, 195*, 972 – 981. 10.1016/j.sbspro.2015.06.363

Levy, O., Beechler, S., Taylor, S., & Boyacigiller, N.A. (2007). What we talk about when we talk about 'global mindset': Managerial cognition in multinational corporations. *Journal of International Business Studies, 38*(2), 231–258. https://www. jstor.org/stable/4540418

Littunen, H. (2003). Management capabilities and environmental characteristics in the critical operational phase of entrepreneurship: A comparison of Finnish family and nonfamily firms. *Family Business Review, 16*(3), 183–197. 10.1111/j.1741-6248. 2003.tb00013.x

Mabey, C., Wong, A.L.Y., & Hsieh, L. (2015). Knowledge exchange in networked organizations: Does place matter? *R&D Management, 45*(5), 487–500. https:// onlinelibrary.wiley.com/doi/pdfdirect/10.1111/radm.12099

Mangabeira Unger, R. (2019). *The Knowledge Economy*. Verso.

Mannor, M.J. (2008). Top executives and global leadership: At the intersection of cultural intelligence and strategic leadership theory. In S. Ang & L. Van Dyne (Eds.), *Handbook of Cultural Intelligence: Theory, Measurement, and Applications*, 91–106. M.E. Sharpe.

Mata, J., & Portugal, P. (2002). The survival of new domestic and foreign-owned firms. *Strategic Management Journal, 23*(4), 323–343.

McDougall, P.P., & Oviat, B.M. (2000). International entrepreneurship: The Intersection of two research paths. *Academy of Management Journal, 43*(5), 902–906. 10.2307/1556418

McGrath, R.G., & MacMillan, I.C. (2000). *The Entrepreneurial Mindset: Strategies for Continuously Creating Opportunity in an Age of Uncertainty*. Harvard Business Press. https://www.amazon.com/Entrepreneurial-Mindset-Continuously-Opportunity-Uncertainty/dp/0875848346

Miesenbock, K.J. (1988). Small businesses and exporting: A literature review. *International Small Business Journal, 6*(2), 42–61.

Milliken, F.J. (1990). Perceiving and interpreting environmental change: An examination of college administrators' interpretation of changing demographics. *Academy of Management Journal, 33*(1), 42–63. 10.2307/256351

Mubarik, S., Jinnah, M.A., Devadason, E.S., & Govindaraju, C. (2020). Human capital and export performance of small and medium enterprises in Pakistan. *International Journal of Social Economics, 47*(5), 643–662. 10.1108/IJSE-03-2019-0198

Neffke, F., & Henning, M. (2012). Skill relatedness and firm diversification. *Strategic Management Journal, 34*(3), 297–316. 10.1002/smj.2014

Neugebauer, F., Figge, F., & Hahn, T. (2016). Planned or emergent strategy making? Exploring the formation of corporate sustainability strategies. *Business Strategy and the Environment, 25*(5), 323–336. 10.1002/bse.1875

Nordman, E.R., & Tolstoy, D. (2014). Does relationship psychic distance matter for the learning processes of internationalizing SMEs? *International Business Review, 23*(1), 30–37. 10.1016/j.ibusrev.2013.08.010

Nordström, K.A., & Vahlne, J.-E. (1992). Is the globe shrinking? Psychic distance and the establishment of Swedish sales subsidiaries during the last 100 years. Paper presented at the International Trade and Finance Association's Annual Conference, April 22-25, Laredo, Texas.

Nummela, N., Puumalainen, K., & Saarenketo, S. (2005). International growth orientation of knowledge-intensive SMEs. *Journal of International Entrepreneurship, 3*(1), 5–18. 10.1007/s10843-005-0350-z

Nummela, N., Saarenko, S., & Puumalainen, K. (2009). A global mindset — A prerequisite for successful internationalization? *Canadian Journal of Administrative Sciences / Revue Canadienne des Sciences de l'Administration, 21*(1), 51–64. 10.1111/j.1936-4490.2004.tb00322.x

O'Grady, S. & Lane, H.W. (1996). The psychic distance paradox. *Journal of International Business Studies, 27*(2), 309–333. 10.1057/palgrave.jibs.8490137

Ojala, A. (2015). Geographic, cultural, and psychic distance to foreign markets in the context of small and new ventures. *International Business Review, 24*(5), 825–835. 10.1016/j.ibusrev.2015.02.007

Onkelinx, J., Manolova, T.S., & Edelman, L.F. (2015). Human capital and SME internationalization: Empirical evidence from Belgium. *International Small Business Journal: Researching Entrepreneurship, 34*(6), 818–837. 10.1177/0266242615591856

Onkelinx, J., Manolova, T.S., & Edelman, L.F. (2016). The human factor: Investments in employee human capital, productivity, and SME internationalization. *Journal of International Management*, 22(4), 351–364. 10.1016/j.intman. 2016.05.002

Ortiz, J.A., Ortiz, R.F., & Ramirez, A.M., (June 30–July 3, 2008). An integrative classification of barriers to exporting: An empirical analysis in small and medium-sized enterprises. *50th AIB Conference*, Italy.

Oviatt, B., & McDougall, P. (2005). Defining international entrepreneurship and modelling the speed of internationalization. *Entrepreneurship Theory and Practice*, 29(5), 537–553. 10.1111/j.1540-6520.2005.00097.x

Pennings, J.M., Lee, K., & Van Witteloostuijn, A. (1998). Human capital, social capital, and firm dissolution. *Academy of Management Journal*, 41(4), 425–440. 10.2307/257082

Peters, M.A. (2009). Introduction: Knowledge goods, the primacy of ideas, and the economics of abundance. In M.A. Peters, P. Marginson & P. Murphy (Eds.), *Creativity and the Global Knowledge Economy*, 1–22. Peter Lang.

Peters, M.A. (2010). Three forms of the knowledge economy: Learning, creativity and openness. *British Journal of Educational Studies*, 58(1), 67–88, 10.1080/00071 000903516452

Rutihinda, C. (2008). Factors influencing the internationalization of small and medium size enterprises. *International Business & Economics Research Journal*, 7(12), 45–54. 10.19030/iber.v7i12.3312

Ruzzier, M. & Konecnik Ruzzier, M. (2015). On the relationship between firm size, resources, age at entry and internationalization: The case of Slovenian SMEs. *Journal of Business Economics and Management*, 16(1), 52–73, 10.3846/16111699. 2012.745812

Ruzzier, M., Antoncic, B., Hisrich, R.D., & Konecnik, M. (2007). Human capital and SME internationalization: A structural equation modeling study. *Canadian Journal of Administrative Sciences*, 24(1), 15–29. 10.1002/cjas.3

Sadeghi, V.J., & Biancone, P.P. (2018). How micro, small and medium-sized enterprises are driven outward the superior international trade performance? A multidimensional study on Italian food sector. *Research in International Business and Finance*, 45(C), 597–606. 10.1016/j.ribaf.2017.07.136

Saghebi, S., Alizadeh, A., Mohammadzaheri, M., & Habibisenobari, T. (2019). Relationships of managers' entrepreneurial perception and internationalization speed in small and medium-sized enterprises (SMEs). *Journal of Global Entrepreneurship Research*, 9(28), 10.1186/s40497-019-0151-9

Sánchez Ramírez, C.M. (2021). *Knowledge Capitalism and State Theory. A "Space-Time" Approach Explaining Development Outcomes in the Global Economy*. Palgrave Macmilan.

Sandberg, S. (2014). Experiential knowledge antecedents of the SME network node configuration in emerging market business networks. *International Business Review*, 23(1), 20–29. 10.1016/j.ibusrev.2013.08.001

Schwartz, S.H. (1992). Universals in the content and structure of values: Theoretical advances and empirical tests in 20 countries. *Advances in Experimental Social Psychology*, 25, 1–65. 10.1016/S0065-2601(08)60281-6

Schwartz, S.H., & Bardi, A. (2001). Value hierarchies across cultures. Taking a similarities perspective. *Journal of Cross-Cultural Psychology*, 32(3), 268–290. 10.1177/ 0022022101032003002

Schwens, C., Zapkau, F.B., Bierwerth, M., Isidor, R., Knight, G., & Kabst, R. (2017). International entrepreneurship: A meta-analysis on the internationalization and performance relationship. *Entrepreneurship Theory and Practice*, 1–35, 10.1111/etap.12280#

Senge, P. (1990). *The Fifth Discipline. The Art and Practice of the Learning Organization.* Currency.

Sousa, C.M.P., & Lages, L.F. (2011). The PD scale: A measure of psychic distance and its impact on international marketing strategy. *International Marketing Review*, *28*(2), 201–222. 10.1108/02651331111122678.

Srinivas, K.M. (1995). Globalization of business and the third world: Challenge of expanding the mindsets. *Journal of Management Development*, *14*(3), 26–49. 10.1108/02621719510078957.

Svetličič, M., Jaklič, A. & Burger, A. (2007) Internationalization of small and medium-size enterprises from selected central European economies. *Eastern European Economics*, *45*(4), 36–65. 10.2753/EEE0012-8775450402

Teixeira, A. (2002). On the link between human capital and firm performance, a theoretical and empirical view. https://wps.fep.up.pt/wps/wp121.pdf

Thomas, D.C., Liao,Y., Aycan, Z., Cerdin, J.L., Pekerti, A.A., Ravlin, E.C., Stahl, G.K., Lazarova, M.B., Fock, H., Arli, D., Moeller, M., Okimoto, T., & van de Vijver, F. (2015). Cultural intelligence: A theory-based, short form measure. *Journal of International Business Studies*, *46*, 1099–1118. 10.1057/jibs.2014.67

Thorgren, S., Wincent, J., & Ortqvist, D. (2009). Designing inter-organizational networks for innovation: An empirical examination of network configuration, formation and governance. *Journal of Engineering and Technology Management*, *26*, 148–166. 10.1016/j.jengtecman.2009.06.006

Torkkeli, L., Nummela, N., & Saarenketo, S. (2018). A global mindset – Still a prerequisite for successful SME internationalization? Key success factors of SME internationalization: A cross-country perspective. *International Business & Management*, *34*, 7–24. 10.1108/S1876-066X20180000034001

Törnroos, J-Å. (2002). Internationalization of the firm – A theoretical review with implications for business network research. Paper presented at *the 18th IMP – Industrial Marketing and Purchasing Group International Conference*, Dijon, France, 5-7 September 2002. http://www.impgroup.org/paper_view.php?viewPaper=484.

Triandis, H.C. (2006). Cultural intelligence in organizations. *Group & Organizational Management*, *31*(1), 20–26. 10.1177/1059601105275253

Voicu, B. (2004). Capitalul uman: componente, niveluri, structuri. România în context european. Calitatea Vieții, XV(1-2), 1–22.

Vătămănescu, E.-M., Alexandru, V.-A., & Gorgos, E.-A. (2014a). The five Cs model of business internationalization (CMBI) – A preliminary theoretical insight into today's business internationalization challenges. In C. Bratianu, A. Zbuchea, F. Pînzaru, & E.-M. Vătămănescu (Eds.), *STRATEGICA. Management, Finance, and Ethics*, 537–558. Tritonic.

Vătămănescu, E.-M., Pînzaru, F., Andrei, A.-G., & Alexandru, V.-A. (2014b). Going international versus going global. The case of the European steel pipe SMEs. *Review of International Comparative Management*, *15*(3), 360–379. http://www.rmci.ase.ro/no15vol3/09.pdf.

Vătămănescu, E.-M., Andrei, A.G., Nicolescu, L., Pînzaru, F., & Zbuchea, A. (2017a). The influence of competitiveness on SMEs internationalization effectiveness. Online versus offline business networking. *Information Systems Management*, *34*(3), 205–219. 10.1080/10580530.2017.1329997

Vătămănescu, E.-M., Gazzola, P., Dincă, V.M., & Pezzetti, R. (2017b). Mapping entrepreneurs' orientation towards sustainability in interaction versus network marketing practices. *Sustainability*, *9*(9), 1580. 10.3390/su9091580

Vătămănescu E.-M., Gorgos, E.-A., & Alexandru, V.-A. (2018). Preliminary insights into SMEs opportunities and vulnerabilities in the European context. A qualitative approach. *Management Dynamics in the Knowledge Economy*, *6*(3), 385–404. 10.25 019/MDKE/6.3.03.

Vătămănescu, E.-M., Gorgos, E.-A., Ghigiu, A.M., & Pătruţ, M. (2019). Bridging intellectual capital and SMEs internationalization through the lens of sustainable competitive advantage: A systematic literature review. *Sustainability*, *11*(9), 2510. 10.3390/su11092510

Wach, K. (2014). The role of knowledge in the internationalization process: An empirical investigation among Polish businesses. In D. Kiendl-Wendner & K. Wach (Eds.), *International Competitiveness in Visegrad Countries: Macro and Micro Perspectives*, 143–158. Fachhochschule Joanneum.

Waldman, M., & Gibbons, R. (2003). Enriching a theory of wage and promotion dynamics inside firms. http://dspace.mit.edu/bitstream/handle/1721.1/3537/4324-03. pdf;jsessionid=E43FCEE7A3F046F64F805EC38B13624A?sequence=2.

Wedawatta, G., Ingirige, B., Jones, K., & Proverbs, D. (2011). Extreme weather events and construction SMEs: Vulnerability, impacts and responses. *Structural Survey*, *29*(2), 106–119. 10.1108/02630801111132795

Westhead, P., Binks, M., Ucbasaran, D., & Wright, M. (2002). Internationalization of SMEs: A research note. *Journal of Small Business and Enterprise Development*, *9*(1), 38–48. 10.1108/14626000210419473

Westhead, P., Wright, M. & Ucbasaran, D., 2001. The internationalization of new and small firms: A resource-based view. *Journal of Business Venturing*, *16*(4), 333–358. 10.1016/S0883-9026(99)00063-4

Wiedersheim-Paul, F., Olson, H.C., & Welch, L.S. (1978). Pre-export activity: The first step in internationalization. *Journal of International Business Studies*, *9*(1), 47–58. 10.1057/palgrave.jibs.8490650

World Bank. (2013). *Knowledge economy*. https://web.worldbank.org/archive/website01503/WEB/0__CO-10.HTM

Zahra, S.A., & George, G. (2002). International entrepreneurship: The current status of the field and future research agenda. In M.A. Hitt, R.D. Ireland, S.M. Camp & D.L. Sexton (Eds.), *Strategic Entrepreneurship: Creating a New Mindset*. Blackwell Publishing.

7 A relationship-centric model of SMEs internationalization
Advancing the 5 Cs

This chapter is the corollary of the previous thematic sections, which have grounded the main research directions in the field of business internationalization, international relationship marketing, and B2B relationships in inter- and cross-cultural contexts. Once the internationalization of small and medium-sized enterprises in the context of the globalization-driven interconnectivity has been presented and analyzed, and once the models of relationship marketing based on interaction and networks have been highlighted, the focus shifts to research themes that are still at an early stage of exploration.

In this sense, the purpose of this chapter is to bring to the fore and integrate in a conceptual model the main facets and dimensions specific to B2B relationships at the international level. Moreover, in line with the vision proposed by Magnusson et al. (2009, 2013), Ivanova and Torkkeli (2013), Vătămănescu et al. (2014), etc., the advanced model focuses on managerial dyads and networks, with managers as key links at the inter-organizational level. Five central dimensions subsumed by B2B relationships from a managerial perspective are addressed, one by one, the conceptual framework organizing – in an organic and unitary formula – concepts and theories recurring in the literature, but which have often been treated unilaterally or linearly, as argued by multiple recent studies.

This chapter aims to develop five interlinked theoretical dimensions, building on strong and consistently valued strands of research by members of the scientific, academic, and practitioner communities. It articulates a new conceptual model (integrating the conditions, contexts, catalysts, consequences, and connections inherent in the construction of international relations), rooted, however, in current topics of debate, which confirms the topicality and relevance of such an approach.

The proposition of the 5 Cs model

The proposition of an integrative relationship-driven model viable in international contexts stands out as an organic step toward a pertinent positioning of SMEs internationalization. Thus, The 5 Cs model of managerial

DOI: 10.4324/9781003432326-9

relationship building (CMR) assumes – at a conceptual level – the interactionist and network-based views advocated by the *Industrial Marketing and Purchasing Group* (IMP), according to which relationships take place at an inter-organizational level, on dyadic foundations within a network, being predominantly reciprocal and interdependent, going through a series of phases characterized by bidirectional learning and adaptation (Fernandes & Proença, 2005; Ford, 2003; Håkansson et al., 2004; Samaha et al., 2014).

The model is based on the resource-based view of the firm – promoted by Barney in 1991 and operationalized by Hunt (2000) into seven specific resource categories, namely: financial, physical and legal resources (constituting tangible resources), and human, organizational, informational, and relational resources (considered to be intangible). From this angle, competitive advantage derives from the development and enhancement of unique and dynamic combinations between heterogeneous resources (Seggie & Griffith, 2008; Vătămănescu et al., 2014). Only by accumulating and allocating the right combinations of resources can one speak of generating sustainable competitive advantages for an organization, and the value of a given resource is calibrated according to its potential to become a differentiator in terms of competitiveness. Furthermore, the model lends credence to the perspective proposed by Magnusson et al. (2009, 2013) who consider human resources – in the sense of intangible resources – as essential to the organization because they are action-oriented and enhance the use of all other resources. In this ideational framework, managers are invested with the greatest capacity to generate and sustain the firm's competitive advantage, their talent and skills positioning them in the zone of success or failure (Griffith & Hoppner, 2013).

This view of things is also supported by Ivanova and Torkkeli (2013) who point out that the main actors involved in any business relationship are the people, as representatives of the companies from which they come, and which mandate them. Individuals, in general, and managers, in particular, are those who interact in different cultural contexts, integrating the cultural background of their reference environments into their approaches and actions.

The theoretical model is designed to integrate multiple facets of relationship marketing and international business relationship management. The scope of each element in the proposed model is addressed in relation to existing research, with previous exploratory approaches that have dealt with the issue in an adjacent manner without relating it to the variables of internationalization. Thus, the focus falls on five main dimensions, namely *convergence, communality, compatibility, credibility*, and *connectivity*, all describing the hypostases of capitalizing on sustainable and multivalent business relationships. In the economics of the model, convergence is the basis for building international business relationships, while communality, compatibility, credibility, and connectivity emerge as mediating factors for increasing competitiveness and profitability that arise from establishing partnerships. Once the convergence of the economic and financial interests of potential

Table 7.1 Summary definition of the dimensions of CMR

No.	Size	Definition
1.	Convergence	The existence and/or emergence of common business interests for several parties, with the aim of strengthening the competitiveness, performance, and development of organizational actors in the market, regardless of the country in which they are located.
2.	Communality	Exploiting business contexts and events of common interest to initiate and develop strong partnerships.
3.	Compatibility	The existence of similar personality, attitudinal, and behavioral traits among the initiators of an international business relationship that facilitate cross-cultural adaptation.
4.	Credibility	Demonstrate mutual trust, commitment, promise, and professionalism in an international business relationship.
5.	Connectivity	Keeping communication channels always open with key business partners, sharing relevant knowledge, and strengthening relationships within a business network.

Source: Developed by the authors.

partners is assumed, each of the mediating factors exerts a distinct influence on the effectiveness of collaboration. Together, the five dimensions form the 5 Cs model of managerial relationship building (CMR), designed to advance a new vision of international business relationships and test their impact on partnership effectiveness (operationalized through the lens of competitiveness, profitability, and organizational development in international markets).

The summary definition of each dimension in the model is given in Table 7.1.

The proposed model is in line with Festing and Maletzky's (2011, p. 192) view that contemporary management and leadership must confront the demands of an international and intercultural context. As different national and organizational cultures interact in the global marketplace, the imperative for businesspeople is to ensure conductive frameworks for interaction, communication, and cooperation. These three processes imply interpersonal and inter-organizational adjustments that can be achieved through coherent strategic projects based on an articulated vision of marketing and relationship management.

Convergence (the condition for building managerial relationships)

The first dimension of the model, *convergence,* is defined as the existence and/ or emergence of common business interests for one or more parties, with the aim of strengthening the organization's competitiveness, performance, and growth in the market, regardless of the country in which they are located. Convergence is thus a basic condition for establishing a business relationship, based on the premise that the conclusion of a partnership is based on mutual advantages and common economic and financial interests. Convergence is rooted in the principle that "the creation and sharing of value can be seen as the raison d'être of customer-supplier relationships" (Anderson, 1995, p. 348). The major premise is that human relationships derive from "subjective cost-benefit analyses that seek to maximise benefits and minimise costs, an analysis that is particularly applicable in B2B contexts" (Palmatier, 2008). Similarly, Kotler and Keller (2006) point out that the goal of relationship marketing is to build and develop relationships at multiple levels – economic, social, technical – provided they are mutually beneficial and profitable in the long term. At this point, the competitiveness of the business internationally is a decisive incentive for the convergence of potential partners – the requirement to stay in the game, to gain or maintain a competitive advantage is a facilitator of collaboration and the adjustment of common interests.

Since the mid-1990s, researchers such as Morgan and Hunt (1994) and Ellram and Hendrick (1995) have argued that businesses are highly dependent on properly developed and managed supplier relationships, which propel the organization ahead of the competition. Further, Wilson and Jantrania (1996) propose conceptualizing the value of the relationship, and hence the commitment of the parties to a business relationship, through the lens of three central dimensions – *economic, strategic, and behavioral (psychological)*. The economic dimension/rationale is concerned with cost reduction, operationalization of technological issues, feasible investments, and competing financial interests of the partners. The strategic dimension/rationale is a projection of the strategic objectives of the organizational actors, manifested in the form of generating competitive advantage, expanding or diversifying the scope of activity or strengthening the position in a given market. The behavioral dimension/rationale is concerned with establishing social ties and cultivating mutual trust. Wilson and Jantrania (1996, p. 66) consider the behavioral elements to be interconnected and dynamic and that "over time, a hybrid culture develops that will support the cementing of the relationship. This culture is likely to integrate the values of both organizations and develop new values not present in either organization." The authors conclude that assessing the value of a business relationship must begin with an assessment of economic value, then strategic value, and finally a qualitative assessment of behavioral value. In other words, two major dimensions have to be considered when the parties decide to initiate, create, develop, enhance, etc. business relationships: technical aspects and social aspects, both of which support and influence each other (Holmlund & Kock, 1995).

Discussing the value of business relationships from a broader angle, Mandják and Durrieu (2000) and Biggemann and Buttle (2012) basically review the reasons behind the convergence or decision of parties to engage in a partnership. In this respect, the catalytic factors fall within a broad spectrum that subsumes: the desirable, perceived, or rational value of the relationship; the value of the relationship from an economic, strategic, or behavioral perspective; the value of the relationship in terms of security, credibility, continuity; the value of the relationship as a projection of trust in a mutually beneficial partnership; the co-creation of value as a result of the unfolding of relational episodes, the sharing of common goals and investments, mutual adjustments, cooperation, and long-term commitment; the co-creation of value as both a direct and an indirect function of the interrelationship.

It follows from the above considerations that engaging in prolific business relationships can give the organization a significant and sustainable advantage in the market in various forms: price negotiation, quality assurance, continuity of flows, risk limitation, reduction of opportunism, knowledge sharing, assimilation of common experiences, more effective coordination, and control, etc. (Kanagal, 2009; Parsons, 2002; Shaladi, 2012).

Following a review of several studies, Palmatier (2008) concluded that "buyer-seller relationships help increase the seller's financial performance, and investments in relationship marketing will result in both short- and long-term financial gains" (p. 52). In the same vein, Kanagal (2009, p. 15) argues that relationship marketing is "one of the underpinnings of systematic action likely to develop into a competitive marketing strategy."

Setting the framework for the debate in the area of small and medium-sized enterprises, the imperative of competitiveness calls for coherent strategies and measures, with expansion into foreign markets being an adaptive approach for the evolution or survival of the organization (Sandberg, 2014; Suh & Kim, 2014). The solution lies in identifying opportunities beyond the domestic habitat in order to generate added value for the organization and increasing profitability and sustainability in the market of reference, by resorting to several main springs: selecting other markets, adjusting policies and products, streamlining operational flows, managing contingencies, leveraging B2B collaborations, B2C, international mergers, distribution networks, franchises, business networks (Hampton & Rowell, 2010, 2013; Hutchinson & Quintas, 2008).

At this level, the longevity of the partnership between individuals is crucial to the success and stability of the organization in the target market. Therefore, selecting an appropriate partner and building a strong relationship are essential (Catulli et al., 2006). Only in this way, international partnerships can be "tools to enhance the firm's ability to compete" (Sheth & Parvatiyar, 1995 cited in Arnett et al., 2003, p. 89), and the establishment of strong relationships with foreign partners can objectify not only a multi-state convergence, i.e., win–win situations at interpersonal but also inter-organizational level: access to cheaper and/or higher quality raw materials, new distribution channels or forms of collaboration, pooling of knowledge and expertise, strategic alliances, etc.

In the logic of the convergence dimension, in order to be validated, SME internationalization projects cannot be assessed only through a socio-cultural filter and, consequently, the use of an economic logic must take place from the first phase of the project cycle, from the articulation of the premises of internationalization. Economic analysis is intended to provide an answer to the question of whether investing in international business expansion represents a real development opportunity for the organization. The approach is part of the managerial economics algorithm that envisages the use of economic analysis to make business decisions through which the organization's limited resources can be used to maximum value (Keat & Young, 2003). It is traced along well-defined courses of action starting from demand analysis and forecasting, cost and production analysis, decision making on price, policies, and practices and continues with profit, capital, and inventory management and ends with the application of game theory, environmental issues, and business cycles (Stengel, 2011).

At this level, profit management is part of the strategic logic of any firm, with profit being a key measure of a firm's long-term success. Profit is often seen as a reward for taking uncertainty and risk, whereas a successful businessman is one who correctly estimates costs and revenues at different levels of the product offered. The stakes are reducing uncertainty and increasing profits for the organization. In this sense, planning and measuring the profit resulting from the internationalization of the SME is a key point on the agenda of management strategy (Stengel, 2011). Several key issues need to be taken into account already at the stage of preparing the internationalization project (Economics and Development Resource Center, 1997): forecast future demands or needs for the organization's products and services; existing sources of supply; the costs of supply and the investments to be made; the project's contribution to meeting market demands and reducing costs; the technological innovation that the organization can bring about; the characteristics of government policies as an enabler or a brake on the organization's objectives.

Given that any business internationalization project is influenced by a specific macro and microeconomic context, investments in this direction should be seen as a gradual transformation of the existing organizational structure. Often the context can be more important than the internationalization strategy itself and, consequently, the attention of the organization's management must be focused on all stakeholders, both external and internal.

Within this framework, SME convergence from an internationalization perspective is based on the analysis of several relevant levels that can significantly influence the internationalization decision, the decision to choose one firm from a particular country over another (Economics and Development Resource Center, 1997): the configuration of macroeconomic parameters – exchange rates, interest rates, and wages; the impact of microeconomic policies, such as special financial incentives for certain investments; customs policies such as import duties and subsidies; the structure of the existing markets in terms of the degree of monopoly over the provision of public utilities; and the level of competition in terms of project outcomes.

Even if the managers of two SMEs are convergent in their vision of international collaboration, both admitting the opportunity and the advantages of establishing a partnership, the existence of high import or export taxes is a major breaking factor. For a partnership to pass the convergence test, it must demonstrate that all resources (which can be accessed) will be used to maximum effect.

The internationalization of the business must take into account the identification, quantification, and evaluation of the objectives and targets of this process, which can be operationalized within a regulated framework based on the systematization of the inputs, outputs, causes, effects, and micro and macroeconomic impacts of the internationalization decision. This provides an analytical framework based on objective criteria and reference indicators for initiating and carrying out the internationalization process.

Convergence analysis from an economic-financial perspective should provide a clear answer to several essential questions concerning the viability of the project and facilitate the systematization and corroboration of the information needed to make an optimal decision on whether or not to proceed with an internationalization approach.

Communality (the context of building managerial relationships)

In the process of establishing convergence between SMEs, the dynamics of international business relations are influenced by managers meeting face-to-face. On this level, *communality* is defined as the exploitation of business contexts and events of common interest in order to initiate and develop strong partnerships. Parties interested in a particular business area can take advantage of specific thematic events, conjunctures, and specific locations to meet businesspeople with common or complementary interests. Commonality is also a characteristic of similar markets, which allows SMEs to progressively internationalize and effectively manage relationships, based on analogy and similarities with the domestic market and the value system of the potential partner.

Communality brings to the fore that international relationship marketing can only be articulated in well-defined contexts that offer a limited spectrum of action alternatives. As argued by various authors (Egan, 2003; Fernandes & Proença, 2005; Fournier et al., 1998; Möller & Halinen, 2000), marketing is context-dependent and thus the emergence of business relationships is conditioned by contextual variables. On this level, relationship managers have the task of observing the new international environment, collecting information about its characteristics and potential advantages by attending thematic events, conferences, fairs, exhibitions, seminars, and workshops. On these occasions, they will consider the opportunity to initiate interactions for the establishment of personal, social, and organizational relationships in their area of activity, with communality acting as a decisive factor toward the realization of the common interests of the parties. Moreover, researchers such as Schein (2009) and Festing and Maletzky (2011) point out that frequenting the same places is a primary indicator of shared interests and facilitates mutual understanding even in intercultural contexts.

Another important aspect subsumed by communality concerns the choices relationship managers make when evaluating potential business relationships. Given that a well-managed business relationship should reduce risk and uncertainty, communality overemphasizes the importance of psychological and geographical proximity between parties in the approach to building an international partnership. Before forming partnerships with diametrically opposed individuals or organizations, relationship managers explore closer organizational actors with whom they have important things in common (interests, expectations, aspirations, beliefs, values). Although in contemporary times, the "born global" manager is no longer bound by physical distances, a gradual approach to internationalizing business and forming sustainable partnerships is still desirable (Kontinen & Ojala, 2010; Moen et al., 2004; Nordman & Tolstoy, 2014; Sandberg, 2014; Suh & Kim, 2014;). In this sense, Etemat and Ala-Mukta (2009) believe that relationship managers will only be able to move to the next level once they gain knowledge about nearby foreign markets and business relationships with similar partners. Only in such a context will businesspeople be able to initiate interpersonal and social exchanges, reinforcing the sense of familiarity with the selected foreign market and progressively reducing the degree of uncertainty (Freeman et al., 2012).

This is where, what Ang et al. (2007) call, the motivational dimension of cultural intelligence comes in. When contextual differences become more pronounced (e.g., when individuals from two completely different cultures interact), they will act to adapt cross-culturally and provide appropriate responses to environmental cues. The motivational dimension will become a catalyst for adjustment in relation to changing cultural contexts, denoting managers' belief that they have the ability to actively and effectively bend to new value coordinates and intrinsic interest in learning about other cultures (Chen et al., 2010; Magnusson et al., 2013). They will mentally assume that the motivations and behavior of potential partners are shaped by the cultural context of reference and will exhibit greater flexibility in their approach.

Discussing the inherent pre-internationalization aspects of SMEs, Khojastehpour and Jones (2014) have highlighted the importance of overcoming psychological distance, a concept that circumscribes differences on many levels (language, culture, education, business principles, and practices, degree of development of the country, etc.). Even if the influence of psychological distance on the internationalization process is often indirect, it has a considerable impact on the formation of business relationships and requires contextual learning and mutual trust building (Johanson & Vahlne, 2009). Consequently, organizations are determined to progressively approach international markets of interest, starting with those closest to them (which offer a minimum level of knowledge through associations and easier access to information). From this point, internationalization will follow the logic of concentric circles that will gradually expand toward markets characterized by greater psychological distance (Freeman et al., 2012; Kontinen & Ojala, 2010).

Compatibility (the catalyst for building managerial relationships)

In the economics of CMR, *compatibility* is defined as the existence of similar personality, and attitudinal and behavioral traits between the initiators of an international business relationship. It acts as an indicator of interpersonal adaptation and intercultural learning. As with the previous dimension – communality – the existence of psychological distance has a strong moderating effect, especially in terms of cultural differences and uncertainty (Freeman et al., 2012; Leonidou et al., 2011). SME activation on the international stage is directly influenced by psychological distance so that "the higher the level of psychological distance, the greater the time and effort for the parties to develop successful business relationships," with the caveat that the effort to fructify the appropriate marketing strategy will also be greater (Conway & Swift, 1999, p. 1392). Similarly, Shaladi (2012, p. 78) argues that "at the stage of initial interactions, the psychological distance will be greater because the differences will be more salient than the similarities between the parties." Important factors such as linguistic, cultural, political, religious variations, beliefs determined by country of origin, social norms, and different values will create structural barriers between potential partners (Khojastehpour & Johns, 2014). In other words, psychological and cultural distance will constitute quasi-intransigent constraints in the relationship-building approach, with social and relational exchanges being altered by the diversity of interpretive horizons, value systems, expectations, emotional and social engagement, information encoding according to culture and country, etc. (Samaha et al., 2014; Shaladi, 2012).

To achieve the goal of compatibility, initial concessions will be necessary. Schein (2009) believes that every culture gives way to well-defined views and inclinations toward other cultures, based on the premise that "our view" is the unconditionally correct one. Similarly, Festing and Maletzky (2011, p. 194) argue that there is an ingrained practice in international or intercultural relations of relying on one's own interpretations and assumptions about the value systems of potential partners. When parties meet, the main obstacle is to find the necessary springs to access compatibility, the alignment of values, behaviors, and opinions with economic interests (Caliguri & Tarique, 2012; Hohenthal et al., 2014). In the same ideational framework, Rodrigues and Wilson (2002) consider perceived structural interdependence as a prerequisite for initiating and enhancing compatibility in a business relationship such that consistent mutual exposure will diminish psychological distance.

In the context of international relationship marketing, communication style, mutual expectations, prioritization of issues, and objectives undergo mutations depending on the negotiators' country of origin (Fischer, 2009; Vătămănescu et al., 2015). Properly operationalized, the cultural dimensions proposed by Hofstede (2001) are likely to enhance success in negotiation and reduce the level of frustration and conflict. For example, in a negotiation between a Chinese and a Canadian manager, the Canadian manager will want to reach an agreement and a signed contract, while the Chinese manager will be interested in spending more time discussing additional, getting-to-know-you issues, emphasizing hospitality, protocol, and the form of interaction with the aim of establishing a long-term relationship.

Here, the metacognitive dimension of cultural intelligence as understood by Ang et al. (2007) is a key concept in explaining the success of SME managers in exploring different cultures. Metacognitive cultural intelligence is especially important because it enhances "(a) contextualized thinking (versus abstract thinking): a style of thinking characterized by high degrees of sensitivity to the cultural strand of human motivations and actions, and (b) cognitive flexibility: the appropriate use of normative schemas and behavioral scripts in response to changing cultural expectations in the reference environment" (Klafehn et al., 2009, p. 319). In addition, Elenkov and Manev (2009) argue that managers with cultural intelligence based on a strong metacognitive component understand business processes better and conduct international transactions more effectively due to the fact that they are able to capture relationship progress, identify potential cultural misunderstandings, and adjust their behavior according to the cultural context.

In agreement with Halinen et al. (2012), episodes of interaction are invested with meaning by relating managers to their past, present, and future experiences, with each personal interpretation of an event having a direct impact on future events (Ford & Håkansson, 2006). Subjective interpretations, often marked by cultural variations, are a construct of major relevance in understanding the process of intercultural interaction (Ivanova & Torkkeli, 2013).

Based on these premises, relationship managers will be in a position to take the catalytic action, to stimulate through both formal and informal interactions the knowledge and acceptance of different cultures, the discovery of affinities and divergences, and the establishment of a relationship marketing strategy useful for achieving common benefits. This stage is decisive for the future of the relationship – "if the relationship dissolves, it is usually at this point during the initial interactions" (Shaladi, 2012, p. 78). The objective of communication, at this stage, is to increase empathy and intercultural openness.

Addressing the issue tangentially, Barnes et al. (2010, pp. 35–37) highlight the importance of avoiding opportunistic behavior in international business relationships. The authors insist that an excessively self-centered approach, without considering the interests of the other party, is a threat to a successful partnership and a dysfunctional factor for long-term cooperation. Thus, relationship managers must be prepared to transcend the limiting nature of differences and emphasize the resources offered by similarity. Dialogical perspectives are key to establishing the negotiating climate in which partners suspend their need to win a debate and focus on win–win achievements and rewards.

Discussing the particularities of intercultural interaction, Rodriguez and Wilson (2002, p. 54) insist that lack of similarity has a substantial impact on business objectives, strategies, and operations. A similar study conducted by Hampton and Rowell (2010, p. 19) brought the same conclusions to the fore, concluding that the internationalization approach of firms must be based on the existence of compatibility between the managers of two SMEs.

A long-term business relationship relies on effective management of compatibility zones, although this variable is often difficult to measure. Leonidou (2004, p. 731) and Testa (2009, p. 78) share this view, nuancing that one source of competitive advantage lies in the harmonization of positions and the creation of added value perceived to be mutually beneficial to the parties. Consequently, controlling psychological distance through appropriate relationship management emerges as a major prerequisite for building sustainable partnerships (Leonidou et al., 2011).

In an overview, analyzing the action of relationship managers through the filter of compatibility will reveal their communication and negotiation qualities and skills, their propensity to seek efficiency in every form of interrelationship, and their assumption of cross-cultural learning (Hilmersson, 2014). In the context of international B2B marketing, mutual accommodation implies absolutely necessary concessions in order to achieve the desired results. For example, in order to develop sustainable business relationships, managers coming from masculine cultures (Japan, Mexico, Germany, United Kingdom) will have to accept and adapt to the cultural model of partners coming from feminine cultures (Sweden, Denmark, Portugal) and vice versa. Only through mutual acceptance and cross-cultural adaptation can long-term, mutually beneficial partnerships be achieved.

Credibility (the consequence of developing managerial relationships)

Credibility is defined as the demonstration of mutual trust, commitments, promises kept, and professionalism in an international business relationship. It is a direct consequence of the processual development of relations between the parties to the extent that international collaboration has followed an agreed path, bringing mutual economic, financial, and socio-cultural benefits. Once the frameworks of compatibility have been established, relationship managers will commit themselves to investing the personal, social, and organizational links created with credibility. If the relationship has not failed in the previous stage, the parties will evolve to the next level; implicitly, the degree of psychological distance will decrease. Relationship managers will

begin to cultivate mutual understanding and strengthen the springs of empathy and loyalty (Filip & Anghel, 2009).

Focusing on cultural differences as a symbolic boundary for international
business relations, Seppänen et al. (2007) highlight their important role on
relational factors in general and trust in particular. The researchers conclude
that the level of trust, and hence mutual credibility of the parties, will increase
with the level of knowledge and understanding of collaborator-specific cultural variables because of close SMEs collaboration.

At this point, it should be noted that the development of the business
relationship and the sequence of episodes between partners is not part of a
linear process since relationships "are continuously recreated over time"
(Halinen et al., 2012, p. 215). The interpersonal adaptation of managers is
a gradual process, and the permeability of the parties' cultural patterns can
only be achieved in the advanced phases of collaboration. Moreover, the
openness of one party to accept the cultural specificity of the partner is a
consequence of a higher degree of knowledge of the other's culture, trust in
the compatibility of the managers' shared value systems and a high level of
perceived interdependence (Weck & Ivanova, 2013). Thus, interactive social
exchanges will become a constant of the interrelationship, with each positive
interaction and shared experience enhancing the relationship and strengthening it through commitment and trust (Catulli et al., 2006; Conway & Swift,
1999; Morgan & Hunt, 1994; Nijssen & van Herk, 2009; Samaha et al., 2014).

Researchers believe that the flows of social exchange are rooted in two
fundamental processes, namely trust and commitment. Trust is central, des-
ignating a party's expectation of the trustworthiness and integrity of the
potential partner, while commitment is a correlative concept, denoting an
organizational approach based on recognition of the importance of the partner
and the stability of the relationship over time. By making a firm commitment,
trust is enhanced, and the business relationship strengthened. Similarly, Ravald
and Grönroos (1996, pp. 24–25) argue that "security, credibility and continuity
contribute to reducing customer uncertainty and are aspects that the customer
sees as essential and highly valuable." The value of the business relationship as
perceived by the parties transcends episodic financial benefits, focusing on the
fulfillment of long-term mutual expectations. In the authors' view, mutual trust
and the credibility of the parties imply loyalty and, inherently, a mutually
beneficial relationship (Athanasopoulou, 2009).

Although addressed in a punctual manner in the literature, there are several reference concepts that the credibility dimension incorporates, some of
which have already been mentioned. In this regard, Khojastehpour and Johns
(2014) focus on trust (confidence in the other party, limiting uncertainty, and
risk), promises kept (mark of commitment in long-term collaborations),
satisfaction (mutual well-being in the relationship), and loyalty (derived from
awareness and confirmation of mutual benefits). Here, the sustainability of
partnerships relies mainly on communication, which is seen as a facilitator for
trust and commitment, experience, and satisfaction.

In support of this, Shaladi (2012) mentions several factors that can strengthen the foundations of sustainable relationships in the context of international business, namely commitment, trust, customer orientation/empathy, experience/satisfaction, and communication. Of all these factors, commitment is considered "the strongest predictor of voluntary decisions to maintain a relationship" (Shaladi, 2012, p. 76), which confirms its defining impact in the long-term development of business relationships.

A comprehensive approach to trust in the context of international relations is offered by Kanagal (2009, pp. 14–15) who argues that "trust ensures the understanding that the relational exchange is mutually beneficial, and the good intentions of the partners are very clear"; moreover, the author argues that "relationship marketing is built on the foundation of trust." Ali and Birley (1998, p. 751) describe two interrelated types of trust, namely trait-based trust, and process-based trust. The former refers to the social similarity between the parties (it concerns similar social and cultural considerations and norms), while the latter is more rational and largely dependent on the experiences and evolution of the relationship. Thus, process-based trust is enhanced by situations where formal commitments cannot yet be regulated and the word of the other party is the basis for starting a business (Shaladi, 2012, p. 77). This calls for iterating good practice in making promises and fulfilling commitments, in demonstrating honesty and respect throughout international negotiations, and in avoiding opportunistic behavior, even when it would lead to greater casual benefits.

Within this framework of debate, Rodriguez and Wilson (2002) speak of a combination of structural and social components underlying relationship building – structural ties refer to economic exchange and negotiation, while social ties refer to accessing the resources of friendship. In other words, relationship strength is dependent on the establishment of a variety of incentives, from eminently economic and financial factors to interpersonal relationships. Similarly, Hohenthal et al. (2014) highlight the idea that overall satisfaction derives from both social and economic incentives, both of which compete toward the viability of international partnerships. At this level, successfully concluded transactions become cornerstones of credibility and promises of continued international partnership. The partnership is defined by the catalytic effect of agreed rules and common benchmarks. Each episode, negotiation, delivery, information exchange, payment, and shapes is shaped by the relationship itself, resulting in the prospect of value co-creation (Shaladi, 2012; Turnbull et al., 1996).

Analyzing the life cycle of relationships, Hampton and Rowell (2013) emphasize the shift in credibility from uncertainty to trust and ultimate commitment. After the primary contact is completed, parties will have some reservations about the viability and professionalism of the new partnership, but following successful operations and transactions, the level of credibility will naturally increase, becoming the driving force behind long-term commitments. At this point, communication has the power to strengthen two-way exchanges, ensuring that information relevant to both parties is shared. As multiple studies point out, although time-consuming and requiring regular efforts, sustained communication is mandatory for ensuring performance in B2B business (Johns, 2012; Leonidou et al., 2011; Tan & Sousa, 2015).

Focusing on the relationship between proven partner credibility and business profitability, Zhao and Smith (2006) and Rehman et al. (2012) conclude that there is a direct and significant relationship between the two variables. Rehman et al. (2012) examine the influence of credibility (a concept that includes trust and commitment) on the profit resulting from business performance. The authors point out that demonstrating managers' credibility in the context of relationship marketing leads to strengthening collaboration and obtaining economic and financial advantages (more competitive prices, longer payment terms, discounts for certain products). A similar perspective is highlighted by Bricci et al. (2016) who, analyzing the service sector in Portugal, conclude that trust, commitment, and satisfaction of business partners considerably influence the loyalty of the parties and, therefore, mutually beneficial long-term collaboration.

Connectivity (the connections for developing managerial relationships)

The fifth dimension of the model – *connectivity* – is defined as keeping communication channels always open with key business partners, sharing relevant knowledge, and strengthening relationships within a dynamic network. The concept describes the connections that underpin the development of relationships between SMEs, highlighting the importance of sustained contact with key business partners and strengthening relationships within an international network structure. The perspective on this dimension is rooted in Gummesson's (2008, p. 15) assertion that "relationship marketing is interaction within networks of relationships" and the IMP group's findings that successful businesses evolve and strengthen through dyadic relationships within a network-based context (Brodie et al., 2008; Ford, 2003; Johanson & Vahlne, 2009). "Network-based marketing is interrelational oriented, but its focus is inter- and trans-organizational" (Hapenciuc et al., 2015, p. 612). Thus, each organizational actor is interested in assuming a position "in a network with varied inter-firm relationships" (Brodie et al., 2008, p. 85).

When talking about the dynamics of today's society, two frames of reference demonstrate their complementarity – the knowledge-based society and the network society. In this context, Nicolescu and Nicolescu (2005) point out that organizing companies as networks makes them knowledge-based and continuous learning-oriented organizations. Organizational networking is based on the stakeholder principle and the interconnection of innovative organizations facilitates the formation of innovative networks, a key feature of the knowledge-based economy. On this level, international networking of organizations is a necessity even for SMEs in the current global context (Nicolescu & Nicolescu, 2012).

Through networks, knowledge is transmitted and shared among all actors who have consented to be part of an interconnected system (Fang et al., 2013; Ferguson & Taminiau, 2014; Wang, 2013; Vătămănescu et al., 2017a, 2017b). Organizational competitiveness of SMEs often means connecting to different forms of knowledge and networks that bring together potential partners in the field of interest, which constantly relate to the fast pace of present socio-economic and cultural flows (Rathi et al., 2014; Uzzi & Lancaster, 2003). In this context, expertise and competences are pooled, allowing their access and exploitation by all members of the business network (offline or online), with information transfer being the catalyst for competitive advantage or even innovation (Filieri & Alguezaui, 2014; Owen-Smith & Powell, 2004; Shu et al., 2012; Valkokari et al., 2012).

A multidisciplinary framework can explain how social networks are likely to influence the achievement of goals within and beyond organizational systems. The dynamic network theory launched by Westaby (2012) proposes new perspectives on goal achievement at the individual, group and business levels, drawing on the advantages of social networks. Networking transcends organizational boundaries in that SMEs develop both intra- and inter-organizational relationships within a highly collaborative macro-environment (Nowicka et al., 2012). What gives value and substance to the network are the strong links between members regardless of country of origin, the shared vision and purpose, and the awareness that each organization is an integral part of the transnational system.

For Carley (2002), the concept of a "multi-agent network" accurately describes the active roles that network members perform within the overall system – they adapt and act, communicate, store and expose information, discover, learn and transmit knowledge, continually reshaping the network configuration. Each actor is simultaneously a creator, a receiver, and a catalyst of knowledge, thus contributing to the advancement, sustainability, fortification, and change of the network and its connections (Westaby, 2012; Vătămănescu et al., 2017a).

The situation presented above is illustrative for industrial SMEs which generally bring together a limited number of potential partners (customers, suppliers, traders, competitors) (Håkansson et al., 2004; Håkansson & Snehota, 2006; Shaladi, 2012). Fernandes and Proença (2005) suggest that industrial networks can be defined as "complex aggregates of relationships that are difficult to plan, predict and manage," while the aggregation process is far from being described as simple or additive.

Network configuration allows for intrinsic dynamics as each entity adjusts and improves its position in the network to successfully meet its business objectives. On this level, Palmatier (2008, p. 19) points out that network theory provides valuable examples of the impact of the structural characteristics of the interaction between multiple entities (e.g., individuals, firms) within an overall network and from an inter-organizational perspective, the theory demonstrates an enlightening point – the quality of the relationship (trust, commitment), the extent of the relationship (network density), and the composition of the relationship (diversity/attractiveness) have a major impact on the development of sustainable collaborations.

Focusing on international business, the role of networks seems to be crucial for the development of relationships, all the more so as "networking is easily achievable given the evolution of technology and communication channels" (Shaladi, 2012, p. 74). On this point, Glavas and Mathews (2014) and Vătămănescu et al. (2015, 2017a, 2017b) highlight the expansion and escalation of online professional social networks which, aligned to certain types of business or industries, are emerging as pillars of cross-border collaboration, in repositories of knowledge and reference contacts for a specific domain. Similarly, Keinänen and Kuivalainen (2015) point out in their study the importance of online social networks in the context of B2B marketing, the perspective of valuing social media in the context of relationship marketing is also shared by Karjaluoto et al. (2015).

In an overall view, exchanges between SMEs through international networks are a prerequisite for growth strategies for each organizational actor. Sustainable competitive advantage emerges at the intersection of organizational resources and the opportunities offered by collective intelligence and pooled expertise. The central node position within the network – facilitated by the constancy and consistency of interchanges – will generate trust capital between SMEs, members of the same network – and increase the cohesion of the whole (Cannone & Ughetto, 2014; Hohenthal et al., 2014).

The same perspective is also supported by the studies of Daou et al. (2013), Jardon (2015), and Wang (2014), researchers highlighting the influence of managerial networking on the economic and financial competitiveness of organizations. Networking directly contributes to increasing the innovative capacity of the network and its component organizations and developing strategic alliances and strong cooperation along the supply chain (Szczepankiewicz, 2013). In addition, according to Lin and Chaney (2007, pp. 577–578), networks catalyze access to relevant information about different business opportunities, helping to reduce the risks and costs associated with establishing new relationships and improving the financial performance of partners. Similarly, Palacios-Marqués et al. (2015) attribute to online networks a defining role in accessing useful knowledge for competitive business development through the fact that they bring together managers with common interests and, implicitly, new information about industries, products, and services of profile.

Corroborating the arguments subsumed under each dimension of the 5 Cs model of managerial relationship building (CMR), this chapter has brought to the fore a new perspective on international relationship-driven approach specific to SMEs. The focus fell on the factors that generate, frame, catalyze, sustain, and strengthen international business relationships and, subsequently, sustainable and profitable partnerships between organizations with converging interests, expectations, visions, and strategies.

The proposed model revolves around multifaceted relationships established as the managerial level in the framework of SMEs internationalization. It builds on the rationale of the existing internationalization strategies and models by laying a special emphasis on the relationship building and development. It digs deeper into the interpersonal relationship dynamics, be they based on social ties or business connections. The chapter opens new research avenues for exploring the importance of relationships in fostering strong international collaborations and welcomes further investigation of the underlying factors supporting SMEs internationalization.

References

Ali, H., & Birley, S. (1998). The role of trust in the marketing activities of entrepreneurs establishing new venture. *Journal of Marketing Management, 14*(7), 749–763.

Anderson, J.C. (1995). Relationships in business markets: Exchange episodes, value creation, and their empirical assessment. *Journal of the Academy of Marketing Science, 23,* 346–350. https://doi.org/10.1177/009207039502300415

Ang, S., Van Dyne, L., Koh, C., Ng, K.-Y., Templer, K.J., Tay, C., & Chandrasekar, N.A. (2007). Cultural intelligence: Its measurement and effects on cultural judgment and decision making, cultural adaptation and task performance. *Management and Organization Review, 3*(3), 335–371. https://doi.org/10.1111/j.1740-8784.2007.00082.x

Arnett, D.B., German, S.D., & Hunt, S.D. (2003). The identity salience model of relationship marketing success: The case of nonprofit marketing. *Journal of Marketing, 67*(2), 89–105.

Athanasopoulou, P. (2009). Relationship quality: A critical literature review and research agenda. *European Journal of Marketing, 43*(5/6), 583–610.

Barney, J. (1991). Form resources and sustained competitive advantage. *Journal of Management, 17*(1), 99–120. https://josephmahoney.web.illinois.edu/BA545_Fall%202022/Barney%20(1991).pdf

Barnes, B.R., Leonidou, L.C., Siu, N.Y.M., & Leonidou, C. (2010). Opportunism as the inhibiting trigger for developing long-term-oriented western exporter-hong kong importer relationships. *Journal of International Marketing, 18*(2), 35–63.

Biggemann, S., & Buttle, F. (2012). Intrinsic value of business-to-business relationships: An empirical taxonomy. *Journal of Business Research, 65*(8), 1132–1138.

Bricci, L., Fragata, A., & Antunes, J. (2016). The effects of trust, commitment and satisfaction on customer loyalty in the distribution sector. *Journal of Economics, Business and Management, 4*(2), 173–177.

Brodie, R.J., Coviello, N.E., & Winklhofer, H. (2008). Contemporary marketing practices research program: A review of the first decade. *Journal of Business & Industrial Marketing, 23*(2), 84–94.

Caliguri, P., & Tarique, I. (2012). Dynamic cross-cultural competencies and global leadership effectiveness. *Journal of World Business, 47*(4), 612–622.

Cannone, G., & Ughetto, E. (2014). Born globals: A cross-country survey on high-tech start-ups. *International Business Review, 23,* 272–283.

Carley, K.M. (2002). Smart agents and organizations of the future. In L. Lievrouw, & S. Livingstone (Eds.), *The handbook of new media,* 206–220. Sage Publications.

Catulli, M., Lavergne, D., & Smart, S. (2006). Testing a relational model across national borders: The case of the library products and supplies industry. In Conference Proceedings, Academy of Marketing Conference. London Academy of Marketing.

Chen, C.-J., Huang, J.-W., & Hsiao, Y.-C. (2010). Knowledge management and innovativeness. The role of organizational climate and structure. *International Journal of Manpower, 31*(8), 848–870. https://doi.org/10.1108/01437721011088548

Conway, T., & Swift, J.S. (1999). International relationship marketing: The importance of psychic distance. *European Journal of Marketing, 34*(11/12), 1391–1413.

Daou, A., Karuranga, E., & Su, Z. (2013). Intellectual capital in Mexican SMEs from the perspective of the resource-based and dynamic capabilities views. *Journal of Applied Business Research, 29*(6), 1673–1689.

Economics and Development Resource Center. (1997). *Guidelines for the economic analysis of projects*. Economics and Development Resource Center.

Egan, J. (2003). Back to the future: Divergence in relationship marketing research. *Marketing Theory, 3*(1), 145–157.

Elenkov, D.S., & Manev, I.M. (2009). Senior expatriate leadership's effects on innovation and the role of cultural intelligence. *Journal of World Business, 44*(4), 357–369.

Ellram, L.M., & Hendrick, T.E. (1995). Partnering characteristics: A dyadic perspective. *Journal of Business Logistics, 16*(1), 41–64.

Etemat, H., & Ala-Mukta, J. (2009). *Growth and internationalization strategies of rapidly growing and internationalizing enterprises from Canada and Finland*. ASAC.

Fang, C., Yang, C.W., & Hsu, W.Y. (2013). Inter-organizational knowledge transfer: The perspective of knowledge governance. *Journal of Knowledge Management, 17*(6), 943–957.

Ferguson, J., & Taminiau, Y. (2014). Conflict and learning in inter-organizational online communities: Negotiating knowledge claims. *Journal of Knowledge Management, 18*(5), 886–904.

Fernandes, T.M., & Proença, J.F. (2005). Relationships and relationship marketing: An interdisciplinary perspective. In F. Wynstra, K. Dittrich, & F. Jaspers (Eds.), Dealing with Dualities, Proceedings of the 21th IMP Group Annual Conference. Rotterdam, RSM Erasmus University, Netherlands.

Festing, M., & Maletzky, M. (2011). Cross-cultural leadership adjustment – A multilevel framework based on the theory of structuration. *Human Resource Management Review, 21*(3), 186–200.

Filieri, R., & Alguezaui, S. (2014). Structural social capital and innovation. Is knowledge transfer the missing link? *Journal of Knowledge Management, 18*(4), 728–757.

Filip, A., & Anghel, L.-D. (2009). Customer loyalty and its determinants in a banking services environment. *Amfiteatru Economic, XI*(26), 288–297.

Fischer, R. (2009). Where is culture in cross-cultural research? An outline of a multilevel research process for measuring culture as a shared meaning system. *International Journal of Cross Cultural Management, 9*(1), 25–48.

Ford, D. (2003). *Understanding business marketing and purchasing: An interaction approach*, 3rd edition. Thomson Learning.

Ford, D., & Håkansson, H. (2006). The idea of interaction. *The IMP Journal*, 1(1), 4–20.

Fournier, S.M., Dobscha, S., & Mick, D.G. (1998). Preventing the premature death of relationship marketing. *Harvard Business Review*, *76*, 42–51.

Freeman, S., Giroud, A., Kalfadellis, P., & Ghauri, P. (2012). Psychic distance and environment: Impact on increased. *European Business Review*, *24*(4), 351–373.

Glavas, C., & Mathews, S. (2014). How international entrepreneurship characteristics influence Internet capabilities for the international business processes of the firm. *International Business Review*, *23*(1), 228–245.

Griffith, D.A., & Hoppner, J. (2013). Global marketing managers: Improving global strategy through soft skill development. *International Marketing Review*, *30*(1), 21–51.

Gummesson, E. (2008). Extending the service-dominant logic: From customer centricity to balanced centricity. *Journal of the Academy of Marketing Science*, *36*, 15–17. https://doi.org/10.1007/s11747-007-0065-x

Håkansson, H., & Snehota, I. (2006). No business is an island: The network concept of business strategy. *Scandinavian Journal of Management*, *22*(3), 256–270.

Håkansson, H., Harrison, D., & Waluszewski, A. (2004). *Rethinking marketing – Developing a new understanding of markets*. John Wiley and Sons.

Halinen, A., Medlin, C.J., & Törnroos, J-Å. (2012). Time and process in business network research. *Industrial Marketing Management*, *41*(2), 215–223.

Hampton, A., & Rowell, J. (2010). Leveraging integrated partnerships as a means of developing international capability: An SME case study. *International Journal of Knowledge, Culture and Change Management*, *10*(6), 19–30.

Hampton, A., & Rowell, J. (2013). An evolution in research practice for investigating international business relationships. *Management Dynamics in the Knowledge Economy*, *1*(2), 161–178.

Hapenciuc, C.V., Pînzaru, F., Vătămănescu, E.-M., & Stanciu, P. (2015). Convergenţa antreprenoriat sustenabil – Practici Contemporane de Marketing în start-up-urile din România [The convergence between sustainable entrepreneurshio and contemporary marketing practices in the case of the start-ups from Romania]. *Amfiteatru Economic*, *17*(40), 938–954.

Hilmersson, M. (2014). Small and medium-sized enterprise internationalization strategy and performance in times of market turbulence. *International Small Business Journal*, *32*(4), 386–400.

Hofstede, G.H. (2001). *Culture's consequences: Comparing values, behaviors, institutions, and organizations across nations*, 2nd edition. SAGE Publications.

Hohenthal, J., Johanson, J., & Johanson, M. (2014). Network knowledge and business-relationship value in the foreign market. *International Business Review*, *23*(1), 4–19.

Holmlund, M., & Kock, S. (1995). Buyer perceived service quality in industrial networks. *Industrial Marketing Management*, *24*(2), 109–121.

Hunt, S.D. (2000). *A general theory of competition: Resources, competences, productivity, and economic growth*. SAGE Publications.

Hutchinson, V., & Quintas, P. (2008). Do SMEs do knowledge management? Or simply manage what they know? *International Small Business Journal*, *26*(2), 131–154. https://doi.org/10.1177/0266242607086571

Ivanova, M.N., & Torkkeli, L. (2013). Managerial sensemaking of interaction within business relationships: A cultural perspective. *European Management Journal*, *31*(6), 717–727.

Jardon, C.M. (2015). The use of intellectual capital to obtain competitive advantages in regional small and medium enterprises. *Knowledge Management Research & Practice, 13*(4), 486–496.

Johanson, J., & Vahlne, J.E. (2009). The Uppsala internationalization process model revisited: From liability of foreignness to liability of outsidership. *Journal of International Business Studies, 40*(9), 1411–1431. https://doi.org/10.1057/jibs. 2009.24

Johns, R. (2012). Relationship marketing in a self-service context: No longer applicable? *Journal of Relationship Marketing, 11*(2), 91–115.

Kanagal, N. (2009). Role of relationship marketing in competitive marketing strategy. *Journal of Management and Marketing Research, 2*(1), 1–17.

Karjaluoto, H., Mustonen, N., & Ulkuniemi, P. (2015). The role of digital channels in industrial marketing communications. *Journal of Business & Industrial Marketing, 30*(6), 703–710.

Keat, P.G., & Young, P.K.Y. (2003). *Managerial economics. Economic tools for today's decision-makers,* 4th edition. Pearson Education International.

Keinänen, H., & Kuivalainen, O. (2015). Antecedents of social media B2B use in industrial marketing context: Customers' view. *Journal of Business & Industrial Marketing, 30*(6), 711–722.

Khojastehpour, M., & Johns, R. (2014). Internationalization and relationship marketing: An introduction. *European Business Review, 26*(3), 238–253.

Klafehn, J., Banerjee, P.M., & Chiu, C.-Y. (2009). Navigating cultures: The role of metacognitive cultural intelligence. In S. Ang, & L. Van Dyne (Eds.), *Handbook of cultural intelligence: Theory, measurement, and applications,* 318–331. M.E. Sharpe.

Kontinen, T., & Ojala, A. (2010). Internationalization pathways of family SMEs: Psychic distance as a focal point. *Journal of Small Business and Enterprise Development, 17*(3), 437–454.

Kotler, P., & Keller, K.L. (2006). *Marketing management,* 12th Edition. Pearson Prentice Hall.

Leonidou, L.C. (2004). Industrial manufacturer-customer relationships: The discriminating role of the buying situation. *Industrial Marketing Management, 33*(8), 731–742.

Leonidou, L.C., Palihawadana, D., Chari, S., & Leonidou, C.N. (2011). Drivers and outcomes of importer adaptation in international buyer–seller Relationships. *Journal of World Business, 46,* 527–543.

Lin, K.-H., & Chaney, I. (2007). The influence of domestic interfirm networks on the internationalization process of Taiwanese SMEs. *Asia Pacific Business Review, 13*(4), 565–583.

Magnusson, P., Westjohn, S.A., & Boggs, D.J. (2009). Order-of-entry effects for service firms in developing markets: An examination of multinational advertising agencies. *Journal of International Marketing, 17*(2), 23–41.

Magnusson, P., Westjohn, S.A., Semenov, A.V., Randrianasolo, A.A., & Zdravkovic, S. (2013). The role of cultural intelligence in marketing adaptation and export performance. *Journal of International Marketing, 21*(4), 44–61.

Mandják, T., & Durrieu, F. (2000). Understanding the non-economic value of business relationships. http://www.impgroup.org/uploads/papers/89.pdf.

Moen, O., Gavlen, M., & Endresen, I. (2004). Internationalization of small, computer software firms: Entry forms and market selection. *European Journal of Marketing, 38*(9/10), 1236–1251.

Möller, K., & Halinen, A. (2000). Relationship marketing theory: Its roots and direction. *Journal of Marketing Management, 16*(1), 29–54.

Morgan, R., & Hunt, S. (1994). The commitment-trust theory of relationship marketing. *Journal of Marketing, 58*(3), 20–38.

Nicolescu, O., & Nicolescu, L. (2005). *Economia, firma și managementul bazate pe cunoștințe [The economy, the company and knowledge-based management]*. Editura Economică.

Nicolescu, L. & Nicolescu, C. (2012). Innovation in SMEs – Findings from Romania. *Economics & Sociology*, 5(2a), 71–85.

Nijssen, E.J., & van Herk, H. (2009). Conjoining international marketing and relationship marketing: Exploring consumers' cross-border service relationships. *Journal of International Marketing, 17*(1), 91–115.

Nordman, E.R., & Tolstoy, D. (2014). Does relationship psychic distance matter for the learning processes of internationalizing SMEs? *International Business Review, 23*(1), 30–37. https://doi.org/10.1016/j.ibusrev.2013.08.010

Nowicka, M., Dima, I.C., & Ştefan, C. (2012). Integrating the IC concept into strategies for the development of regional network systems. *European Journal of Business and Social Sciences, 1*(6), 21–33.

Owen-Smith, J., & Powell, W.W. (2004). Knowledge networks as channels and conduits: The effects of spillovers in the Boston biotechnology community. *Organization Science, 15*(1), 5–21.

Palacios-Marqués, D., Soto-Acosta, P., & Merigó, J.M. (2015). Analyzing the effects of technological, organizational and competition factors on Web knowledge exchange in SMEs. *Telematics and Informatics, 32*(1), 23–32.

Palmatier, R.W. (2008). *Relationship marketing*. Marketing Science Institute.

Parsons, A.L. (2002). What determines buyer-seller relationship quality? An investigation from the buyer's perspective. *Journal of Supply Chain Management, 38*(2), 4–12.

Rathi, D., Given, L.M., & Forcier, E. (2014). Interorganizational partnerships and knowledge sharing: The perspective of non-profit organizations (NPOs). *Journal of Knowledge Management, 18*(5), 867–885.

Ravald, A., & Grönroos, Ch. (1996). The value concept and relationship marketing. *European Journal of Marketing, 30*(2), 19–30.

Rehman, S.U., Shareef, A., & Ishaque, A. (2012). Role of trust and commitment in creating profitable relationship with customers. *Interdisciplinary Journal of Contemporary Research in Business, 4*(1), 606–615.

Rodriguez, C.M., & Wilson, D.T. (2002). Relationship bonding and trust as a foundation for commitment in U.S.-Mexican strategic alliances: A structural equation modelling approach. *Journal of International Marketing, 10*(4), 53–76.

Samaha, S.A., Beck, J.T., & Palmatier, R.W. (2014). The role of culture in international relationship marketing. *Journal of Marketing, 78*, 78 –98.

Sandberg, S. (2014). Experiential knowledge antecedents of the SME network node configuration in emerging market business networks. *International Business Review, 23*(1), 20–29. https://doi.org/10.1016/j.ibusrev.2013.08.001

Schein, E.H. (2009). *The corporate culture survival guide*. Jossey-Bass.

Seggie, S.H., & Griffith, D.A. (2008). The resource matching foundations of competitive advantage. *international marketing review, 25*(3), 262–275.

Seppänen, R., Blomqvist, K., & Sundqvist, S. (2007). Measuring inter-organizational trust – A critical review of the empirical research in 1990-2003. *Industrial Marketing Management, 36*(2), 249–265.

Shaladi, B. (2012). Business relationship development and the influence of psychic distance. *Innovative Marketing, 8*(3), 73–80.

Sheth, J.N., & Parvatiyar, A. (1995). The evolution of relationship marketing. *International Business Review, 4*(4), 397–418.

Shu, C., Page, A.L., Gao, S., & Jiang, X. (2012). Managerial ties and firm innovation: Is knowledge creation a missing link?. *Journal of Product Innovation Management, 29*(1), 125–143.

Stengel, D.N. (2011). *Managerial economics: concepts and principles.* Business Expert Press.

Suh, Y., & Kim, M.-S. (2014). Internationally leading SMEs vs. internationalized SMEs: Evidence of success factors from South Korea. *International Business Review, 23,* 115–129.

Szczepankiewicz, E.I. (2013). Concept of using the InCaS model to identification, measuring and presenting relational capital of a network enterprises. *Management, 17*(1), 136–152.

Tan, Q., & Sousa, C.M.P. (2015). Leveraging marketing capabilities into competitive advantage and export performance. *International Marketing Review, 32*(1), 78–102.

Testa, M. (2009). National culture, leadership and citizenship: Implications for cross-cultural management. *International Journal of Hospitality Management, 28*(1), 78–85.

Turnbull, D.F., & Cunningham, M. (1996). Interaction, relationships and networks in business markets: An evolving perspective. *Journal of Business & Industrial Marketing, 11*(3/4), 44–62.

Uzzi, B., & Lancaster, R. (2003). Relational embeddedness and learning: The case of bank loan managers and their clients. *Management Science, 49*(4), 383–399.

Valkokari, K., Paasi, J., & Rantala, T. (2012). Managing knowledge within networked innovation. *Knowledge Management Research & Practice, 10*(1), 27–40.

Vătămănescu, E.-M., Pînzaru, F., Andrei, A.-G., & Alexandru, V.-A. (2014). Going international versus going global. The case of the European steel pipe SMEs. *Review of International Comparative Management, 15*(3), 360–379.

Vătămănescu, E.-M., Dumitriu, D.-L., Andrei, A.G., & Leovaridis, C. (2015). Networking intellectual capital towards competitiveness: An insight into the European higher education institutions. *The Electronic Journal of Knowledge Management, 12*(3), 157–168.

Vătămănescu, E.-M., Andrei, A.G., Nicolescu, L., Pînzaru, F., & Zbuchea, A. (2017a). The influence of competitiveness on SMEs internationalization effectiveness. Online versus offline business networking. *Information Systems Management, 34*(3), 205–219. https://doi.org/10.1080/10580530.2017.1329997

Vătămănescu, E.-M., Gazzola, P., Dincă, V.M., & Pezzetti, R. (2017b). Mapping entrepreneurs' orientation towards sustainability in interaction versus network marketing practices. *Sustainability, 9*(9), 1580. https://doi.org/10.3390/su9091580

Wang, C.-H. (2014). How relational capital mediates the effect of corporate reputation on competitive advantage: Evidence from Taiwan high-tech industry. *Technological Forecasting and Social Change, 82*(1), 167–176.

Wang, X. (2013). Forming mechanisms and structures of a knowledge transfer network: Theoretical and simulation research. *Journal of Knowledge Management,* *17*(2), 278–289.

Weck, M., & Ivanova, M. (2013). The importance of cultural adaptation for the trust development within business relationships. *Journal of Business and Industrial Marketing, 28*(3), 210–220.

Westaby, J.D. (2012). *Dynamic network theory: How social networks influence goal pursuit.* American Psychological Association.

Wilson, D.T., & Jantrania, S. (1996). Understanding the value of a relationship. *Asia – Australia Marketing Journal, 2*(1), 55–66.

Zhao, Y., & Smith, L. (2006). How supplier involvement influences, buyer satisfaction and trust: A study of industrial markets. *Innovative Marketing, 2*(2), 110–121.

8 Back to the future
Instead of conclusions

By intertwining seminal studies to topical developments, the book has advocated that relationships stand out as the fabric of small- and medium-sized enterprises (SMEs) internationalization, progressively weaving multi-layer strata for international business performance. We proposed a manifold analysis of the role of managerial relationship building and development and SMEs internationalization, considering that, in the networked economy, relationships are the invisible golden threads that link organizations and support business growth across borders.

All the chapters converge toward the final one which puts all the elements together in a unitary model. The lynchpin of the book is woven of all sort of relationships: macroeconomic relationships from the SMEs internationalization standpoint, interpersonal, social, business relationships as inferred by the existing internationalization models, particular business relationships in a specific region as determined by the historical, geopolitical, political, and cultural circumstances, relationship marketing and network-based marketing in the context of B2B internationalization, relationships development based on managers' global mindset versus psychic distance and the corollary of managerial relationships as powerful drivers of internationalization.

Stage by stage, macro- and micro-organizational realities and trends affecting the SMEs internationalization were brought forward, adjointly providing phenomenological overviews of context-driven approaches (i.e., the internationalization of SMEs in the Central and Eastern European (CEE) region considered as a living research laboratory). By doing so, we aimed at advancing a comprehensive conceptual framework of the underlying threads of SMEs internationalization coupled with a fresh discussion of current phenomena which would help the reader achieve a more pertinent image of the topical business environment.

The first part of the book, titled *Relationships and the internationalization of SMEs: A zoom-out perspective*, comprised three chapters that elaborated on the key topics pertaining to relationship formation and growth during the internationalization process. Their goal was to address the principal characteristics of the current international environment, ranging from multi-dimensional macro causes to phenomenological overviews of the

DOI: 10.4324/9781003432326-10

idiosyncrasies of SME internationalization in particular locations (i.e., CEE countries). It provided an overview of the contemporary civilizational transformations brought about by the emergence of the Fourth Industrial Revolution and the energy shift toward adopting more sustainable sources and modes of consumption, as well as a variety of demographical, social, behavioral, cultural, political, and geopolitical changes that are currently occurring. The book continued by addressing the key characteristics of the current international business environment and by presenting globalization as the force that creates growth opportunities for the most numerous companies on the planet – the SMEs – while at times posing insurmountable barriers to their development. Focusing on SMEs and their international development, the next subchapters described the elements that support SME internationalization, the internationalization modes, and the current metrics of SME performance in international contexts. Based on these foundations, the final chapter of the first part of this book argued that it is pertinent and necessary for researchers in the International Business field to examine the business realities specific to Central and Eastern European countries due to the complex transition process that these nations have undergone over the last few decades, following the fall of communist regimes and during and after their transition to becoming members of the European Union.

The second part, entitled *Relationships and the internationalization of SMEs: A zoom-in perspective*, highlighted the uniqueness of establishing connections within the context of the internationalization process. The three chapters in this part focus on the significant role that human capital plays in the internationalization of SMEs, demonstrating that the psychological, social, and cultural equation of the manager is of the utmost importance to the success of SME internationalization. Based on these principles, the first chapter of this part proposes that B2B relationships have been treated in the literature through the interaction-based B2B relationship marketing model and the network-based B2B relationship marketing model. The chapter acknowledges that, on a larger scale, culture and country of origin may impact international B2B relationships, anticipating that studying the managerial mindset, cultural intelligence, and personal value perceptions regarding psychic distance are key instruments for predicting the company's ability to leverage on relationships with local, cross-border, and cross-cultural partners. The following chapter provides insight into the aforementioned concepts, emphasizing the catalytic effect that the manager's mental models and global mindset have on the success of SMEs in international activities, while also acknowledging the role that the human capital embodied by the entrepreneurs (who may not be managers of the company at a given time) and by the employees plays in either encouraging or discouraging the internationalization of the SME. The concluding chapter of this part introduces a new theoretical model for understanding managerial relationships in the transorganizational context: the 5 Cs model of managerial relationship building. The model articulates conditions, contexts, catalysts, consequences, and connections inherent in the construction of international relationships. It is based on the major theoretical streams in the fields of business internationalization, B2B marketing in inter-cultural and cross-cultural contexts, and international relationship marketing.

From a bird's eye view, this chapter advances a novel framework which is developed and argued step-by-step across the previous chapters. Each chapter stands out as a backward-looking toward the road ahead, advocating for a certain dimension or sub-dimension of the model and linking it to various relevant factors. *In nuce*, all chapters tackle SMEs internationalization through the lens of various acknowledged models (progressive, contingency, network-based, etc.), ever going deeper into the phenomenology of initiating, developing, and enhancing international relationships in manifold ways. It is a processual approach which delves into specific phenomena with a view to finally interconnect the elements within an articulate picture. Subsequently, the ultimate goal of the book is achieved: one small step for the internationalization models of SMEs, and one giant leap for un-weaving the fabric of business performance via managerial relationships.

Index

Printed in the United States
by Baker & Taylor Publisher Services